Noah Adams on
"All Things Considered"

Also by NOAH ADAMS

SAINT CROIX NOTES:
RIVER MORNINGS, RADIO NIGHTS

NOAH ADAMS
on
"*All Things Considered*"

A Radio Journal

by

NOAH ADAMS

W · W · NORTON & COMPANY · *New York London*

The text of this book is composed in ITC Modern 216 Light
with the display set in ITC Modern 216 Medium
Composition and Manufacturing by the Haddon Craftsmen, Inc.
Book design by Jacques Chazaud

Library of Congress Cataloging-in-Publication Data

Adams, Noah.
    Noah Adams on "All things considered" : a radio journal / by Noah
Adams.
        p.   cm.
    1. Adams, Noah—Biography. 2. Radio journalists—United States—
Biography. 3. Radio journalism—United States. I. Title.
    PN4874.A2806   1993
    070'.92—dc20
    [B]   92-11871

ISBN 0-393-03043-1

W.W. Norton & Company, Inc., 500 Fifth Avenue, New York, N.Y. 10110
W.W. Norton & Company Ltd., 10 Coptic Street, London WC1A 1PU

1 2 3 4 5 6 7 8 9 0

for Grace, Edith, Neenah.

Contents

Foreword
by Susan Stamberg

Sometime around 1977 it all began to blur. "All Things Considered" had been on the air since 1971. We'd gotten through the end of Vietnam and Richard Nixon, the beginning and middle of Jimmy Carter, the annual recitations of budget and State of the Union, wars, coups, countercoups, countless new movies and books and plays and performers, and a moment arrived at which it became impossible to know whether the John Irving interview had been last year or the year before, whether the campaign financing discussion had been before or after Senator X got reelected in Pennsylvania.

That's how it is with daily journalism. That "big picture" we all aspire to gets painted in Seurat-like dots of days. Once enough days pass, you ought to be able to step away and see patterns emerge, big shapes. The problem, though, in daily journalism, is that every time you try to pattern-hunt, a new day pops up and cracks your concentration. The pattern eludes. What's left is the blur. It's as if, as host of a daily news program, you're on a fabulous bullet train, whizzing though unfamiliar landscape. Scenes flash past the window, but the train never stops long enough for you to really be able to see the sights. The ride is exhilarating but frustrating. Or so it seemed to me, toward the end of my first decade as host of "All Things Considered."

With this book Noah Adams, toward the end of his first decade as host of "All Things Considered," stops the blur, slows it down. Clarifies. He takes a single year on "All Things Considered," and chronicles it day by day, dot by dot. He brakes the train, climbs down and studies the shape of the place, notices how it smells and what there is to eat there. (Has any broadcaster ever taken such profound and simple pleasure in American cooking? Even the redoubtable Julia Child has competition from Noah when it comes to sheer appreciation for the fragrance and texture of food. Country food's his favorite. Good bread and apple butter. Nothing fancy that you can't pronounce.) He takes a year of news and events, people talking, places visited, and lets us hear it in print.

And what a time he's chosen, 1989 to 1990! The year of Tiananmen Square *and* the death of the Ayatollah Khomeini *and* the crumbling of the Berlin Wall *and* the ensuing domino spill of Communist countries across Eastern Europe *and* the release of Nelson Mandela in South Africa, *and and and* . . . And there is Noah, charting the developments, connecting listeners to them, by radio.

No one, it is my sincere belief, takes his radio connection more seriously than the author of this book. After seventeen years of working with him—first when he came to National Public Radio and edited my taped interviews, later when we conducted interviews and hosted "All Things Considered" side by side (his rise was not exactly meteoric but it was utterly justified), later still when I moved into reporting while he remained at the anchor desk—I have come to see in Noah the conscience of the work we do. His is the most genuine, uncontrived voice in broadcasting. The conviction shines through the words he writes, and the quiet and very powerful way in which he speaks. He is a quiet, careful man,

a craftsman in his work, his seriousness softened by a twin-
kle in the eye, an occasional goofy grin, and the daffodils
he'll bring into the studio on an especially tense or stuffy
day.

In this book Noah writes something absolutely astonish-
ing. He's riding a train in North Dakota to do some stories
about the old Great Northern Railway. And he says, "I don't
like going up to strangers to talk." That statement, from a
man of absolute and perpetual sincerity, is the rock bottom
truth, than which there is nothing truer. Noah Adams hates
to talk to strangers. He is profoundly shy. And yet this reti-
cent, singular man has chosen a profession that depends on
such conversations. Not only chosen it, but succeeded bril-
liantly at it.

Talking to strangers is Noah Adams's job description. But
no one who talks with Noah remains a stranger for long. His
careful, caring respect helps others to open up.

This book revisits people and places that were once
strange to all of us. It also gives dimension to some familiar
"All Things Considered" voices. In doing all that, it also re-
forges the links between them and him and us.

These strong radio links helped us get through that event-
ful year, 89-90, and all the other years in which Noah Adams
has been broadcasting. Now, in print, they make sense for us
of the past, remind us of where we once were, and show just
how well cared for we have been.

Introduction

I think our dogs turn up the radio and dance when there's no one home. You recall the scene in the movie *Risky Business*? Tom Cruise—wearing only a shirt and underwear and white socks—comes sliding across the floor, pretending he's Bob Seger, singing about that "Old Time Rock and Roll"? That would be Bonny, the terrier. Will, the older dog, is less audacious, but he likes to bark in encouragement.

The dogs will bark back when they hear a dog on the radio, and if a doorbell should ring on the radio, they'll run to see who's come to visit. But they pay no attention to *me*. The familiar RCA symbol—the dog Nipper, head cocked to one side, listening to "His Master's Voice" on the phonograph—is only a fanciful image in our house; I'm told there's not a flicker of dog recognition at five o'clock, when the ATC theme starts and my voice says hello on the radio.

The voices work for me, though. And some moments from the radio are now like shining windows into the past. I'd sit at the kitchen table late at night, listening to Waite Hoyt on WLW, broadcasting the road games of the Cincinnati Redlegs. He didn't travel with the team; he was in the studio reading the teletype, using his imagination, and a block of wood and a crowd noise record to recreate the action. One day I came home from junior high school and went up to my room and turned on the radio and heard "Heartbreak Hotel"—they said it was Elvis Presley. I was working at a CBS Radio affiliate the day John F. Kennedy was shot, and the bulletin came through from Dallas. On NPR, I've heard the simple, joyful sounds of a baby's cries, just at birth; the voice of E. B. White, reading from *Charlotte's Web;* and the quiet pride of the young people who helped create a new Czechoslovakia. And we had quite a scare from Deborah Amos, on the second night of the war in the Persian Gulf. There was a missile alert in Saudi Arabia, at the base at Dhahran. We didn't know how bad it could be: Did the missiles have chemical warheads, even nuclear? Deborah managed to call in from Dhahran and was describing the activity at the base when ... her voice went away. With a PFF ... FT sound. It was quiet. And I remember hoping that her mother and father weren't listening to NPR at that moment. (Deborah called back some time later, and we learned that the satellite phone technicians at Dhahran had simply turned off the transmitter, afraid that the signal could be a target for incoming missiles.)

I'm working for the radio program I'd like to be listening to. I can remember when I first heard "All Things Considered," back in Kentucky. The sound was invitational rather than exclusionary; the people doing the program seemed to believe their listeners had some intelligence, common sense, a wide range of interests—and they made you want to hear about tomorrow.

Tomorrow comes at 9:45 in the morning. I'm usually a minute or so late for the meeting, others have been in for an hour, checking AP, UPI, Reuters; talking with the overnight foreign editor, the Washington desk. Fifteen people at the table; some a couple of years out of college, several who joined NPR in the seventies.

Cups of coffee, a carton of juice, someone has a bagel, a banana. Newspapers, printouts of wire stories, articles torn from magazines, notes on the backs of envelopes. Ideas float through the air to be grabbed or waved away. Attention spans are short; you can be arguing one minute and drift off reading *Doonesbury* the next. Our meetings are more grumpy and more cynical than our program, and more fun—the world can get to be absurd when you chase after it every day. But there's ninety minutes to fill. Foreign news? National stories? How can we advance "Morning Edition"? Sports? Any music ideas? Anything *interesting*? A long day with an often-frantic conclusion stretches ahead. A few on the staff might go out for a run at noon, but some days there's not time for lunch.

I sit at this table with women and men who have journalism degrees and language skills and years of experience (both Linda Wertheimer and Robert Siegel, my co-hosts, have worked in New York and London). I dropped out of college and started in radio as an announcer (I still tend to read *Time* magazine from the back to the front). Others have quite different backgrounds: music, film, print; it doesn't matter—the *mix* is what's important.

I'm told that radio could have more of a future than a past. Digital CD-quality radio. An infinite number of satellite signals. Intensely personalized: your car radio could know that you want to hear (1) traffic updates, (2) local happenings, (3) business features, (4) news from Europe and Southern Africa, (5) just the baseball scores, (6) country music only, please—anything by Garth Brooks, and (7) no more stories this week about the presidential primaries.

But good radio will still be a simple matter of voices, in our home towns and from around the world. The voices of the people in trouble, the voices of fear, of wisdom, of wonder, of joy.

What follows is a highly edited, very idiosyncratic *remembering* of one year's programs, one year's travels—looking for stories, making friends. Thank you for listening.

N.D.A.
April 1992

Noah Adams on
"All Things Considered"

Sunday, June 4, Washington, D.C., 1989

I'm up at 6:00 A.M., reading *The New York Times*, waiting for *The Washington Post*. It's a warm, sunny morning and I sit out on the porch reading about China. At nine o'clock, CBS's "Sunday Morning" comes on television and Charles Kuralt tells us the Ayatollah has died in Iran. In Moscow, the People's Congress of Deputies is talking about democracy, and Poland is seeing the first free elections in forty years. Kuralt says this is a morning "on which you can feel the world change. And China weeps."

The numbers go up quickly. Perhaps thousands of Chinese have been killed. CBS has lost touch with Richard Roth and his cameraman. We hear Roth—on tape from the night before—as soldiers approach and knock the camera down. Roth is yelling, "Oh, no—", before the connection to New York is broken. Kuralt asks Dan Rather, in Beijing, to explain what it all means, and I find I can't pay attention. CBS always brings Rather on as an expert and it bothers me that Kuralt should have to be asking him questions. Then word comes that the Chinese police have released Roth and his colleague, Derek Williams.

"This Week with David Brinkley" on ABC has videotape flown out to Hong Kong (no uplinks now from Beijing). Bodies being taken by troops to be cremated. Soldiers telling hospitals to withhold care from students. Fears that troops will go into universities to kill students. ABC now has Jackie Judd in China; she's an old friend and was once my co-host on weekend "All Things Considered." Other former NPR people on ABC today: David Ensor, from Poland, Bob Zelnick, from the Pentagon; and the Brinkley show uses Cokie Roberts, our congressional correspondent.

In the afternoon my wife, Neenah, and I finish putting in
our garden, and then clean up and drive over to Maryland to
buy some wild bird food, then on into downtown Washington to Tower Records. Neenah wants one of Bonnie Raitt's
first albums, now out on CD. We've talked about going to a
Jerry Lee Lewis–Bo Diddley concert tonight, but decide to
stay home and watch the Tony Awards.

I go out for a long run, between five and six o'clock, listening to "All Things Considered" on headphones. They talk
with a BBC television correspondent, Kate Adey, in Beijing,
who was hurt slightly by gunfire the night before. Her description of the shooting in the square, and the panic, is
vivid and matter-of-fact. She was in the streets all night and
then went around to the hospitals trying to make estimates
of the dead and wounded.

Monday, June 5, Washington, D.C., 1989

We have a power failure at NPR and it feels like a holiday.
No one else in the building, dark hallways and stairs. The
standby generators provide enough power for a couple of
studios, the newsroom, and Master Control. The NPR offices
and studios take up the first four floors of an eight-story
glass-and-steel building on M Street, downtown. The White
House is about ten blocks away, the CBS Washington Bureau just across the street.

The Beijing story goes well. There is speculation that a
civil war is imminent in China, or at least a confrontation
between the 27th Field Army and the 38th. The 27th reportedly did most of the killing. The estimates of thousands
dead, however, are now being revised downward. The troops
of the 27th have moved into a defensive position—the term
is "disposition," and Neal Conan, our executive producer,
wants the word used on the air. He has specialized in military matters (as well as sports) and sometimes can overdo

these things, but "disposition" sounds like the right term, if it's pronounced with just a slight emphasis, almost verbal quotation marks.

Neal is close to forty, with red hair and beard and an Irish intensity. Working with him is like playing half-court basketball at the YMCA—he pushes himself and everyone else to be better; sometimes you can almost hear him growl.

In March 1991, at the end of the war in the Persian Gulf, Neal got a bit closer to the Iraqi military than perhaps he wanted to be. He and Chris Hedges of *The New York Times* were among forty Western journalists held by the Republican Guard in southern Iraq. Neal was in good company; Chris Hedges speaks Arabic, and this is the sort of thing he does for a living—he gets in Jeeps and drives around looking for trouble.

They were trying to get to Basra; the fighting was finished in Kuwait and a rebellion had started inside Iraq. Neal and Chris were stopped at a roadblock, then taken to an Iraqi Army command post. Eventually the troops brought them along to Baghdad: they were caught on Monday, released on Friday. Early Tuesday morning, after we were convinced Neal was missing, I went over to spent the morning with Liane Hansen, Neal's wife. They're both old friends (she's the host of "Weekend Edition Sunday"). I took along some doughnuts and we read the papers and watched all three networks and CNN and listened to NPR and answered the phone every three or four minutes. NPR management was working fast, asking the State Department for help, and key members of Congress, even the White House.

The rumors that day were bad: stories that some of the journalists had been hurt, some even killed. And it was a long, frustrating week at work. I spent hours at my computer terminal searching for news and clues amid all the various wire services and all the stories coming out of Iraq. By Thursday, I was upset with the computer itself, I wanted to shake it and bang on it as if somehow there was information about Neal hidden inside. Then on Friday the calls from the Red Cross, and CNN people in Atlanta—They're all fine, they'll be free soon, your man's on the list. On Saturday, they were driven to the border with Jordan. Neal took a taxi from there to Amman; he had some cash hidden inside his N.Y. Yankees baseball cap. He called Liane from the hotel, started filing stories that evening about the fighting inside Iraq.

In a few days he was back in Washington and we all got together for lunch. He told us about the worst time—the second night. The Guard convoy entered a village and came under fire from the rebels. Neal and Chris and the soldiers dove face down into the mud, and then spent the night in the vehicles, expecting a rocket attack at any moment. So much for the "elite" Republican Guard. A friend told Liane after Neal was freed, "It's every reporter's dream to be captured, held for four days, and then released." This is akin to what Winston Churchill said: "Nothing in life is so exhilarating as to be shot at without result."

It was difficult for many of us, during the war in the Gulf, to avoid using personal pronouns on the air. It could seem natural to talk about "our" troops and to ask, what do you think "we'll" do next, instead of "U.S." troops and "coalition" forces. I've heard people from the Canadian Broadcasting Corporation, and the BBC as well, admit to this same problem, their newscasters and presenters going on about "our chaps" overseas. This usage is especially jingoistic during a war and probably should always be avoided. I never felt comfortable, for example, talking about "our" strategic nuclear missiles as compared to "theirs." A lot of our what's-the-right-word discussions involve governments and soldiers: the difference between "invasion" and "incursion," "freedom fighter" and "guerrilla."

An NPR editor wrote, at the time of the Camp David Accords, that "Israel and Egypt have now put an end to years of enmity." I argued that "enmity" really wasn't one of *my* words, that it would be unfamiliar to the audience; he felt it was the right word and perfectly understandable in this context. He agreed to a change but now I think he was right. Once I had another editor change my script at the last second, cutting out some words. The story was about the last business day for the Community Services Administration— the anti-poverty agency once called the Office of Economic Opportunity. I went over to CSA headquarters to interview some of the long-time employees. And I wrote at the end of the story:

> The office party later spilled out into the streets, past all the boxes and files that someone will have to come and pick up. There was music outside—in the sunshine, and a few speeches and many memories. [then the part that the editor cut] *And left behind in the hallway upstairs, written in crayon on the wall: "The O.E.O.—1964–1981. Conceived in compassion by John F. Kennedy, put into law by Lyndon Baines Johnson, kneecapped by Richard Milhous Nixon, coldly ravaged by Ronald 'Bonzo' Reagan."*

Another time an editor cut out a reference to razor blades in a story about piano students at the Juilliard School in New York. I'd interviewed several pianists about their training for upcoming performance competitions, and I asked a young woman if it was true that Juilliard students had sometimes placed razor blades, upright, between the keys of the practice pianos. She laughed and said, no, that's just an old myth, and then went on to talk about the friendly nature of the competition. And that's the way the story ran on "All Things Considered." But later it was re-fed to the stations as part of an arts package, and an editor took it upon herself to cut out the story about the razor blades. She said, when I complained, that it was "gratuitous violence."

Tom Friedman of *The New York Times* had a far more serious problem reporting from Lebanon in August 1982. He filed a story about Israel's "indiscriminate" shelling of Beirut. The story appeared the next morning in the *Times* without the word "indiscriminate." Friedman later wrote in

his book *From Beirut to Jerusalem,* "At the time, my editors felt the word was 'editorializing'; I felt that it was an
exact description and that its omission was editorializing. I
still feel that way."

I've been lucky, though—I've done more than ten thousand interviews and stories and had only a few arguments
with editors; the process is far more collaborative than com-
bative, and they've saved me from making a thousand mistakes.

Just before today's ATC editorial meeting at ten o'clock, I
type out a short essay, about reading the news from China,
yesterday morning. I carry it around for most of the day,
rewrite it once, and finally show it to Neal. He thinks it's a
day too early, but then the essay does go on the air, at the
end of a half-hour, after six stories from and about China.
The next morning Neal kids me about it, saying it wasn't
until he heard it on his way home in the car (a later feed of
"All Things Considered" is carried by WAMU in Washington—WETA takes the first, at five o'clock) that he realized I'd
mentioned a dog in the essay. He always accuses me of trying to sneak dogs on the air. A couple of weeks ago I ended
an interview with Glenn Gould's biographer, Otto Friedrich,
by asking him to tell the story about the pianist's dream of
starting a puppy farm, up in the Arctic. Gould left half of his
estate to a fund for deserving animals. I just figure that any
time I have the words "puppy farm" on tape I should try to
get that tape on the air. I usually point out that half the
households in the United States have dogs and 70 percent of
those dogs are said to sleep on the bed with their owners.

Once for a story about goose hunting, on Maryland's Eastern Shore, I interviewed Sam Leonard, one of the guides in
the town of Cambridge. We were out in Sam's blind at sunrise, waiting for geese, and then went to his house in the
evening for a quieter talk. His Chesapeake retriever, Cindy,
was on the porch, and I asked that she come inside to be
with Sam while we talked in front of the fire. I had a great
deal of admiration for Cindy; she spent the morning in the

cold water bringing back close to a dozen geese. During the interview Cindy sat happily by the fire, her tail thumping whenever she heard her name mentioned. Afterwards I remarked to Sam that the dog seemed quite pleased with herself, and he said, "She ought to be, this is the first time she's ever been in the house."

NOAH: By late Saturday night, we had heard and seen most of the story from Beijing. We watched television for a while before bedtime, just watching anything, to have friendlier images in our minds as we slept.

I got up early the next morning and made coffee and went out to the front porch to wait for the paper. *The Washington Post* usually arrives late on Sunday in our neighborhood. It's delivered by two young boys, with a lot of help from their mother who drives the station wagon. There's a small brown dog who comes to supervise. The boys ride along on the tailgate, and at each stop they're off in different directions.

On this Sunday morning their little sister was helping out, and she brought my paper right up on the porch to my chair. She was barefoot, with blond hair, wearing a pink-and-white checked sunsuit. She couldn't have been more than three years old. She seemed shy but she was smiling and said good morning and looked right at me as she handed me the paper.

I knew what the headlines said, and was happy that she was too young to read. After she left, I looked at the front page:

TROOPS ROLL THROUGH BEIJING TO CRUNCH PROTESTORS,
HUNDREDS FEARED KILLED AS CHINESE TROOPS FIGHT BACK

You could not really be *away* from this news. On Saturday, people were talking early at breakfast, about trouble in China, Tiananmen Square, on CNN. Then the radio newscast stories, with finally an absolute tone

that had not been heard during the seven weeks of
reporting about the student protests in Beijing. Some
people, I guess, try to stay away from the news
altogether, most of the time. Why listen to the stories
of cruelty and greed? Once I heard an argument that if
you had been deep in a cave during the decade from
1965 to 1975, the only story of true importance you
would have missed was Nixon's secret bombing of
Cambodia.

And I've heard a producer say that the news is
important to people in concentric circles, moving out
and away from your home. We always ask, "Am I safe?"
"Is my family safe?" "Is my neighborhood safe?" "My
town, my state, my country—the world?"

The very young child who brought my newspaper
does need to know the news from China, that there are
men capable of this, that her neighborhood is possibly
not as safe . . . now.

But she doesn't need to know about it on *this* soft
Sunday morning, with sunshine and her brothers
laughing, and her mom and the dog waiting for her in
the car.

Tuesday, June 6, Washington, D.C., 1989

I leave for work at 7:00 A.M. in order to phone Ross Terrill at
his hotel in Beijing, before his bedtime. We've talked with
him often in the past: Terrill's written several books on
China; he speaks Chinese, and is in close touch with several
Party members. On this trip, he arrived at the Beijing airport Saturday evening—at the very time when everyone
else was trying to get out. His descriptions—calmly delivered in his matter-of-fact Australian accent—of the two
nights he spent out in the streets were chilling.

Our reporter in Beijing, Vicki O'Hara, says that troops are
being brought from other regions of China, and that foreign

embassies are making evacuation plans.

Today we try to find something a little lighter to put on the program, and someone remembers a story left over from last week. A new section of Interstate 90 has just been completed; the entire road is almost finished and now the only traffic light from Boston to Seattle is in downtown Wallace, Idaho. We decided to call there and see what was going on. I talked with a waitress at Kellmer's Coffee Shop, busy at lunchtime. Audrey Smith is happy in Wallace and explains why. One of the best reasons—left out of the edited interview because of time—she's a member of the local summer theater. They're doing *Dracula:* she's playing a professor who shows up to investigate some strange proceedings.

My first question, though, was about today's lunch special.

SMITH: A fried ham and swiss cheese with mushroom sandwich on a wonderful French roll and homemade chicken noodle soup.

NOAH: Any homemade pie?

SMITH: Homemade pie, apple, Washington nut, sour cream fudge, coconut cream.

NOAH: That sounds pretty good.

SMITH: We have wonderful homemade food here. Fresh-brewed iced tea.

NOAH: Well, that's worth stopping for, I would think.

SMITH: That might just bring you right down.

NOAH: Now, besides the lunch there at Kellmer's Coffee Shop, what else is of note in Wallace, Idaho?

SMITH: Well, we have a wonderful museum, a mine tour that has tied for number one in the state for the top tourist attraction. We have the old depot which has been turned into a railroad depot and is a magnificent building, it dates from 1902. We are one hundred five

years old here and the entire town is on the National
Historic Registry.

NOAH: You like living there?

SMITH: I love it. I came home in 1972. I was in southern
California for about twenty-two years and I came home
on three weeks vacation from the *San Diego Union
Tribune* and never went back. Well, I tried a trip in '80,
but I couldn't... I came home.

NOAH: Now in 1991, I guess, there's going to be a bypass
opening that will go around Wallace, and there will no
longer be a stop light on any of this Interstate.

SMITH: That's right. There'll probably be one heck of a
party. Wallace is noted for its great parties.

NOAH: That's kind of sad, though.

SMITH: Well, in a way, but I know when I travel, if I want
to stop, I stop, and we have built up quite a tourist
trade... I just had a couple in here a while ago having
coffee... they were just driving through and they
stopped and are spending the day looking around.
They think it's "totally charming" was the word she
used. And a family from Australia, about seven from
Australia the other day, and they are touring the
United States and the lady said this was the most
beautiful little town that they had ever seen. I thought
that was quite a comment being as they came from
across the ocean and all over.

NOAH: Thanks, Audrey Smith.

SMITH: Well, thank you so much. We appreciate your
interest. Come and see us sometime.

I suppose we should do an update interview, to find out
how things are going in Wallace, Idaho, now that Interstate
90's opened, bypassing the town. I did hear, though, that

Kellmer's Coffee Shop closed. Most of the staff went down the street to work at Sweet's Café, where the food's said to be just as good. And Audrey Smith retired—now she has more time for acting.

Thursday, June 8, Washington, D.C., 1989

On Thursdays we read some letters from listeners on the air, and I usually try to go through all the mail, helping choose the seven or eight letters from which we'll quote. The most intriguing letter today is from Joe B. Clarke, Jr., in Louisiana; it's about an interview with Ian Frazier, author of the new book called *Great Plains*. I had talked with Frazier mostly about the settlement of Nicodemus, Kansas, by blacks from Tennessee. And Mr. Clarke writes:

> Nothing remarkable here except that again you choose to deal with minorities. I have traveled all over the West and can assure you that there are many exciting and interesting things to have written and commented about except this aborted settlement by blacks. Take the matter of apartheid. You regularly beat this subject to death, quoting Tutu at every opportunity, covering every excess of the South African government. There are a lot of interesting and wonderful things going on in this world and you consistently fail to tell us very much about them. Does National Public Radio have a charter for social change?

I noticed during war in the Persian Gulf that you could divide our mail up into two equal piles, without even opening the envelopes. Half the listeners supported the war, half did not, and it would be easy to find equally divided opinions about our coverage.

I wrote an essay to close one program at the end of February, just when the war was over, mentioning that perhaps it would now be possible to notice the arrival of spring. Catherine Larson, of Eugene, Oregon, said, "I was stunned by your comments. . . . How can you be so ready to celebrate springtime in the wake of such destruction? Why are you celebrating only minutes after reporting that hundreds of soldiers were incinerated by bombs as they fled down a highway?" And Tony Doyle of Gonzales, California, wrote, "Just heard your closing thoughts on the Friday broadcast. I could only think, what a decent man, what a gentleman—I have no higher compliment to offer."

Much of the criticism of our reporting was thoughtful, detailed, and often accurate. Dennis Funnemark, of Niceville, Florida, who signed his letter as a "retired fighter pilot," complained about the way the TV networks, and NPR, covered the conflict, demonstrating, in his view, little knowledge of weapons systems and tactics, bomb-damage assessment. Mr. Funnemark wrote: "Each network has its pool of military experts and analysts who answer the questions asked, but the interviewers frequently seem to lack sufficient knowledge of the subject to ask the questions to give their audience an accurate description, or to pry out information the press keeps claiming the military is holding back."

He could have been talking about me. I know our correspondents, in Washington as well as the Gulf, were well prepared and quite conversant with weapons systems and military doctrine, but I didn't feel ready for the war, even though we had six months warning. I guess I just didn't think it was actually going to happen.

Our listeners send critiques, encouragement, songs, poetry—and when we have a contest, entire mailbags full of entries. If we forget to specify "postcards only," it's going to take somebody a day or so just to open the envelopes. The term "contest" is used quite loosely; we offer no prize other than recognition. Usually we try contests to solve a problem or provide a name for something. In December of 1980, it was this: let's make up a word that could mean "a mingling of pleasant aromas." I'd been trying to write part of a story about the island of Martha's Vineyard, off the coast of Massachusetts, trying to describe the smell of the wild roses and sea air in the early mornings. I needed a noun that didn't exist, so we had a contest.

More than two hundred new words were submitted. Eugene Ehrlich of the Oxford American Dictionary chose "osmyrrah" (oz-mur-AH). The winning neologist, Thomas Cowdry of Tucson, Arizona, explained the etymology: it comes from two Greek words, *osmee,* meaning "to smell," and *smurna,* meaning "to mingle with." The "h" on the end adds typographical balance and a sense of pleasant emotion. Cowdry demonstrated how John Milton could have used "osmyrrah" at one place in *Paradise Lost* (Milton could only think of "smell"), and then he used the word in a sentence of his own devising: "Trapped so long beneath the surface in darkness thick with sulphur fumes he winced at the brightness as they brought him forth and gasped in the osmyrrah of the living earth."

We were pleased with Thomas Cowdry's creation and encouraged listeners to use it as much as possible: Eugene Ehrilich told us that a word only gets into a dictionary after it finds common usage. We heard, then, about a restaurant in Florida called "Osmyrrah," and a dress shop using the name, and even an old lobster boat renamed the *Osmyrrah* (for the smells of the boat, rope, hot coffee, and sea air, the owner said)—but I guess we're still a long way from a lexicographer's offical notice.

Friday, June 9, Washington, D.C., 1989

The week ends with Beijing still tense. Deng Xiaoping has praised the soldiers for the actions in Tiananmen Square. I talk with Yang Gui-Lin, a Chinese student leader at Notre Dame. Yang wants President Bush to take a tougher stance with the Beijing leadership. Bush has "deplored" events

there. Yang wants Bush to "condemn" them. There are demonstrations in U.S. cities in support of China's pro-democ-
racy movement, with replicas of the Goddess of Liberty
statue that the students paraded in Tiananmen Square. The
Goddess was a symbol of freedom attacked by the government; over the next two years we were to see the icons of
tyranny falling in the name of freedom. The most spectacular—in Moscow, the statue of Feliks Dzerzhinski, the
founder of the Soviet KBG.

There's time to run an interview that I did yesterday with
Penn Jillette. Neenah and I saw Penn & Teller's show at the
National Theater. It was great fun, and some classic magic:
Teller's trick called "Shadows" is said to be one of the finest
effects ever developed in America. It's a lovely, elegant moment: a vase, a rose. The shadow of the rose is shown on a
screen . . . Teller, with a shining sharp knife, touches the
shadow of a single petal. And from the rose, the real petal
falls.

Penn Jillette comes into the studio with a can of Diet Coke
and pleasantly answers questions. He and Teller—the short
one, who doesn't use his first name and doesn't talk on
stage—have been together for about fifteen years now. They
have a magic show which is also sort of an anti-magic show:
by watching closely, you could learn how to do some simple
tricks, but you'll also see things that are wonderfully as-
tounding. Much of it is done with the help of volunteers
from the audience, and Penn Jillette believes these people
should be treated with great respect.

> JILLETTE: I mean it's really Puritan work ethic stuff, it's
> my job. . . . I'm not some sort of *king* that's there to
> push them around; I am in some sort of way, pretty
> direct way, working for them and they should be made
> to look good and comfortable and that we should do
> fake miracles for them. (*Laughs*) That's essentially our
> job.

NOAH: There's one point, though, in quite a long piece, where Teller is in water, he's holding his breath, and the volunteer from the audience, the man that I saw, couldn't get the key into the lock because it was the wrong key—did he not have the feeling, and has it happened in other cities, that Teller was going to *die* here? Did you whisper to him and say don't worry?

JILLETTE: No, I don't think you have to do that. You'd be surprised at how much they know about theater, and I think people are much more aware of the levels that are going on than you like to give them credit for. You'll find a lot of DJs—your morning DJs—saying, "Isn't Teller in a lot of danger there?" and I think that people, like when they're on a roller coaster, they get that feeling in their guts but they don't really believe they're going to die.

NOAH: What I was thinking about, it was a movie that I saw when I was a kid; we have seen Tony Curtis playing Harry Houdini not come up out of the water, the locked box down under the river.

JILLETTE: The *truth* is that Houdini never did anything even slightly dangerous; he never did anything more dangerous than sitting in his living room. Houdini was a pro and he knew that it was very important not to injure yourself. Houdini actually died being punched in the stomach by a college student—he used to have people punch him in the stomach to see how strong his stomach muscles were. And he had a college student who was coming in to interview him, and he was dozing on his couch in his dressing room, and the college student came in and punched him in the stomach while he was asleep and ruptured his appendix. He died two days later on Halloween. Which is why we have a rider on our contract that says there

should be Diet Cola beverages in the dressing room,
that Teller should have peppermint tea, and that no
college students will be allowed backstage while we're
sleeping (*laughing*). It's just an important thing, you
know, better safe than sorry.

NOAH: How do you feel about the argument that your
show is more about show business than it is about
magic and I have this feeling—you break some tenets
of show business; you mingle with the crowd during
the intermission, many of the things you do, you're not
supposed to do in the theater, yet, I feel, especially in
the end, when you sit on a darkened stage, with a
candle burning and you talk about fire-eating, which
you then do, and you talk about your respect for those
who did it for a living and did it all day long and
wound up with lighter fluid in their stomachs and
poisoning their livers, I think it's then your testament
to show business, to the theater, more than magic.

JILLETTE: The sideshow thing at the end is kind of about
show business, but it seems more important to me
than that. I mean, I remember I was about nine or ten
and I went to see the "World's Smallest Couple." Two
midgets, in a sideshow. And I walked in and they were
sitting in chairs, easy chairs, old easy chairs, and the
wife was eating an apple. They were about the age of
my parents. And they were watching TV.

Now, the TV was kind of where we were, so that they
were facing us. And as we walked in they stood up, to
show how small they were, and answered a couple of
questions and then sat down. And it was an amazing
experience. Teller often says, "The show is what we do
to give ourselves and the people an excuse to stare at
us, and each other," as we bring them up from the
audience. And that image, of that midget couple just
sitting watching TV, living just like my parents, very
similar easy chairs, just eating an apple, has always

been what show business is to me. You know, there's just the humanity of—here are other people, and treating people on stage that same way, giving people a chance to stare, is very, very important, and then *you do really cool things*, so that people have an excuse to come to the theater.

Friday, June 16, Washington, D.C., 1989

We now have two reporters, an engineer, and a producer in China. Anne Garrels, from Beijing, says the government is issuing conflicting accounts of the shootings. Our academic friend, Ross Terrill, who's still there, says it's all part of "politics as theater" in China.

There's trouble starting in the Soviet republic of Uzbekistan, between the majority Uzbeks and the minority Meskhetians. A desk assistant locates an Uzbeki expert, Bill Fierman, at the University of Tennessee. We have two desk assistants; they work long, difficult days setting up interviews. The producer says, "Find us someone in Bulgaria. I need somebody who'll criticize [or praise] the President's crime package. What about Beijing? [forgetting China's thirteen hours the other way]" Then, as just exactly the right person is located and convinced to do the interview, the producer decides there's no room in the show. The gentle people we are lucky enough to hire for these jobs are usually young and extremely overqualified. Extra languages help. And energy and patience and a confident presence on the telephone. I usually tell applicants that we're asking for two years only—after that they'll want to move on to a job where they can take time for lunch. Cadi Simon, our Foreign Editor, began as a desk assistant. Also Deidre Berger, who's now a reporter in Bonn, and Dan Morris, who works for ABC's "Nightline."

The job has gotten a bit easier over the years because

we've become so much better known. If we call the Uzbeki
expert in Knoxville, chances are he's a listener, pleased to be
called, and helpful. I no longer hear the desk assistants trying to explain who we are ("well, it's sort of like Public Television").

There's a classic Desk Assistant's Worst Fear story: An
ATC host, Sanford Ungar, went into studio five prepared to
tape an interview about tractors in the Soviet Union. He was
connected with our New York studio; a cellist was waiting
there to be interviewed by someone else at NPR Washington. Sandy starting talking with the cellist about New York
and the weather and then about tractors in general and Soviet tractors specifically: the cellist, believing the host was
joking, then pretended to know a thing or two about agriculture and the conversation continued, until Sandy was
forced to ask, "Are we talking about the same thing here?"

There's time today on the program for an interview with
Tess Gallagher, Raymond Carver's widow. She's edited a new
collection of his poetry. We talked a few weeks ago when she
was in New York. It was a long, quiet conversation about her
husband, and his dying, and the new book. I've been editing
the interview in my office, trying to bring the length down
to about ten minutes. It's pleasant work: I like the honesty
and amusement in her voice. The original interview was
about twenty minutes long. (The interview with Penn Jillette was six minutes out of twenty-five.) Real time, real conversation, is not very interesting on the radio, and in theory,
we allow each interview to find its own ideal aesthetic
length. In this case, we actually did. Only a few ATC interviews are live. Some are taped and heard at virtually their
original length, but most are edited by between 30 and 50
percent.

NOAH: Raymond Carver died last August of lung cancer
at a time when he was being celebrated as one of
America's finest writers. he is best known for his short
stories, but he turned to poetry for the last work of his

life. The collection of poems entitled *A New Path to the Waterfall,* published this week, was mostly written when Carver knew he was dying, and that was a time shared almost in seclusion with Tess Gallagher, his wife, at their home in Port Angeles, Washington. And both Gallagher and Carver began then to reread the stories of Anton Chekhov, and some of their favorite passages have been included in this new book. Tess Gallagher explains:

GALLAGHER: We saw that there was a kind of tonal element that Chekhov was providing if we used these sections next to his poems, it gave the book another kind of dimension, so that there was this time dimension of the time of troikas and bull's-blood soup, and so on, that kind of thing coming into contact with Ray's poems. The brutalities of childhood in a working-class family, this alcoholic experience he had had, fighting alcoholism for ten years and that having been a part of what destroyed his first marriage.

NOAH: There's a wonderful story in the Introduction about the thought that perhaps there would be too much Chekhov in the book and it would be too much borrowing from someone else's art. It's a story about Tchaikovsky as regards Beethoven. Would you tell that story?

GALLAGHER: Yes. We were watching television one night and these two composers were on the television set, and they were talking about this and saying that Tchaikovsky had lifted huge passages of Beethoven, just taken them, and incorporated them into his work, and there was this question of how could he do this, and Tchaikovsky had said, well, I love him, therefore I have a right. And Ray took notes on this—I saw him write it down on a piece of paper—and I found it later in his desk. I think that he also was exercising the

right of love, because he had been so fully involved
with Chekhov's work. And there's a lot made of Ray's
connection to Hemingway, but he was far closer to
Chekhov, I think.

NOAH: Would you read please the Chekhov passage on
page 93?

GALLAGHER:

> FIVE O'CLOCK IN THE MORNING
>
> As he passed his father's room, he glanced in at the door.
> Yevgraf Ivanovich, who had not taken off his clothes or
> gone to bed, was standing by the window, drumming on
> the panes.
> "Goodbye, I am going," said his son.
> "Goodbye . . . the money is on the round table," his fa-
> ther answered, without turning around.
> A cold, hateful rain was falling as the laborer drove
> him to the station. . . . The grass seemed darker than ever.

NOAH: And "Hummingbird," on [page] 96. I think of them
together, in a way.

GALLAGHER:

> HUMMINGBIRD, for Tess
> *Suppose I say summer,*
> *write the word "hummingbird,"*
> *put it in an envelope,*
> *take it down the hill*
> *to the box. When you open*
> *my letter you will recall*
> *those days and how much,*
> *just how much, I love you.*

NOAH: That's wonderful. There is on . . . the beginning of
one part of the book a quotation from Robert Lowell,
which says, "Yet why not say what happened," and I
don't know really what is meant by that, but to me it
means, this is a very honest year that you and Ray

spent with his dying and with the poetry, and is that what's meant by that Lowell quotation?

GALLAGHER: I think one of the pleasures Ray had in his poetry was working so close to the life that you really ... there's just a very thin membrane separating life and art. And the "Why not say what happened," when Ray was telling me that he'd discovered this line, he said, he sort of misquoted it, he said, "Why not say what really happened," and he added that word "really," so that sense of art and life coinciding, and yet of course we know that the art did inflect the life.

NOAH: And too, so often people ... I can't think of other examples of people writing about the ... knowing it is the last year of their life and actually confronting it, not denying it, and going ahead and writing about it.

GALLAGHER: That's right. And he covers the whole range of the experience, you know, even from hearing the news from the doctor and then that assessment of the past in that poem "Gravy," which was published in *The New Yorker* shortly after his death. He talks about our marriage, which is one of the things we decided, we had been together eleven years in a relationship which was very close and we finally decided on June 17 to get married.

PROPOSAL

I ask her and then she asks me. We each
accept. There's no back and forth about it. After nearly eleven years
together, we know our minds and more. And this postponement, it's
ripened too. Makes sense now. I suppose we should be
in a rose-filled garden or at least on a beautiful cliff overhanging
the sea, but we're on the couch, the one where sleep
sometimes catches us with our books open, or
some old Bette Davis movie unspools
in glamorous black and white—flames in the fireplace dancing
menacingly in the background as she ascends the marble

staircase with a sweet little snub-nosed
revolver, intending to snuff her ex-lover, the fur coat
he bought her draped loosely over her shoulders. Oh lovely, oh lethal
entanglements. In such a world
to be true.

A few days back some things got clear
about there not being all those years ahead we'd kept
assuming. The doctor going on finally about "the shell" I'd be
leaving behind, doing his best to steer us away from the veil of
tears and foreboding. "But he loves his life," I heard a voice say.
Hers. And the young doctor, hardly skipping a beat, "I know.
I guess you have to go through those seven stages. But you end
up in acceptance."

After that we went to lunch in a little café we'd never
been in before. She had pastrami. I had soup. A lot
of other people were having lunch too. Luckily
nobody we knew. We had plans to make, time pressing down
on us like a vise, squeezing out hope to make room for
the everlasting—that word making me want to shout, "Is there
an Egyptian in the house?"

Back home we held onto each other and, without
embarrassment or caginess, let it all reach full meaning. This
was it, so any holding back had to be stupid, had to be
insane and meager. How many ever get to this? I thought
at the time. It's not far from here to needing
a celebration, a joining, a bringing of friends into it,
a handing out of champagne and
Perrier. "Reno," I said. "Let's go to Reno and get married" . . .

Raymond Carver goes on in the poem to describe their
wedding; Tess had a green cotton dress he'd bought for her
in Bath. "Proposal" is as open and honest as poetry is likely
to get, and Tess's reading is clear, without affectation. I
interviewed Carver a few years ago—we talked about short

stories and his earlier problems with drinking—and once we spoke briefly at a party in Minneapolis, the year before his death. I wish I had known him better.

Tuesday, June 20, Washington, D.C., 1989

Discussions today about Fang Lizhi, the astrophysicist and China's best-known dissident, who entered the U.S. Embassy when the crackdown started in Beijing. My co-host Linda Wertheimer and I decide to start a campaign to make sure that Li Shuxian receives better attention in these stories. If she is mentioned, the news copy usually reads: "Fang Lizhi and his wife, Li Shuxian, a well-known dissident in her own right."

And an interview about mule diving. It's another "critter story," as someone on our staff started calling them, just a good conversation with a laconic judge out in Iowa. We've developed attitudes about certain categories of stories. Fires, beloved by TV news, are almost impossible for us to cover. Floods are tough, and generally we stay away from weather stories altogether. When a plane goes down we do our best to report what happened, and then stay with the safety issues of the crash. All of us like the "boy-returns-cash-refuses-reward" stories, and the interviews with triumphant survivors—the very best radio is when all we have to do is ask, "And then what happened?" During his time producing the program, Neal Conan developed a way to evaluate the potential of any story. He wants to have something going on. "Where's the tension?" he'll say. A child rescued from a well in Arkansas is a great story, but a child who is still down in that well is a better one. A city council argument about a ban on handgun sales is far more interesting in its unresolved state.

Here's a story I didn't get on the air, didn't even bring it up:

I guess the tension was all out of that story, and probably the mule-diving story as well. A judge had already ruled that the diving mule act at the All-Iowa Fair could continue—the Humane Society had wanted the court to stop it. Actually, it was a pony and two mules and a dog, jumping thirty feet down into a pool of water. Linn County Judge William Eads said he had some serious personal reservations about this kind of entertainment but didn't have a legal reason to stop it. He didn't see the act in person—he watched videotapes instead.

NOAH: Well, what was the logic that you were using, was it indeed that you said, that you'd never seen a mule that you could make do something that it didn't want to do?

JUDGE EADS: There was evidence of that, I didn't say it, but there was expert witnesses who testified that they were stubborn and could not be made to dive if they didn't want to. They simply didn't prove their case that there was cruelty to the mule. When they jumped, they got right out and seemed to be none the worse for wear. When you kind of think of it, I suppose that the alternative wouldn't be very good for the mules, they're not going to keep them as pets. If they couldn't dive, I suppose it would be the glue factory or fertilizer plant as possible alternatives.

NOAH: Yeah, no way the mules, though, could use that information as part of their decision-making process.

JUDGE EADS (*laughs*): No, they couldn't.

NOAH: Have you talked with any of the local Humane Society people; are they disappointed with the ruling?

JUDGE EADS: The president of the Humane Society that brought the action said he thought it was a fair decision.

NOAH: Judge Eads, if you felt that indeed it was a mindless activity, why wouldn't you just take advantage of the opportunity to say, why do this at a fair, why have animals do these strange things, jumping off a diving board into six feet of water?

JUDGE EADS: Well, I can't force my taste onto the general public. Judges are not to be doing that sort of thing, it's either legal or illegal. Or its illegality has not been proven. If we got rid of every mindless activity, there probably wouldn't be enough judges in the country to adjudicate all the cases involving them.

Thursday, June 22, Washington, D.C., 1989

I had more than a moment's hesitation about an interview with a young artist. You could hear it as good public relations for the Chinese government—Wang Yani's trip was officially sanctioned by Beijing; she has exhibitions scheduled in Washington, D.C., Kansas City, and San Francisco. Her permission to travel was not withdrawn. But she's a wonderful artist, only fourteen years old, and the events in Tiananmen Square are far away from her world. Wang Yani lives close to the Li River in the Guangxi Province in southern China. She began painting at age two, working with watercolors and large brushes on paper scrolls on the floor.

Also today an interview with Michael Smith, from the BBC studios in London. I've interviewed Michael before, about his music, especially a song he wrote called "The Dutchman," the story of an elderly couple in Amsterdam, and he sang the song on one of our "Good Evening" programs from the World Theater in Saint Paul, broadcast

every Saturday during 1988. I'd been asked to come to Minnesota to design a program that would replace Garrison
Keillor's "A Prairie Home Companion," same time period,
same theater. It was a great chance to work with actors and
storytellers, singers, musicians, and to be on stage with nine
hundred and fifty people in the audience and thousands
listening at home—and to begin to understand the special
feeling of absolute communication that a performance can
sometimes achieve. When Michael Smith played the opening notes of "The Dutchman" on his guitar, the audience
became still, many knew the song, remembered the story of
the retired sea captain whose mind was now failing, recalled
the chorus, "Let us go to the banks of the ocean / where the
walls rise above the Zuider Zee / Long ago I used to be a
young man / and dear Margaret remembers that for me." I
was standing just off stage; something quite powerful was
happening. The audience lost itself in emotion, both sadness
and joy. Michael told me later that he felt himself floating
out into the theater during the song, becoming a part of
memories in the dark. When "The Dutchman" was over,
there was hardly any applause, it would have broken the
mood.

I've always had much the same reaction to the McGarri-
gles' "Talk to Me of Mendicino"—I always want to cry, and
certainly did when Kate and Anna came down from Canada
to sing on "Good Evening." And once I saw perhaps hundreds crying in the audience. We booked the Bulgarian
State Radio and Television Female Vocal Choir. They had a
surprising hit record, *Le Mystère des Voix Bulgares,* and
came through Saint Paul on a U.S. tour. We introduced
them with what's known in theater as a "reveal." We normally didn't use the curtain on our program, performers
just walked right out on stage. But for the Bulgarian Choir
we closed the curtain before they were introduced, and they
started singing in full, resounding voice as they were revealed, twenty strong women from Bulgaria, all wearing the
vivid costumes of their home provinces. There was an over-

whelming glory and beauty to this that *hit* the audience, and many were immediately in tears. I heard Mickey Hart, The Grateful Dead's drummer, talking once on "Morning Edition" about The Dead concerts and the special moment "when the magic goes down." The band would wait for it, and then, "Here it is again, the dragon's coming out."

And these must also be the moments that keep performers going when they don't seem to be actually getting anywhere. Michael Smith had been in and out of music as a career and was working as an accountant in Chicago when the Steppenwolf Theatre Company asked him to help with *The Grapes of Wrath*, the stage adaptation of John Steinbeck's story of the Dust Bowl and the Depression. The production began in Chicago, then moved to San Diego's La Jolla Playhouse and last night opened with the original American cast at London's National Theatre. Michael's the play's musical director and sings most of the songs; he's on stage with three other musicians.

The play was an opening-night hit in London.

> SMITH: It went wonderfully. Folks were very, very
> emotionally involved and they stood up at the end.
> This lady I talked to who had been going to the
> National Theatre for twenty years said this is the first
> time she'd ever seen a standing ovation. I pride myself
> on trying to keep away from that sort of thing, but I
> was really entranced by the way they reacted.

I was happy we were on radio—you could hear the excitement and pride in Michael's voice as he told us about the party after the performance and the reviews in the morning papers. All this of course would happen again for the cast of *The Grapes of Wrath*, as the play opened on Broadway the following year.

Usually it's a mistake to try to interview performers right after a play or a concert—they're too charged up, too easily distracted. It's also impossible to find a quiet place back-

stage. The absolute worst deal is the dressing room at the
intermission of a two-show performance. I got stuck with
Randy Newman in just this situation. We had spent months
trying to set up an interview and this was the best his record company would offer. Sometimes the PR people can be
tough, acting as if they're paid to keep people away. I knew
the between-show interview wouldn't work, but I stopped
by anyway. Turns out Randy Newman is fond of NPR and
would have been happy to come to our studio for an interview. "Why didn't you call?" he said.

We usually try to interview musicians the day after the
concert, around noon so they have a chance to wake up.
They stop by our studio, have some coffee, talk for a while.
Just please don't ask them to sing, thank you—it's a conversation, not a performance.

Wednesday, July 5, Washington, D.C., 1989

An interview today with John Jerome, a writer I've long
admired. Although we've talked before, I've not met
Jerome—as they say back in Kentucky, "we've howdied but
we haven't shook." For this conversation, he's in the studio
at one of our member stations in Massachusetts.

My favorite literature is contemporary nonfiction, books
that explain things: Verlyn Klinkenborg's *Making Hay,*
Tracy Kidder's *House,* Gretel Ehrlich's stories about ranching in Wyoming, *The Solace of Open Spaces.* I think the
books make good interviews—the audience learns something, as new subjects open up in appealing ways (fiction on
the other hand can be frustrating, as the conversation tends
to be about people the listener doesn't know or have any
reason yet to care about).

John Jerome is attracted to matters of competency and
learning—he just needs one good idea every other year or so,
and he usually finds it. He wrote a whole book about fixing

up a 1950 blue Dodge pickup truck. He's written about mountains (on mountain climbing, which began in Britain: "The English have a long history of inventing new games, teaching them to foreigners, then getting soundly whipped at them") and skiing, and—how far into middle age can you continue to improve as a swimmer? All my Jerome books are full of underlined sentences, and now I'm learning about the building of stone walls. *Stone Work: Reflections on Serious Play and Aspects of Country Life* is the title, and for most of the book John Jerome is in the fields near his home in western Massachusetts trying to figure it all out. There's only one piece of instruction usually offered to the beginner.

JEROME: You want to overlap the stones as you see in any brickwork, so the gap between any two stones is being covered by a solid stone above, and the economical, New England way of saying that is "one stone on two, two stones on one." If you put two stones on the ground, then you put one stone to cover the gap over those two. Then if you put three stones on the ground, two stones cover those gaps, then you'll need three on top, and so on.

NOAH: Now that turns out to be about the only practical advice you can get out of a book or even talking with people there.

JEROME: Yeah, they tell you things like string out strings to keep your lines straight and how deep to make the footings and that sort of thing, but basically the advice is: "Don't hurt your back." (*Laughs*)

NOAH: You met, worked a bit with a stonemason named Linda Mason. Her advice was not to talk about it too much. It's as if it's somehow metaphysical.

JEROME: She didn't actually say that. I just couldn't get her to talk about it. I kept expecting her to lay some

profundity on me about this elemental process we
were going through and she just didn't seem very
interested in talking about it. What you're thinking
about the whole time is the shapes of the stones, and
there isn't language to describe that adequately. You're
not going to sit around saying, well I had one that was
kind of oblong on one end and flat here and . . . it
doesn't support a great deal of conversation.

NOAH: Did you find stone fences back in the woods and
wonder about them, almost as if they contained a
presence of the person who put them together?

JEROME: Oh, definitely so. I happened to be fortunate
enough to have walls on my land back in the woods
that were serving no useful purpose, and when I saw
stones that really fit together well, when I saw a neat
piece of work, you know, it would roll my eyes back in
my head at the workmanship that was going on. Also,
there happens to be one wall on my land that goes
straight down the fall line of a steep slope, and I
discovered that after I had tried to dismantle another
wall that was on a milder slope and I found out how
much trouble it was to work on a side hill, how much
harder it made it to get the stones off the wall and into
the wagon and get the wagon parked and get . . .
everything's trying to get away from you all the time;
the work is three or four times harder if there's any
slope at all. And these guys somewhere back there, a
hundred and fifty years ago, had built one right down
the fall line of a very steep slope. It broke my heart to
see it, thinking of the labor that went into it. It's just
so much harder.

NOAH: You describe the physical pleasure, and it's
pleasurable in other ways, too. One would be the time
when you first pry up a big heavy stone from the
ground, when it just begins to move, and the second is

when it is going into place, when you're lowering it into place and you sort of like to drop it so it will have a percussive effect. Why is that?

JEROME: Well, in the first place, you drop it so you don't smash your fingers. But, yeah, if you're trying to get loose a big stone, the first time you get it to move and you realize, yes, you are going to be able to move it, because if you can budge the thing at all, eventually with rollers and pry bars and so forth you can get it where you want to ... there's a great breakthrough there, but it doesn't compare with the satisfaction of having it fit snugly into place. Of course, they very seldom do, and then that means you pick it up and move it a little bit and pick it up and move it a little bit—that's where it gets tedious.

Thursday, July 6, Virginia, 1989,

Up at 5:00 A.M. for a trip down to Virginia to cover the United Mine Workers' strike against the Pittston Coal Group. I'll meet Melissa Block, a producer, at National Airport. I've been promising myself to stop taking these early morning flights out on assignments. I never can sleep the night before, worried about missing the flight, worried about the next day's interviews.

The Washington Post has a story about the UMW's Fourth of July rally down in Saint Paul, Virginia. Cesar Chavez came to speak. It rained; they had five thousand people, they were hoping for fifteen thousand. Coal miners in Alabama, Tennessee, Pennsylvania, Ohio, Indiana, and Kentucky have joined in wildcat sympathy strikes over the past month, and many of them came to Virginia for the rally. It was an important event and could have been interesting to cover, but it would have meant working over the holiday

and I felt like I needed the time off. Also, we would have
recorded the music at the rally, including the labor songs,
and then we'd be tempted to use some of it in our story. I've
been, I think, guilty in the past of romanticizing the people
I've talked with in Appalachia, especially the miners and
their families. They speak in their harsh and lovely accents;
I write some copy about the mist coming in over the mountains as it gets dark, then we play some lonesome-sounding
music that fades out as the story ends. Sometimes crickets
chirping.

Once, several years ago, I almost gave up trying to do any
reporting in the mountains; I went to Letcher County in
East Kentucky to do a story for "All Things Considered"
about depressed conditions in the coal fields, and I met a
twenty-four-year-old out-of-work miner, talked with him at
his house one afternoon outside of Whitesburg. We stood in
the yard and talked about the weather for a while, then he
took me in the front room and asked his family to all stand
up so I could see them. His wife, their three kids, his wife's
father bent and ill with black lung disease. The young man
said, "This is why I'm a coal miner, this is my family. And
that's all I ask, is a chance to work." I left the house and left
the county and the story behind, saddened by this moment
of absolute honesty. And I recall, too, the stories from this
area during the War on Poverty in the 1960s. The reporters
and TV crews would go into the mountains for a day or so to
"get some poverty stuff." In 1967 a Canadian filmmaker was
killed in Letcher County, at a settlement called Jeremiah.
He had been photographing some poor families and their
houses; the landowner arrived and started shooting.

I'm determined this time to bring back just a straightfor-
ward story of the coal strike. I did notice later, though, that
the word "mist" found its way into my script. It's one of my
overused words. Also, it was our private joke that we were
going to call this story "Guerrillas in the Mist," because of
the striking miners in their camouflage clothing.

highway sounds

NOAH: I went looking for the coal strike last week, drove
up into Wise County from the airport. The hills got
higher, the valleys more narrow. I began to see the
signs in gas stations, grocery stories—signs in support
of the United Mine Workers.

We passed through Banner and Coeburn and Saint
Paul, turning north in Russell County on State
Highway 63, which runs alongside the railroad tracks.
And every few miles or so you'd see the coal
communities, about ten or fifteen small frame houses,
side by side, some abandoned, some nicely painted,
white, light green, with gardens out back. These once
were company houses, close by the company general
store and the post office.

Our first interview, in the parking lot of the store at Dante,
was so good that I thought later we should have just turned
around and gone back to Washington and used the full
eight minutes on the air. I had just asked Thermon Sproles
for directions, showing him my map, and he said, "Now
honey, I don't need no map to tell you how to get over to
Carbo." Men around here will often call younger men
"honey."

Sproles signed up with the union in 1942.

SPROLES: Before we got organized labor, I went out to
work on many a morning at six-thirty or six o'clock,
and I'd be there at nine o'clock that night, still running
coal through the cleaning plant and get paid for eight
hours, $3.60 for eight hours.

And I shook 'em up good back in March down here
in Haysi—they organized this here Ladies Auxiliary,
you know, union auxiliary? That's the nicest thing
that ever happened. But some of the men made the

remark that their wife wasn't going to get on that
picket line, wasn't going to go out and show their
ignorance, so I burnt them up in the union meeting.
Said if my wife was here, she'd be right by the side of
me.

The part of the interview that we used on the air was fine,
his comments about the union—but here's something he
said that we didn't use and I can't forget. He was talking
about his wife, who died in 1987, on his birthday:

I was seventy-two years old on the fourteenth of January
and I seen the biggest snow I ever seen in my life. I had
thirty inches of snow. My yard's as level as that road, and it
was thirty inches deep. About nine-thirty that morning,
called the hospital my daughter did. Said, well your mother
seems to be all right. Said, she eat a pretty fair breakfast.
They had her in ICU. She was a diabetic. And twenty 'til
four the phone rung, and I's in the basement and when my
daughter answered the phone I just picked it up. I had one
in the basement where I could keep in contact with my
wife because she's blind you see and I had to stay pretty
close. So if I's out in the yard or in the basement
somewhere and she needed something she'd just dial
through her number onto my number and get ahold of me.
So when the phone rung I picked it up and it said she went
into cardiac arrest and they couldn't bring her out of it.
And if she had lived until the twenty-fourth day of June
we'd've been married fifty-three years.

Thermon Sproles talked fast, and you could hear the
melodies of England and Scotland in his voice. I have to be
careful in this part of the country, that I don't slide back
into my own native accent. I'm from East Kentucky, and
years ago lost what I now consider to be too much of my
Appalachian way of speaking. I grew up pronouncing the
letters "i" and "o" as "a's." I would say "far tar," for example,

instead of "fire tower." Most of this accent went away during
my first year in radio, on WIRO, Ironton, Ohio. Or as I used to
say, "Arntn, Ohia." Young people going into radio and television should be encouraged to sound as if they actually come
from someplace; you can still hear North Carolina in Charles
Kuralt's voice or Texas when you listen to Bill Moyers. And
consider Fiona Ritchie. Born in Scotland, she came to Charlotte, North Carolina, as an exchange student. She liked the
sound of WFAE; she thought she might want to volunteer,
perhaps she could be on the air, maybe she was even dreaming of her own radio program. The station manager said,
"But my dear, with your accent you'll never get on the air
here." She persevered: "The Thistle and Shamrock," her program featuring Celtic music, is now carried by 240 public
stations.

When Garrison Keillor's "A Prairie Home Companion"
was offered to National Public Radio—it had been broadcast
in Minnesota for ten years—Frank Mankiewicz, then NPR's
president, said, after listening to the sample programs, "No,
it's too provincial." The people in Minnesota said, "We think
it's worthy of a national audience, we'll distribute it ourselves, we'll put together a network." "A Prairie Home Companion" became a phenomenal success, and American Public Radio became NPR's chief competitor. (Mankiewicz is
now an executive with Hill & Knowlton, usually referred to
as a "high-powered Washington public relations firm.")

We spend the afternoon talking with striking workers, and
union supporters, and watching the state police try to help
the coal trucks—with nonunion drivers—get through.

people by the road chanting: U-M-W-A

NOAH: Maybe seventy-five men and women wearing
camouflage jackets and T-shirts and hats are standing
as close to the road as possible, being kept back by the
state police, and the police have the traffic blocked
both ways.

yelling, horns honking

MAN DESCRIBING SCENE: I'd say they're probably going to bring scab trucks through.

ANOTHER MAN YELLS: They'll never break this union. We're a hundred years old next year—they'll never break this union.

AND ANOTHER MAN: This is just like a month ago with China when all the students got killed. The only difference here is they haven't used their weapons yet, but they've got them on.

NOAH: The miners are frustrated, having to stay out of the road. Early in the strike they were sitting down in front of the nonunion coal trucks and being arrested, two thousand of them. Then they've been trying rolling roadblocks; they get on the narrow roads and drive as slowly as they can in both lanes. They've been arrested for that, too. At the moment, all they're doing is yelling as the trucks go through.

MINER: Go ahead scab, come on through scab. Come on scab, come on.

NOAH: A convoy of coal trucks goes on past—you can hardly see the drivers. Sheets of Plexiglas cover all the windows of the trucks to protect against rocks and worse, but the miners seem to be more angered by the state police and the Pittston security cars that are escorting the coal trucks. They raise their arms in a Nazi salute as the police pull out.

And in the evening we drive up into the hills to find one of the miners' camps. It resembles a bluegrass festival—families have come from several states with pickup campers and tents; they're sitting out in lawn chairs, gathering around campfires. But no one's having any fun. Melissa and I wander about trying to find someone to interview. "We don't trust the media," they say. "Just go on and write whatever you want," someone says.

I've never heard striking union members react this way, but I think it's mostly because we've come into their territory, at night. They're making plans for tomorrow morning; one miner does tell us to be sure and be out on the roads early, as if to suggest there'll be some action.

It's eleven o'clock when we have supper at the Pizza Hut in Coeburn. The food's good—the *Batman* music's too loud on the speakers. At the Holiday Inn in Norton, we notice that a state policeman is standing guard outside, and we drive around the parking lot slowly and count twenty-five or thirty police cars, most of them unmarked, heavy, gray four-door sedans with blackwall tires and extra antennas. We see the policemen at breakfast, out of uniform, four of them more than filling a booth. In journalism you do perhaps notice more things—it's like those magazine features when you were a kid, "What's Wrong with This Picture?"— but you're also more paranoid, and I tend to be melodramatic, overinterpreting what I see. Not too much wrong with this unless you let it get on the air. Many of my suspicions while working on stories in the past have involved guns: could those guys in the car following us too close have a shotgun? Is there really somebody behind that tree with a rifle? Do you think he's got a pistol in the next room and is he really mad at us?

Friday, July 7, Virginia, 1989

bell ringing

NOAH: This bell was saved from an old church in the area. It stands now out in front of the Binns-Counts Community Center on Route 63. The center is a gathering place for the strike; the miners from out of

state coming by for breakfast and lunch and supper.
The food's donated—it's cooked by the Ladies
Auxiliary.

The Reverend Donald Prange took some time to talk with
us. He's a Lutheran pastor and has worked as a community
organizer in Appalachia since the early seventies. He says
the people in the area are becoming empowered by the
strike, standing against the coal company.

REV. PRANGE: Just the fact that there are people who are
in this one community center who've never been in
this community center before. In fact, there are times
when people were even suspicious of this particular
community center because they knew it was
church-related in some way, but it didn't somehow fit
church as church was understood. But there's a greater
understanding of what's going on—

sirens in distance, getting louder

REV. PRANGE: It sounds like the boys are coming.

NOAH: Word comes back down Route 63 that a miner on
the picket line has been hit by a coal truck. Other
versions of that story circulate around the county for
days.

When I was trying to write this story back in Washington,
I kept thinking of the civil war in El Salvador: the rebel
soldiers out in the hills, the army setting up roadblocks,
outside economic forces at work. I mentioned this to a couple of people. They frowned, and they were right—the anal-
ogy was inept; many, many people have died in El Salvador,
and I've never been there, don't have any idea what it's like.
One paragraph of the coal story, though, did result from the
imagery.

NOAH: There is an intensity about this strike in the coalfields. It's in the air, like mist from the mountains at night. The out-of-state miners sleeping in tents in their camp up on the ridge, wondering about their own jobs at home. The coal company wondering about the union. The striking miners wondering about the security force the company has hired, and the state police, who must feel they are caught in the middle; and the nonunion miners, replacement workers, called scabs, who have crossed the picket lines to work, are wondering about everybody.

As it turned out, it was a reasonably quiet day. About the same number of arrests, for driving too slow on the roads. We stayed around the community center for a while, talking with the volunteers, accepting coffee but saying no to ham biscuits and Krispy Kreme doughnuts. Melissa finds a phone and finally is able to arrange a time to talk with a replacement worker. When you're covering a strike, it's important to interview someone who chooses to cross the picket line; but they've got a lot to lose by talking with you, and trust is hard to establish. Melissa has talked with Billy Adams several times—she'd been calling from Washington—and now he agrees to give us directions to his house. Field producers must get tired of the telephoning—sometimes more than a hundred calls for a story, only a few of them really productive. Some NPR producers like to travel with a cellular phone—calling from the car, or trying to set up the next interview while the current one is being taped.

Billy Adams is getting ready to go out to work; two of his friends come by to pick him up—all three will work double shifts, sixteen hours—he wants to leave his car in the driveway so it'll look like he's home. He says dynamite's gone off in his yard, and his car's been shot at. He has an arsenal in the house now; never even had a gun before. He comes home from the mines usually about one o'clock in the morning and sits up in the front room with a rifle, waiting for first

light. Billy Adams tells us something that later we decide
not to use on the air: "I aim to shoot to kill."

As Adams talks with us, his wife stays with the kids in the
kitchen. He has thought through the issues of the strike;
he's read the contract that the union turned down, thinks
the union is wrong, but mostly he just wants to work, and
now he's caught up in it, as people are choosing sides.

> ADAMS: I've got good friends that are standing there with
> picket signs and yes, it's broke this community up.
> Some of my wife's friends, and some of our friends
> have, you know, chose to shun us and give us a rough
> time because they think the UMWA is being so
> mistreated, this, that and the other. I've even run into
> situations where I know people that have never
> worked in the mines, would never work in the mines,
> have never been affiliated with the union, they don't
> really know what's going on, but just because of the
> fact that, you know, if they can put a little camouflage
> streamer on their antenna or camouflaged hat or
> something like that, people come around and pat them
> on the back and say, you're fightin' for what's right.
>
> Kind of reminds you of what went on in the sixties, a
> lot of people really didn't know the issues of what was
> going on with Vietnam, but anybody that was willing
> to walk up, put a pair of bluejeans on and a peace sign,
> he was cool. He was took right in. It's the same thing
> around here now with camouflage. It don't matter if
> ninety percent of those people over there on the picket
> lines never did like you before, if you'll come over
> there with them now, they'll like you.

Our last interview is with Mike Odom, president of Pittston Coal. During the strike, he's been holding a news conference every day at two o'clock. Five reporters join him in a
Pittson conference room. He's in a good mood, joking, wearing a white shirt with no tie, glasses, he's about forty years

old. I have some extra questions after the others leave, and I'm just a little apprehensive. I've heard that Odom didn't like a previous NPR report on the strike. But he's not at all difficult to talk with, as he outlines Pittston's position on the labor issues, and explains that people don't understand how hard it is to compete in an international coal market.

We get to the airport in plenty of time, and during a change of planes in Charlotte I find, surprisingly, a copy of the new *People* magazine. In Washington, *People* isn't on sale until Mondays, and it's one of the magazines I feel I have to read, so I'm ahead of the game by the time we land at National.

Those of us in the news business are our own best customers. I read *Time* and *Newsweek* at the office on Mondays. Sometimes *U.S. News & World Report, The Economist, The Progressive, Business Week, Advertising Age*. In the mail at home: *Sports Illustrated* (I've been reading it since 1956), *Premiere, Outside, Esquire, GQ, New York, The New Yorker, The Village Voice, Rolling Stone,* and *Columbia Journalism Review*. Also *Entertainment Weekly*, which is doing well after a shaky start.

My favorite magazine is *Musician*. The articles can be highly technical but I don't need to understand everything in life. I like going to see Chris Isaak in concert, and then later reading what he's said about his 1950s and 1960s-influenced music: "I think people relate my stuff to that era because my vocals are on top of the mix and there's a real clear sound to Jimmy's guitar. I like the big notes and Jimmy [Wilsey] likes to bend and twang." I also like learning, for some reason, that Isaak uses "Gibson L-5 and J-200 guitars, strung with medium-gauge Ernie Ball strings and played with .73 Jim Dunlop Tortex picks through a Fender Twin Reverb amp." On the fifteenth anniversary of the magazine a contributing editor declared, while explaining why the name was *Musician* rather than *Music* magazine, "Why? Because musicians are interesting and everything else is boring. Well, okay. Music is intensely interesting when listened to. When written about, it is boring."

This may be true for music, but certainly not for baseball. Think of Roger Angell's spring recountings of the previous World Series in *The New Yorker,* intensely interesting writing about the game, not the players.

I don't have much musical ability, but I do have a good ear. One time, late at night, Ronee Blakely asked me to sing to her. She's Juilliard-trained, the star of the movie *Nashville,* and was in Washington appearing at The Cellar Door. She came by for an interview and I went to see her show, and afterwards she said, "I'll bet you can sing. You have such a nice voice." "No, I can't sing," I said. "Absolutely not." But she insisted and put a quarter in the jukebox and played "Hey Nineteen," by Steely Dan, and I sang along for a verse and then a chorus and Ronee stopped me and said, "You were right. You can't sing."

And I've even proven that on "All Things Considered." I had been working on some stories in New York and found time to stop by a recording studio for a quick feature on "sing-it-yourself" music. You provide the vocal. The instrumental tracks are already recorded; you simply sing along, and for fifty dollars you walk out with a cassette to give to your girlfriend or send to your mother. I sang the Eagles' "Take It to the Limit." Someone told me later it was a tough song even for the Eagles' Glenn Frey to sing, and it was impossible for me. Laughable. I brought the finished version back to Washington and played it for Susan Stamberg in our studio, recording her reaction. Then we put that tape on the air. It was painfully embarrassing but I have to admit it was funny. There was also a serious response from listeners. Letters saying, "I was getting ready to drop out of law school and we were thinking about getting a divorce but if you have the courage to stand in that studio and sing that song and play it for Susan on the radio, then I know we can do anything we really set our minds to." Hundreds of letters came in, far more than for any news story I've done.

I'm lucky to be working for a program that pays attention

to music and literature and sports, as well as news. It means I can read as much and as widely as I want to without feeling guilty. I've always read a lot of magazines, even years ago when I was doing construction work, although I couldn't afford subscriptions then and had to find most of them in the library. In terms of what you need to know for "All Things Considered," you'll use only about one hundredth of a week's reading. But it's a crucial one hundreth, and you never know which one it's going to be.

NPR is often accused of being "East Coast–centric," having a bias toward the news from Washington, New York, Boston. I think that's true, but it's by circumstance, not by design or philosophy. We know we have to work harder to find stories out in the country—it's easy just to stay in the East Coast big-media vortex, chasing the news around the world and around the clock. We watch ABC's "Nightline," *The Washington Post* listens to "All Things Considered," the MacNeil/ Lehrer NewsHour people read *The Wall Street Journal . . .* and the rest of the world goes by. I read the *Post* and *The New York Times* at home and *USA Today* on the subway ride into work. Then I'll search through the regional wire stories on the computer. My favorite interviews are with people in Kansas, or Colorado, any state people who are doing interesting, important things, making a real difference in their community, who don't know who you are and who couldn't care less about being on the radio. In Washington we deal with "professional talkers," members of Congress or think-tank or trade association people. This is efficient but frustrating, and it's easy to miss the real stories out in the country.

A small wire-service item some years ago turned into a half-hour report for us because we were able to spend some time following it up. A young couple had been arrested at a religious commune called Stonegate, in West Virginia, and charged with manslaughter in the death of their two-year-old son. The boy had been spanked for hours, he'd gone into shock, and was dead by the time he was taken to the emer-

gency room. We sent a producer out to Charlestown, West
Virginia, to do some research and to get to know some people in the community, and when I arrived on the weekend
we were able to go into the Stonegate commune and interview many of the members, and Dot McClellan, the group's
leader and founder.

They all said the death had been an accident, but that
they did believe a child must be taught to be obedient to his
parents if he is to grow up and be obedient to God. In this
case, the boy was being disciplined and he refused to say he
was sorry. Most of the young people in the group had been in
trouble before, with alcohol or drugs, and they said Stonegate was the only real home they'd had. Before we left, some
of them wanted to sing some bluegrass songs for us. Later,
the boy's parents were convicted, and Dot McClellan eventually served a prison sentence as well; she was found guilty of
conspiracy to commit manslaughter. I got pretty close to
this story. I have trouble with people who proclaim they
have the answers for everyone else—the murder/suicide at
Jonestown is another example—and I found it difficult to
imagine how young parents could be convinced to punish a
child in this way.

Monday, July 17, Washington, D.C., 1989

Every summer about this time it's fun to call one of the
MacArthur winners—the people who'll receive the so-called
"genius grants." The MacArthur Foundation, based in Chicago, awards a number of no-strings-attached fellowships
every summer; artists, dancers, scientists, and so on. On announcement day the list comes out in the morning and
there's time to find someone who's just been notified and is
still surprised and excited. Today I talked with Baldemar
Velasquez, a farm labor organizer in Toledo, Ohio. His
MacArthur fellowship—$265,000, he says—is for persist-
ence rather than genius.

We also try to cover some of the Nobel Prize announcements, again getting the news early enough to be able to find one of the recipients by air time. The same is true for the Pulitzer Prizes: we like to watch the complete list come in over the newswire and try to figure out which of the winners would make the best interview. I can't recall any stories about the Academy Awards or the Tony Awards—those ceremonies are always covered by "Morning Edition," since they don't happen on "our watch."

Another fun call today is out to Colorado: the subject is cannibalism. James Starrs, a forensic scientist at George Washington University, is involved in an archeological adventure—trying to find out if Alfred Packer was indeed guilty of cannibalism. Five men, gold prospectors, have been buried up in the San Juan Mountains since the winter of 1874. Today their gravesite was disturbed. The scientists will try to find evidence that Packer was telling the truth when, in court, he admitted killing one of the men and eating the remains of all five. Professor Starrs says Packer was the only person who claimed cannibalism, and that Packer was, irrefutably, a pathological liar.

STARRS: He could have lied when he said he ate them only to get some kind of a oneupmanship before the jury as to his starvation conditions.

NOAH: Kind of an interesting lie when he said—if he's being quoted accurately—"the breasts of man"—

STARRS: No, that's not an accurate quote.

NOAH: —"would be the sweetest meat I've ever tasted."

STARRS: That's not an accurate quote. That's part of the myth and the fable and the fiction of the case. So much of that exists; I hope some of it we can put to rest.

Thursday, July 20, Washington, D.C., 1989

There was a bad plane crash yesterday evening in Iowa, at
the Sioux City airport. A United DC-10—more than a hundred killed, but there were a surprising number of survivors, and after we were off the air I recorded a conversation
with one of them. Our coverage today includes reports from
Howard Berkes, who went to Iowa last night from his home
base in Salt Lake City (if it's a major news story in the Midwest or Northwest, Howard is probably already packing
when the call comes in from the assignment desk in Washington; he'll get on a plane, get to the story, and work
through the night for "Morning Edition," and "All Things
Considered" the next afternoon, plus hourly newscasts in
between), and Wendy Kaufman, NPR's aviation expert, re-
viewing the DC-10's safety record. Then we played the tape
of my talk with the survivor, Bruce Bennum. His home is
near Denver, he was going to Chicago on business. His only
injury was a cut on the forehead. When I called Bennum at
St. Luke's Hospital in Sioux City, I was thinking about those
on board the plane. Did they hear the engine explode? Could
they tell the plane was hard to control? What did the pilot
say to them? And what was it like as the plane started
down?

> BENNUM: They really didn't indicate a crash landing. They
> indicated that the landing was going to be far from
> normal and very rough, okay. And they had worked
> with us on bracing and bracing procedures, putting
> your head in your lap and so forth, also what to do in
> the event of an emergency evacuation, you know, be
> sure to locate your exits and all this other kind of stuff.
> Like those things were so turned upside down that you
> couldn't tell which way was up ... we just knew we
> were upside down.

NOAH: Were you thrown out?

BENNUM: No, sir. I was still in my seat. The portion of the plane that I was in, of course, in the middle of the plane, went for some period of time fairly level, though we could tell we were scraping on the ground, and then it began to roll and turn and so, you know, we were upside down and all kinds of things when it finally came to a stop. And so we had to disconnect our seat belts and we dropped to the ceiling, of course, which was now the floor.

NOAH: Then you scrambled out.

BENNUM: Most people in our area were able to begin to evacuate.

NOAH: Had you wondered before ... it seems that most people who fly have a moment from time to time in which they think about a plane going down. Had you been one of those people before? Had you sort of thought about it before?

BENNUM: Yes, I did.

NOAH: And how was it different in actual practice, when it actually happened?

BENNUM: Well, I'd always envisioned that if I ever were in a plane crash, it would be over, just because you don't hear too much of survivors in plane crashes. I guess I would say that, you know, I envisioned that it would be, you know, a sudden falling out of the sky and then a massive explosion, but since we were ... you could feel that the plane was damaged and since we were heading for a crash landing, it was very anxious, fearful, a lot of emotions run through your mind and you think about a lot of things, but mainly hoping that things work out okay and it's not as severe as what it might be. It was pretty scary.

NOAH: And how were the people around you?

BENNUM: Calm, for the most part. I think we were all
pretty much within ourselves at that point in time. We
had some discussions with folks and folks were I think
nervously chattering and talking to one another,
trying to convince each other that things weren't as
bad as what they might be. So there was a lot of that
nervous kind of talk, but people were pretty collected
and seemed to be realizing that they just had to hang
in there, I guess, is a good way to put it. Very little
panic; I thought the flight crew did an excellent job
preparing us for it, and doing their best once we had
impact and once we were trying to evacuate, and I
could hear flight crew people saying we've got to get
out of here and proceed to the back of the plane and,
you know, those kinds of things. It was directed well
by them.

NOAH: There was always the thought in your mind that
you were going to make what could have been just
simply a pretty rough landing there at Sioux City.

BENNUM: Yes, that's what I quite honestly was hoping for
was that we'd be getting off the plane, probably
somewhat shook up a little bit because he said it was
going to be a rough landing, but you know, walking off
to the side and seeing the damage to the tail and
saying, oh, that's what it was. Hopefully going about
our business and maybe making it to Chicago tonight,
all those kinds of things. So I was very hopeful and had
a lot of faith that things were going to turn out okay.

Thursday, July 27, Washington, D.C., 1989

A day at home, mostly worrying about equipment. Our dining-room table is covered with audio gear, and batteries and
cassettes. I'm waiting on word from Alaska that it's time to
get on a plane and fly to Anchorage. A whale researcher,

Craig Matkin, has agreed to take me out into Prince William Sound. I've been wondering about the effects of the Exxon oil spill—it doesn't seem right to call it the "Alaska" oil spill—on the whales that come into the Sound in the summer months; I'd seen a small news story about dead gray whales, beached on an island out in the Gulf of Alaska.

If you start making phone calls about whales in Alaska, you'll wind up with Craig Matkin's number, in Homer, a small town on the Kenai Peninsula at Kachemak Bay. Matkin has a contract this summer to run a new census of the humpback and killer whales, the Orcas, but he makes his real living as a fisherman and now it's salmon time in the Sound, so our trip has to be scheduled around the fishing days. Also I've had to promise that I won't reveal any of his early findings. All the researchers who've signed on with the government to survey the oil spill damage have agreed to keep their data secret until the final reports are ready. But other than that, sure, he says, come along. (This restriction on the data remained in place for more than three years, but—according to a 1992 preliminary report—it appeared likely the oil spill had harmed the whale population. Out of one group of thirty-six killer whales, thirteen had died in the year following the spill. It was, in the terms of the researchers, a "totally unprecedented" mortality rate. There's speculation the whales died from the effects of inhaling the oil and fumes.)

Matkin could only take one extra person on his boat, so I'd have to do my own sound recording. Probably couldn't have found the money for an engineer anyway; this is a $2,000 trip, and NPR usually runs short of money in late summer—if you want to have an expensive project approved, it's best to schedule it for October, the beginning of the new fiscal year. (NPR's total news budget is about $15 million a year; the ATC budget is $2.3 million. And that's cheap when compared to television. We used to estimate that a year of "All Things Considered" would cost about the same as just one week of "NBC Nightly News.")

I have a good cassette recorder, and a short, "shotgun"

microphone; I'd need it for recording on the deck of a fast-moving boat, chasing after whales. Shotgun mikes are usually long and thin, with very tight sound-gathering patterns; you'd use a shotgun at a football game to pick up the quarterback's signals from the sidelines. The mikes do look a little threatening; you don't want to go waving one around during a street demonstration, for example, where the police could mistake it for a weapon. They also show up suspiciously on the airport X-ray screens.

NPR, of course, owns lots of good microphones, and expensive Nagra reel-to-reel recorders, but they don't let reporters use them, only engineers. I've fought against this policy over the years, arguing that reporters should (with proper training) be using better equipment (if NPR is really about state-of-the-art audio) and also that technicians should be doing more producing and reporting (if NPR is really about innovative journalism). It's wonderfully reassuring to go out in the field with NPR techs and a producer, and their work becomes vital to the story, but many times you're sent on assignment by yourself. And we don't see often enough, in radio, the equivalent of a photojournalist—an experienced reporter using first-rate equipment, working alone.

That thought always reminds me of my one true growing-up ambition: I wanted to be several steps back from the scene, observing more than reporting. I wanted to be a *National Geographic* photographer, to load up with those super Nikon lenses and motor drives and hundreds of rolls of film, and head for the airport and a distant land. Maybe someday I could find a photographer who really wanted to be in radio—perhaps it's not too late to make a deal.

Friday, July 28, Alaska, 1989

Arrived in the evening after a day of flying—Anchorage is five hours and nineteen minutes away from Minneapolis–

Saint Paul. The flight was on a Northwest 757; people at the airport were talking about avoiding the DC-10s. After the crash at Sioux City last week, another DC-10 went down in Libya. As we flew over the Canadian Rockies and on over to the Gulf of Alaska, I remembered a night at the airport in Seattle, twenty years ago. The people who were lined up to get on an Air Alaska flight—women, men, children, and dogs—had a wonderful aura of adventure; they were healthy and excited and were leaving stories behind for more interesting ones ahead. I thought for a moment I would join them. I'd come to Seattle to try to talk a girl-friend into coming back with me to Kentucky, but she re-fused to even see me, and I spent a sorrowful weekend in a hotel room staring out at the fog in Puget Sound, eating cheeseburgers and waiting for the phone to ring (they told me at the desk the Beatles had once stayed at this hotel, as if that might cheer me up). So by Sunday night at the airport I was certainly a good candidate for a new life. But I got on the plane that went east instead of north: we make choices, and then spend years wondering.

Broiled halibut, and fresh horseradish, and sourdough bread and a good beer made in Juneau, called Chinook—it's a fine meal at an Anchorage seafood restaurant, Simon and Seafort's. Marilyn Dalheim and I watch the sunset and the waters of Cook Inlet and talk about whales, or rather, she patiently answers my questions. She wants a day or so to think about one of them: if we know, say, 90 percent of what there is to know about elephants, how much do we know about whales?

Marilyn is with the National Marine Mammal Laboratory in Seattle; it's her department that has ordered up the whale survey in Prince William Sound, and she's going out on the boat with us tomorrow—she and Craig Matkin have worked together in the past. She's an oceanographer, her specialty is underwater acoustics, and her fascination is with whales. The answers she's looking for could be important. A few years ago the CIA tried to hire her for a research project—

they wanted to study the differences between biological sounds, made underwater, and mechanical-electrical ones. Whales or submarines.

The *Anchorage Daily News* has a front-page color photograph: a humpback whale in Prince William Sound, the flukes of the tail glistening as the whale dives. The picture's reassuring—that's what we're going out to find.

Saturday, July 29, Alaska, 1989

"Nothing shittier than Whittier," they say about this dreary and unusual small town, which is trapped between the mountains and the water. Whittier is on Prince William Sound, but there's no road, only a railroad tunnel. So we drive south from Anchorage, lock the car, take the train through the mountain (we heard a dandy bear story on the train: they found a pair of boots with the feet still in them), and go down to the dock to locate the *Lucky Star*. We've brought fresh fruit and vegetables and coffee. No alcohol— Craig Matkin runs a "dry boat."

There's a yell and a wave and Craig's found us. They've unloaded their salmon, taken on diesel fuel, and soon we're off, down along Passage Canal, then out into the main body of Prince William Sound—it will take the better part of two days running at good speed to reach the first whale camp. The *Lucky Star* carries a fishing crew of three, and if they're indeed lucky, fifteen thousand dollars' worth of salmon in her holding tanks. They're allowed—by the state of Alaska— to fish only in certain places, and on designated days. The oil spill has practically stopped everything so far, but Craig is expecting another fishing "opening" in a few days, and it's possible he could be out for the entire month of August. It could be thirty days straight without touching land. You fish eighteen hours a day and all the days of the week; a supply boat, a "tender," comes out to take off your catch and bring groceries. And then you put your boat up for the winter and go home and sit in the tub until the snow comes.

Just one day in Alaska and you can hear the words "oil whore." If a boat stayed afloat and ran, you could rent it to Exxon for use in the cleanup. A purse seiner like Craig's would go for $3,500 a day—without a crew. It got tempting not to fish. Although it's Exxon, indirectly, that's paying for this summer's whale research, Craig has stayed away from the big oil money. He thinks the cleanup has been worse than the spill, it's created greed and waste and noise. He hates hearing the "southern voices" on the radio. But the National Marine Mammal Laboratory wants to know how the whales are doing after the spill, which killer whales are still in the Sound, which humpbacks have come from Mexico and Hawaii for the summer feeding, and the laboratory is keeping track of all the extra expenses, expenses that Exxon is expected to pay. Craig Matkin has a master's degree in marine zoology and a deep, pragmatic curiosity about whales. He's put together a small research organization, mostly volunteer work, to help establish a whale census.

Late in the afternoon, after hours of slamming through some heavy, choppy water out in the Sound, we pull alongside the *John C. Cobb,* a National Oceanic and Atmospheric Administration research vessel. There are several government scientists on board, and we all sit around in the warm, spacious galley drinking coffee. I'm sort of dozing, but I do hear one of the researchers say, well, all this is going on Exxon's account number anyway. Marilyn knows the captain of the *Cobb,* they've worked up in the Bering Strait together, and she asks for some of his special chocolate chip cookies to take back to the *Lucky Star.* The captain also has whale news for us—they've seen thirty-five killer whales out catching salmon. And they were singing so loudly you could hear it without a hydrophone, the sounds coming up through the hull of the ship.

Sunday, July 30, Alaska, 1989

In my sleeping bag, tucked away in a bunk underneath the bow of the *Lucky Star,* I awoke before first light and listened to the wind, and the water moving. We anchored close by the *John Cobb,* giving up on the weather early, and had grilled red salmon for supper. I asked Craig the question that Marilyn wanted extra time to answer: What percentage of the whole is our current knowledge of whales? Earlier in the day Marilyn had told me 30 percent. And that's the same estimate Craig now gives—they are both delighted to learn their answers matched.

We are still hours away from the first whale camp. It's gray and misty out. Prince William Sound is vast—on a cloudy day it could be an ocean. We watch a sea otter, floating by—"cruisin' and snoozin'," Craig says. (The sea otter, on its back with its head and feet in the air, and a quizzical, whiskered look, is the cutest creature in the Sound and a standard feature of every television report about the spill's cleanup.) Craig sits up behind the stainless-steel wheel of the *Lucky Star,* his coffee cup at hand, watching the water ahead, and the radar screen. He's about forty, tall, curly blond hair and a beard, he's wearing jeans and a green and white wool sweater, also a blue nylon jacket that has a polypro hood, and a built-in flotation device—if you fall overboard, you pull a cord and a CO_2 cartridge fires, inflating the back of the jacket. "The newest thing in the fleet," Craig says, and it's saved a few lives already—quite often fishermen have never learned to swim.

We idle up into the inlet at Point Nowell. The two young researchers are waiting, with smiles and stories about bears and whale sightings. Craig brings their supplies ashore— food and film and batteries, and fuel for their outboard motor. The whale watchers spend most of their time out in the Sound, hoping to find whales to photograph. Marilyn checks through their log books—at summer's end all the field data will be collected and analyzed at her offices in Seattle.

Then all of us go out, on two boats, for a whale search. The *Lucky Star* cruises through Knight Island Passage, the smaller craft, in touch by radio, ahead about a mile and off to the left, to port. The cameras are readied; Nikon 8008s with 300mm autofocus zoom lenses, Ilford 400 black and white film. Craig makes some lunch—a chunky clam chowder and cold salmon sandwiches—and just then Kelly Balcomb calls in with a sighting. Killer whales. We launch the *Lucky Star*'s inflatable boat, and for the next hour we travel with the whales of A-B Pod, moving at good speed out into the open Sound. Craig's taken pictures of these whales before—about forty are in the group; they're identified by patches of white on the dorsal fin and the "saddle patch" just behind the fin. The killer whales are small in whale terms, they are truly dolphins—"super dolphins," they are called. But they can be thirty feet long and weigh up to five tons. They are fast and smart, navigating by echolocation, cresting through the water in parallel arcs, leaping in the air, zooming in swerves under the boat. Craig believes many of the Prince William Sound whales recognize his boat, and they come alongside as if to play.

MATKIN: Oh, a beautiful breach by the mother. A full breach out of the water. That white on the bottom of the belly is incredible. Always moving, killer whales are always moving. The only time I've seen when they haven't moved very much is when the oil came around this spring—well, no, there's two instances where I've watched them and they don't move, they stay in one spot. One is when they're waiting at a black cod buoy for somebody to come and pull it and, of course, when the fisherman comes to pull the buoy they eat the fish off the lines, and then this spring when the oil moved

down the passage and it was on both sides of them, I
watched them in an area where they just stayed
basically in one place for a period of time, but
otherwise, killer whales are always on the move.

I'm trying to watch and record the sound at the same
time; I'm using the shotgun microphone on Craig, who's taking pictures, and Marilyn, who's driving the boat, trying to
pick up their comments, and the shutter clicks and the
splashing of the whales, and once when I'm *not recording,* a
whale jumps straight up out of the water not four feet away
from us. It hangs in the air, sleek and powerful white and
black—I can see its bellybutton. Marilyn screams with delight. The whale drops back into the water with a crash. A
4,000-pound juvenile female, they say. Craig stops the boat
for a minute and drops a hydrophone over the side, so we
can listen to the eerie, liquid voices—the whales of A-B Pod
calling to one another, and possibly to us.

Later, Marilyn asked me if I plan to mention our lunch in
my radio story—the hot mugs of Craig's chowder and the
sandwiches tasted wonderful out in the chilly air. I think
she was concerned that this exciting time with the whales
could appear to be fun, and not work, not science.

That night on the *Lucky Star,* two more of the whale researchers join us for supper. And Kelly Balcomb tells me
about his camp and the nearby "rubbing beach"—a favorite
spot for the killer whales. They come into the shallow water,
rubbing their bodies along the small stones on the beach.
Why do they do that, I wonder?

BALCOMB: It feels really good. They're very sensory
    animals, and in this case they're rubbing on the rocks
    and small smooth stones and it just must feel really
    great.

This gathering on the *Lucky Star* is sort of a staff meeting
for the whale watchers and their supervisors. And soon

there's an argument. Whale watcher Eva Saulitis has published a letter in the *Anchorage Daily News* highly critical
of Exxon's cleanup efforts in the Sound—huge, noisy floating cities, fuel leaks from the work boats. And once she
towed a discarded and filthy oil boom across the Sound to an
Exxon headquarters ship. She also brought along a bag containing the body of a sea otter, killed by the oil. No one on
the ship would talk with her. Eva's letter-to-the-editor embarrassed some of her higher-ups. Marilyn Dalheim tells her
the message from Seattle was that she should "put a sock in
it," that speaking out now could jeopardize the whale research project. Dalheim's point concerned timing—every
one agreed they had a responsibility to speak out when they
saw something wrong.

This was quite a debate, between idealism and pragma-
tism, and I was surprised they were having it in front of me.
I wasn't recording, clearly, and I wondered if they thought
their comments would be off the record if I wasn't holding a
microphone. Actually, I could have been recording. I
brought a small PZM (pressure-zone microphone) that could
have been taped to a wall without anyone's noticing; it just
looks like a flat piece of black metal. The PZM would have
easily picked up all the voices in the *Lucky Star's* cabin.

Monday, July 31, Prince William Sound, 1989

The next morning I'm invited to a banana pancake breakfast at Eva's camp, across the water of Knight Island Passage. A small island, a rocky beach, a white canvas tent,
twelve feet by ten. Inside, a wood-burning stove, bunk beds,
bookshelves, a view of glaciers and the Kenai Mountain
Range. Eva Saulitis lives and works here, along with her
assistant Matt Hare. She's spent several summers on Prince
William Sound and she's a graduate student now, working

with killer whale acoustics. She described an encounter
with a single killer whale.

> SAULITIS: He was really active at the surface, just by
> himself, in his own little world, laying over on his
> back, slapping his flippers, both flippers at the same
> time, slapping his tail, just kind of lazing around in the
> water and he came, as we approached him to take the
> photograph, he came and he swam directly under our
> boat, real slowly, and you could watch his body—it was
> huge, bigger than our boat. He went underneath us
> and then as he was passing the boat we started to hear
> the sounds coming up through the hull of the boat and
> so we dropped the hydrophone and he just was making
> beautiful long calls and loud and clear—it was just a
> really interesting feeling to me to encounter because
> he was by himself.

> *killer whale calling, underwater, far away, then closer*

> Usually you see them together, but it was like he was
> just . . . having a good time. Then he started heading
> out into Montague Strait and heading north and kept
> calling. He could come up to the surface and be silent
> and then he'd go back down, and as he was down under
> the water for about eight or nine minutes, he would be
> calling continuously, and he kept repeating that cycle.
> When he was a mile and a half away, we were still
> getting calls loud and clear on the hydrophone. It was
> just really unusual. We couldn't follow because the
> weather was getting awful, but we just watched him go
> and listened.

I borrow Eva's cassette player to make a direct copy of the
whale calls she'd recorded that day. And after breakfast I
ask her to tell me about the dirty oil boom and her encounter with the Exxon officials. I want to get the story on tape
just in case.

Then Eva and Matt and I go out in search of humpback whales. They've seen them almost every day, taking pictures to send down to the National Marine Mammal Laboratory in Seattle. I'll have a chance to go down there to see the photo-matching procedure—a computer and a video disc player with eighty thousand photographs of whales. When a humpback dives, you can see the white and gray patterns—highly individualistic—on the underside of the tail.

We're in a small blue and white cabin skiff, taking along sleeping bags and sandwiches and a thermos of tea. Matt is driving, Eva sitting on the bow with the camera. I was already feeling lucky, because of yesterday. It would have been tough to go back to Washington without seeing any whales at all. And now I needed the sound of the hump-backs spouting. The conditions were close to perfect.

NOAH: The water is flat, green, with sheets of white mist. There are mountains around, unseen for days.

boat idling

We spot some whales, from a distance. The humpbacks forty to fifty feet long with big white flippers. They roll heavily through the water, the tail flukes descending. Eva takes a few pictures, but I am hoping for a chance to hear the blowing of the humpback whale, the spouting from the blowholes, the nostrils really, that have evolved to the back of the whale's head. The breath of the whale—pressurized water vapor, carbon dioxide, nitrogen. It is said to have a musky smell.

quiet water sounds

The boat drifts. I'm hoping a whale will come close enough. There is a wind down from Icy Bay, chunks of glaciers in the water. You can hear stories about ghosts on Prince William Sound, of mummies in the sea caves

on the islands. And the blowing of the whale, when it
comes, *is* an ancient sound.

The boat stops. I aim the microphone where I've seen the
plume, turn up the gain ... try not to breathe. And there it is.
And again. I had to record it, I realize, it's a sound that I
couldn't describe. Back in Washington when I was putting
this story together, the engineers worked carefully with
these few seconds of tape, to make the sound louder, darker,
more present. It was enchanting, even frightening. You are
trying to make it real, calibrating the recording to your
memory of the sound.

On the way back up Perry Passage, heading back to Whittier, we stop by a cleanup site in Herring Bay. Barges and
cranes, and sprays from high-pressure hot-water hoses.
About forty workers are there, some busy, some standing
around. It looks like awful, discouraging work. Two men are
lifting barbells, another is fishing off the side of a barge.

Farther on that night, at anchor in a cove, we go out on
deck for a while, still hoping to see the stars, and Eva leans
over the side of the boat and waves a paddle in the water to
show us the luminescent plankton. The water's black, until
you disturb it, then it sparkles and glows like thousands of
wet, cool fireflies.

Tuesday, August 1, Seattle, 1989

I call home from a phone booth in a shopping center south
of Anchorage. "I'm back, I'm safe," I report. And I'm proud
that I'm having some slight difficulty in balance on dry
land, my legs remembering the roll of the boat. Coming in
this morning, the wind was up before we turned for Passage
Canal, and Craig was trying to make up time so the *Lucky
Star* was bouncing and wallowing at the same time. I asked
for a couple of pieces of dry toast, and stood out on deck with
my face in the cold rushing air.

Craig talked with the Whittier harbor master by marine
VHF radio, and learned that the fishing opening—the event
we've been rushing back for—is postponed. They've found
oil in the water near Esther Island. So the morning slowed
down, and we unloaded and said goodbye, taking the train
ride back through the tunnel in the mountains, to drive to
Anchorage and the airport.

In Seattle, going off to sleep at last in a bed, I thought
mostly about the first thing I had seen that morning—
about a hundred yards away, through the silver-blue fog. A
black bear, a big one, with a rolling, almost prancing walk
along the green banks of a salmon stream, spilling into
Prince William Sound. There is one piece of tape that I'm
missing, for this story—I don't have anyone talking in any
sort of wistful, anthropomorphic, metaphysical sense about
the whales. The scientists don't bother to romanticize the
whales; it isn't necessary. Still, I can't resist ending my story
with a quotation from the Heathcote Williams book, *Whale
Nation.* The poet is writing about the fact that most of the
earth is water:

> *From space, the planet is blue.*
> *From space, the planet is the territory*
> *Not of humans, but of the whale.*

I also add just a little music from the Paul Winter Consort,
to complete the story. At a listening some months later, I
realize the music *is* a bit much. There's come to be a certain
public radio sound over the years, lovely music that's been
overused: Paul Winter's soprano saxophone, and anyone's
hammered dulcimer.

Most every story I've done could have benefited from a
day's rest and a second hearing, before broadcast. We're usually working too fast for that to be possible, and there's also
what William F. Buckley, Jr., has called the "liberation of the
deadline"—if it doesn't have to go on the air, it won't get
done. Certainly that's the way I work and I've only known

one producer—Robert Montiegel, working at NPR in the 1970s—who could finish a project early. He'd put a documentary on the shelf and forget about it for months, and then one afternoon he'd invite some colleagues into his office for a glass of Sherry and a listening session. You can never really hear your program or a story until you listen to it with someone else in the room, someone for whom it's absolutely new and fresh. Robert would ask for comments, take a few notes, and perhaps then make a couple of changes in his program for the air date.

I like most of my stories better after years have gone by, although at a delayed hearing they usually seem to run longer than necessary. And that's always a surprise because when I'm working on a story, the last-minute cutting is the most painful part of the process. And usually when I go home that night after the broadcast, I'm discouraged and worried over what I had to leave out.

A panicked, twenty-second cut from an "All Things Considered" interview once caused all of our phone lines to light up with frustrated callers asking, "What happened to that guy?" I remember being scared myself: we taped the interview earlier in the week, with the lights off in the studio. I was talking with a man who had been chased by a grizzly bear. The listeners heard him describe how he climbed up a tree to escape, but then was followed by the bear. The bear's claws grazed the bottom of the man's boots . . . Then, all of a sudden, the interview was over. Our producer had been desperate, the program was running long and she needed to find a cut. She did. The tape that went on the floor contained this exchange:

NOAH: Gosh, then what happened?

MAN: Nothing, the bear just went back down the tree and walked away. I was really lucky.

The listeners who called didn't even stop to think about the fact that the storyteller had to be alive, and quite likely, uninjured. That apparent logic probably encouraged the producer to make that particular cut, but listeners, deep into a story, don't have time for logic, and that's the joy of radio. The stories are compelling because a listener fills in all the details, the colors, the smells—the fears—from his or her own imagination. The highest compliment our listeners pay us—and we do hear it often—is, "You know, I didn't even get out of the car when I got home, I just sat there in the driveway until that story was over."

The sounds of a radio story can be startlingly convincing as well. Once I was walking along a busy street in Washington, listening on headphones to a *kuntzkopf* recording that a radio producer had sent from West Germany. *Kuntzkopf* is a binaural recording system: stereo microphones are placed in the ear canals of a dummy head; the idea is that the mikes pick up sounds in the same way as we normally hear them. The recordings are then played back through stereo headphones and you *hear in 360 degrees.* If, during the recording, someone walks behind the dummy head, whistling, you'll hear the movement. If someone spins the dummy head, the listener can get dizzy. The tape my friend sent me was of an audio tour of Berlin, but when an airplane suddenly roared dangerously close over my head, I was already flat on the ground before I remembered that it was only an airplane in Berlin.

Monday, August 7, Washington, D.C., 1989

Robert Siegel talks with Sandy Gillis of "The Tonight Show, Starring Johnny Carson." We've heard they were having trouble finding "light" stories for their program. It's a problem we've noticed too lately. Not enough lighthearted feature stories. We call them "enders"; they most often serve to close each half-hour segment. The conversation about enders ends "All Things Considered" tonight. The story just before, about a ballooning accident, was quite serious. A hot-air balloon that should not have been flying in the first place fell three thousand feet and killed the pilot, Robert Mock. This happened at a competition in Louisiana. On the way down Mock was talking with his wife by radio, warning her that it didn't look good and to clear the people out from underneath. We called an air-safety investigator who had seen the accident.

ARMOND EDWARDS: The balloon opened up right at the, not the very top, but the panel next to the top—the, what we call "load-carrying tape" at the seam peeled open for about a length of nine feet.

NOAH: If you divide that balloon into pie wedges of fabric, how much of it would have come apart?

EDWARDS: Maybe one quarter, maybe a little less. The upper portion of the envelope.

NOAH: It just came apart?

EDWARDS: Yeah, it just ripped right down the seam.

Edwards said the balloon was a bit old—it was built in 1977—and that some sections had deteriorated, damaged by overheating and ultraviolet rays. Balloons scare me a little. I've only been up once; when we were broadcasting from Alaska about ten years ago, we went up on a flight early one morning. Three of us: the pilot; Flawn Williams, our engineer; and myself. The idea was to tape an opening segment for that day's program. A wicker gondola, it turns out, is a lovely studio, a thousand feet in the air. It's quiet (when the hot-air burner's not blasting) because the balloon is moving with the wind. The sounds of Anchorage at sunrise drifted up from the ground: a dog barking, a truck starting. We didn't see much, though, because I was trying to write and then record a two-minute essay and Flawn was only watching the Nagra's VU meter, and so we were a bit shocked when the pilot, who had donated his time and balloon, said, well, we're going to have to land and it could be rough. Just make sure you stay with the basket!

I had the idea it wasn't all that safe up there anyway for a balloon, even just after sunrise. Lots of Cessnas zipping around over Anchorage—and 747s, too, cruising in from Tokyo, Hawaii, New York. But I hadn't realized the landing site would be so arbitrary; the pilot explained later that he doesn't really have much control over where the balloon goes down. I should ask Flawn sometime if he was recording as we started losing altitude. We came pretty close to some electric wires as we slid in sideways to land in a vacant field. I was proud of the pilot and pretty happy to be on the ground.

"All Things Considered" consists of three sections—"thirds"—and, by tradition, the first third and the third third usually have the serious news of the day. Longer features and softer news stories are likely to be in the second third. Each third begins hard and moves to light, but increasingly it seems there's a need to have news and analysis take up the entire first and third thirds. In the early years of the program it was tough to fill the ninety minutes each night. The interviews were long and often rambled. Reporters could do almost any story they chose, at any length; we used a lot of material from the BBC, and, especially in the summertime, we reran quite a bit of material. But two things have changed: we've given several minutes of each third back to NPR's member stations, for local news and announcements; and, at last, there's now a fair-sized staff of reporters and producers in Washington and around the world, as well as reporters in various bureaus and member stations around this country. So we're trying to put many more stories into a smaller program, and the news will always win out over the more lighthearted stories; when things are happening out in the world, the book reviews and interviews with musicians stay on the shelf.

Many listeners do seem to want a more serious program

these days, at least many who write say that. But then you'll hear complaints that "All Things Considered" isn't as warm as it used to be, isn't as personal.

Reader's Digest, for the January 1984 issue, asked permission to print a transcript of a discussion that Susan and I had on the air one evening. I remember it for two reasons: they paid us a dollar a word, and I think it's an example of something that you wouldn't hear on our program today.

Susan Stamberg and Noah Adams, co-hosts of National Public Radio's "All Things Considered," muse about what you focus on when you're out in the cold and have to get home—what thoughts keep you going until you can get inside the door.

ADAMS: I always think about a nice hot bath and a cold drink and Mozart and clean, dry, white socks to put on and just-washed bluejeans. And then later a chilly bedroom, sleeping under a down comforter without setting the alarm clock, some reading that can make you feel less sorry for yourself, like Jack London's short story "To Build a Fire." Do you know that?

STAMBERG: I don't know it. But it sounds warm to me. Now I would have chosen a fire, too, for my list—a very snapping one in front of which a large, furry Golden retriever has been sitting for at least an hour. I would also think about a steaming pot of mulled wine with the definite ingredient of cinnamon sticks, a bowl of chili with extra-hot peppers in it, a terrycloth robe that somebody—not me—has just pulled out of the clothes dryer, and finally—to come in out of the cold to—a hug!

ADAMS: A hug. That's a nice, warm thought to close on.

Our cold-weather conversation seemed fine in the winter of 1983–84, but now it would be too sweet, too soft. Now it's even more of a challenge to find light material: "Where's the fun?" people will say around two o'clock. If we're not careful we'll have a somber program, a lot of foreign news on scratchy phone lines, a lot of men talking to men about political repercussions. Just more worry for our producer, Michael Sullivan. He's in charge of the daily program; tomorrow is not his concern. Michael spends his afternoons listening to tapes, watching the newswires, answering the phone, staring at a large white board—the "roadmap"—trying to fit in all the reporters' stories, three or four of the host interviews, a movie review, a commentary, adding up times in his head, muttering to himself, and throwing Magic Markers at the roadmap.

That's for fun. We also have visible reminders of intense frustration: two office walls with good-sized holes, one kicked in, the other caused by a fast-moving doorknob, and those are only the ones that haven't been fixed. Art Silverman was the producer doing the kicking; he was trying to get a story on the air too fast—it was, he remembers, something about an enormous chair that had been set up on the Mall by a Buddhist organization. The story had a lot of sound and several interviews, and he finished the first three minutes but couldn't find an open studio in time to mix the last four. He missed the deadline—he'd never been late before. Robert Siegel had to ad-lib his way to the end of the feature. Art went back to his office, kicked the wall in, and then covered it up with a map of Vietnam—just the right size.

We've had about fifteen ATC producers over our twenty years. Each of them, at the end of almost every day, would be unhappy with the program they had just put on the air. Producers are too close, they can only see the compromises. Ideally this would be a job for a twenty-five-year-old who's been reading *The Economist* since junior high school and who goes off to sleep listening to the BBC World Service on shortwave and wakes up to "NBC News at Sunrise." Someone

who runs five miles after work to release the frustration.
Michael Sullivan didn't fit into quite all of those categories,
and probably that's why after doing a great job for three
years he decided, in the summer of 1991, to go off to London
to be a reporter and worry about just his own work for a
while.

NBC-TV recently hired Jeff Zucker, twenty-six, to be executive producer of the "Today" show. *The New York Times*
noted that "Zucker vaguely remembers President Richard
M. Nixon's resignation as the first news story that made an
impression on him." He was nine years old. I hope Mr.
Zucker is a runner.

Monday August 14, Maine, 1989

> NOAH: In a report to the U.S. Lighthouse Board, 1868, this
> sentiment: "Nothing indicates the liberality, prosperity
> or intelligence of a nation more clearly that the
> facilities which it affords for the safe approach of the
> mariner to its shores."

A quick plane trip, a short drive, and we're happy: lots of
things to make noises and someone to tell us about them.
We start the tape recorder and Ken Black rings a ship's bell,
he clatters a telegraph key for us, the Coast Guard would be
signaling the lightkeeper. A fog detector makes a steady
tick, tick, tick, sending out a beam of light to be intercepted
by water droplets in the air. When there's enough water in
the air, the foghorns are turned on automatically—invent
the fog detector and you don't need the lightkeeper.

The Shore Village Museum is in a neat, gray-shingled
house, a few blocks from the harbor in the town of Rock-
land. The museum is a haven for lighthouse fans and lighthouse artifacts.

brass bell ringing loudly, reverberating

BLACK: This particular bell system came from a lightship called, well, it was a relief lightship, our number was the 536. I was captain of it, so I'm kind of familiar with it. Here's the code, that's the military code: One bell means go ahead; two to stop; three to go back; four to go full, in the direction in which the propeller is rotating. So, visualize—you'd be steaming along and have to make an emergency stop, two bells to stop her; three bells to go back; four bells to go full. Nine bells, you can live or die nine deaths while you're ringing nine bells.

Ken Black, thirty-two years in the U.S. Coast Guard, now a museum director, is helping us along our way on a quest for sound, of lighthouses and the ocean. And our story is to be recorded, edited and mixed, and broadcast digitally. It's the editing and mixing that's new—we've played digital music recordings on "All Things Considered," and an occasional interview, and lots of stories that have been recorded in digital and then transferred—dubbed—to analog tape for editing, but we've never produced a feature story that was digital from start to finish. A computer now makes this possible, but as we learn, only barely so. We do think it's worth the effort to determine the state of the art at the moment, and the results can be satisfying. Digital production versus regular analog would bring to radio the same quality difference that CDs offer over vinyl records or cassettes.

Kevin Rice is the engineer. He's young, tall, with red hair and a special fascination for computers and their potential for use in radio production. He's brought a Sony—a DAT recorder, Digital Audio Tape. The tapes—which are just a bit larger than regular cassettes—last for two hours of recording. The batteries go fast, but they're rechargeable in a motel room overnight.

Melissa Block is our producer; she's in her late twenties

and is intense—it's her fast schedule that we're on. It finds
us, after our tour of the museum and an interview down by
the docks, out in the harbor—flying—in a Coast Guard boat,
chasing the sounds of buoy bells. The outboard motors are
Yamaha 70s and the young Coast Guard ensign has the ta-
chometer needles pushed just to the edge of the red section.
Kevin was trying to record and he couldn't use his hands to
hang on and I was afraid that both our engineer and our
rented DAT machine were going to bounce over the side
into Penobscot Bay.

Then a trip up Highway One, along the bay, just past Cam-
den to the Lighthouse Motel. Mostly we've come to interview
Cliff and Dorothy Shattuck. But it's a place you would have
picked to stay anyway, just driving past. Neat white cabins
with blue trim, chairs outside on the porches, a good view of
the water. And as to lobster? Cliff served only breakfast. His
recommendations? "No. Don't go there. If you do, you'll be
asking me for the Kaopectate in the morning. Go to the one
across the road from there, you'll like it." And we do. One-
and-a-quarter-pound lobster, $9.95. And strawberry short-
cake. After supper, we have a talk with the Shattucks.

    bell ringing, in channel marker

NOAH: The Lighthouse Motel. In the office, original
    paintings of all eighty-three of Maine's lighthouses.

DOROTHY: I think my favorite is Boone. It is just a barren
    hunk of rock, and the lighthouse rises up out of the
    rock. We went out there one time and I took a
    chocolate cake out to the Coast Guard fellows who were
    serving out there at that time. And, as you come upon
    it, it's just so barren, and no matter where you look,
    there's nothing but rough sea all around it, and you
    think of how desolate it is and it really gives you the
    true meaning of what a light really is put out there for.

NOAH: What's happened to it?

DOROTHY: It's automated.

CLIFF: The blizzard of '78 did it in.

NOAH: You mean, destroyed it?

DOROTHY: The water came in through the house and went out through the other side of the house, and it demolished some of the oil tanks and took away the boathouse, did a lot of damage.

NOAH: So they said, let's automate it, after that?

DOROTHY: They said, let's automate instead of rebuilding.

CLIFF: After a hundred and sixty-seven years, it was automated.

DOROTHY: When that storm came, the men were driven to the top of the tower. My husband went out with the Coast Guard in the helicopter to rescue them. They were up in the top of the tower with the dog. He was scared, I remember you telling how frightened he was.

NOAH: The dog, oh, I'll bet.

DOROTHY: The men were, too. They were up there in the tower a day and a half before they were rescued.

Noah: Cliff Shattuck has written a couple of books on the lighthouses of Maine and has climbed to the top of all of them. Shattuck is quite critical of the way the Coast Guard has torn down lighthouses in the past, ripping down history, he says, and he believes everybody should make more of an effort to save them. The Coast Guard does have a leasing program available now for many of the automated lighthouses. You promise to maintain the property, the Coast Guard continues to service the light and the fog signals. Some towns have taken over lighthouses and historical societies. Also individual owners.

Cliff: We have seven here in Maine that are privately
owned summer homes now. And they are fine
expressions and examples because the people are
proud of them, they take care of them, and they are
rapidly emerging as the best examples of lighthouses
left in the state.

NOAH: You'd like to see that done again?

CLIFF: I'd love to see that done again.

NOAH: But couldn't somebody go in and put a fast-food
restaurant in a lighthouse?

CLIFF: What's the matter with that? Two of them are
bed-and-breakfasts right now. Why, what's the harm in
it? If McDonald's wants to put the arches over a light
facility, so what? I dare say it'll be pretty and painted
for many, many years. That's a lot more than the
government has done to it.

   foghorn sounding

Tuesday, August 15, Maine, 1989

It was still dark in the morning when we drove back down
the coast. We had to leave without Cliff and Dorothy's breakfast, featuring "Maine's most scrumptious blueberry pancakes," and didn't find coffee until we were down to Rock-
land. I'm afraid I sat in the back seat and grumbled a bit.
Melissa and Kevin wanted to record as early as possible—if
we get out before dawn, the wind's down and the boats
aren't out making a racket.

   Then we drive around by Owls Head Light, leave the car,
walk up the road, and start to get excited—you can *hear
scenes!* There's a heavy fog, and the signal is on: the foghorn—a soft, low, resonant blast every ten seconds or so—

and there's a higher-pitched horn, in the distance at Rock-
land Harbor. There's some wind in the trees, and waves on
the rocks below, and the fog seems to amplify all of the
sound, holding it in the air. And these are the only sounds
we hear—just a lighthouse on a cliff by the ocean early in
the morning in Maine. Kevin records from several perspectives, for about thirty minutes, he's smiling, his eyes intent
on the VU meters.

One day ten years ago in Kentucky, as part of a story
about Thomas Merton, we climbed the steps of the belltower
at the Trappist monastery, the Abbey of Gethsemani, to record the monks at Vespers, their voices echoing through the
cold limestone chapel. For a frightening documentary on
Jim Jones and his People's Temple in Guyana, we used some
actual recordings from the "services" in the jungle, Jones
threatening and haranguing his followers, and their unified
primal screams in response. Someday I hope to do a story
about the mission churches of northern New Mexico, and
use the soft, vibrant, early morning sounds of the birds
chattering under the *portales* around the plaza at Santa Fe.

These are scenes that work for radio; too often we're stuck
with sounds that could happen anywhere: traffic going by
on the street, and the town hall bell (which is now more
than likely to be a recording itself). Radio producers have
been known to argue about the relative honesty and purity
of a sound. Can you, for example, use a tape of West Coast
surf for an East Coast story? Surf is tough to record, so I
think I would, but in a nonspecific way: I wouldn't say, "This
the sound of the surf at Nags Head, North Carolina." (A producer once taught me that if you have to say, "This is the
sound of . . . ," then you've got the wrong sound.) Can you use
out-of-state birds? Or out-of-season birds? Probably
shouldn't unless you want to answer some mail; people
know about birds. We all have favorite sounds: if a dog barks
someplace when I'm doing a story, it's going in. I know a
reporter who is fond of footsteps on gravel and car-door
slams. Other devices can become tiresome: I can't stand to

hear a phone ring in a story, because then I know I'm going to hear someone answer it and say something like, "Citizens for Clean Water, can we help you?" I've almost given up recording in churches on location; it's a scene that's used far too often.

Later in the morning Melissa makes some calls, arranging permission to record the huge old foghorn on the lightship *Nantucket,* at dock in Portland. The *Nantucket* is decommissioned, now privately owned—a traveling exhibition. We're lucky she's in home port.

NOAH: Mike Perry is the *Nantucket*'s engineer. He starts up the air compressors below deck. The diaphone signal is very low frequency, very high volume, 104 decibels. It is said to be capable of knocking seagulls out of the sky. All of the diaphones have been replaced by electronic signals. The *Nantucket*'s horn is half a century old. The three compressors run for ten minutes, building up air pressure. And Engineer Perry sounds the horn.

long, loud blast across the harbor

It's a fierce, blatting sound, ripping across the water and the city, and rolling out into the countryside. Two long notes, the higher one dropping off . . . WEEEEEEEEE—OOOOOH. Kevin was taping on shore about a half a block away, and Mike Perry lets me pull the lanyard to blow the horn a second time. Yesterday, Ken Black had told us what it was like, serving aboard the lightships.

BLACK: You learn to talk through the fog signal, and in very short order you learned to talk, and you'd talk along as we're talking now and . . . stop while the foghorn had been ringing, just wait while it blows and then keep on going. After the first night, I slept—my cabin, the captain's cabin, was twenty feet away from the foghorn and after the first night, no problem. You couldn't put a clock or a barometer on my bulkhead in the cabin because the vibration would ruin it.

Our appointment with a lightkeeper was rescheduled, so we actually had some free time. We drove to Two Lights State Park, for lunch at a lobster shack on the beach. I had forgotten how rich a food lobster is and that you really don't have any business eating it for lunch if you just had it for dinner the night before, and sure enough I soon got sick. The air turned hot, the sunlight gritty, and the sound of the surf bothersome, and I felt shaky on the ride over to Portland Head Light, and weak as I walked around the lawn for a while. The keeper was upset with us for missing our earlier appointment, although he seemed to be fine when Melissa called him. Now he was surly. He'd done a lot of interviews, he said. And, in fact, I had seen him on television just a week ago, on the anniversary of the Lighthouse Act; it was two hundred years ago that Congress approved the money to build the first lighthouses. Portland was the first to be completed; Davis Simpson is the twenty-ninth and the final keeper, the lighthouse has just been automated, he's planning to retire.

And no, Simpson says, he won't take us up to the top of his lighthouse—he now realizes that all media people ask the same questions anyway, so why bother. We're not having fun here, and this is the first time I'm about to throw up on someone I'm talking to. The keeper doesn't realize this, and certainly doesn't know that at the moment, I just don't care if he's in a bad mood. We both, though, have jobs to do, and soon he's talking comfortably, and I'm nodding like I'm paying attention. About ten minutes of tape, and we can say goodbye and we're sorry, and head for the airport.

Saturday, August 19, Washington, D.C., 1989

Studio two at National Public Radio. The control room is dark, mostly, except for a large Radius computer screen. The first one minute and thirty seconds of our lighthouse story has been mixed, very painstakingly, by Kevin and Melissa— they've spent most of four days in this room. I've come by this morning to listen to what they've finished. Kevin touches the computer's keyboard . . . and through the studio's JBL monitors I hear the waves smashing against the cliff, the foghorn of Owls Head Light, and the lighter note of the faraway horn. I can shut my eyes and the feel of the fog against my skin returns, and the scent of the roses. When you listen to digital tape on good speakers, you can almost get up *inside* the sound.

waves against rocks, a distant foghorn

NOAH: It takes only a moment, standing on a cliff on the coast of Maine, watching the fog swirl in, listening, a moment to slow down, for your thoughts, even your breath to arrive and settle and depart, along with the waves on the rocks below.

waves

And then climb the path to the top of the hill to the Owls Head Light, built in 1826, high on a point over Penobscot Bay.

foghorn louder, echoing

The lightkeepers are gone now, but early this morning the light is on, the fog signal is working, and you can hear another one, too, from the harbor to the north.

both fog signals sounding

The goldenrod is in bloom and you can smell the wild roses, the grass is seacoast green, a mourning dove is calling. It *would be* some place special, and it's easy to imagine a century ago, a ship out on the ocean in bad weather, the mariners hoping to see the faintest flash of a light.

There are some wonderful sounds in this story, but what we're learning about digital editing and production is that NPR isn't ready. And neither is the technology, really, although there is a digital work station, I'm told, that could do all of this much faster; but the hardware would cost half a million dollars.

It's the editing that takes time: Kevin displays a particular sound, or sentence, on the monitor in the form of a wave pattern. Melissa decides if she wants it shortened, or to have a word taken out of the middle, and that's done by computer command, using the Macintosh keyboard, and the Mouse. You get to hear the sounds as you're seeing them on the screen. You can change the volume; you could change the pitch, add reverberation, do almost anything, but it's slow going.

Last Thursday, I finished writing and came down to the studio to record the narration. My voice became another wave on the screen. You could use sixteen stereo tracks of sound—all arrayed horizontally across the screen. The actual mixing of the completed story took only a minute or so, laying it out on the screen, but waiting for the computer to make the edits took endless hours. I found it too frustrating to watch, and didn't want to spend any time in the studio at all.

The story sounded great on the air, though (we played it from a digital machine, and used digital to record "All Things Considered" for the later feeds of the program, going out at 6:30 and 8:00 P.M. EDT). There was some argument

about our mentioning—at the end of the story—the specific
audio equipment we had used. Why bother with that, our
editor said. It sounds pretentious, someone else thought.
But I believed some in the audience would be interested, in
the same way you might take note of a photo credit—the
camera and lens, and film. Also, it was a way to let the audience know they had heard a complete digital production.

> NOAH: The sounds of our visit to the lighthouses in Maine
> were recorded in stereo, with a Sony PCM digital tape
> recorder, and mixed with a Diaxis digital work station,
> controlled by an Apple Macintosh II. The microphone,
> Neumann RSM-190.

Monday, August 21, Washington, D.C., 1989

It's a delightful thing about this job—you get to talk with
your heroes. I'd always wanted to meet David Lewiston, a
producer for Nonesuch Records. I didn't actually see him, he
was in New York, but it was a very satisfying conversation.
Lewiston is a musician and composer, but most of all a recording engineer, with great energy and curiosity and love
for the music of the world: Java, Tibet, Pakistan, India,
Bolivia, China. And now he's returned to Bali after twenty
years to make a new tape and compact disc. He recorded the
music in the pavilion of an art gallery in a village called Mas.

> *Balinese music, bells and percussion, fades*

> LEWISTON: Balinese music is meant to be played or
> listened to outdoors. Also, Bali doesn't have a really
> good indoor recording space, so recording outdoors is
> the logical way to go. The problem is that there are
> packs of stray dogs howling, especially at nighttime.
> Bali is infested with these stray dogs and they make it

very difficult to find a quiet enough place for recording. Also, motorbikes have invaded Bali. There are people on really noisy, little 125cc motorbikes, on even the smallest lanes in Bali, so they go everywhere, even to the remotest villages, and you can imagine what that does to recorded sound.

NOAH: And the microphones?

LEWISTON: I used a pair of mikes which are designed for outdoor work, in fact I'm sure in your interview work you must have seen them—Electrovoice RE-50s, which are designed for hand holding. And I think that to the astonishment of all of us, they are more than adequate for the rather demanding music of the gamelan.

NOAH: My technician behind the glass here is making a surprised face because the RE-50 is a standard broadcast interview microphone.

LEWISTON: It's a very simple mike.

NOAH: *Gamelan—*?

LEWISTON: *salunding,* from Tenganan, music of the Bali Aga, and they are most unusual people. These are the original Balinese and they have the—they claim that this is the real Balinese music. They feel that the other is heavily enculturated with what the Japanese brought when they came in the fifteenth century.

music plays for a time, mostly chimes

LEWISTON: What gives the gamelan its magical shimmering sound is the fact that the same note on a different instrument will be tuned to a slightly different pitch, and it creates beats, and the essential shimmer of the gamelan comes from—if all the instruments were tuned identically, it would sound very dull.

NOAH: In the song that sounds like frogs . . . ?

LEWISTON: Yes, "Frog Song." And that has to be the froggiest frog song that I've ever heard. I was working with Pak Artika and his group, and they had these instruments which essentially are just pieces of bamboo with slits carved in them, so that the slits are blown across much in the manner one would blow across a reed of some kind, and that creates the sound.

NOAH: What is the name of the instrument?

LEWISTON: *Enggung.*

NOAH: You have twenty-eight recordings for Nonesuch?

LEWISTON: I think that's the latest count, yes.

NOAH: What's the one that you put on late at night, the one that is really special to you after all these years?

LEWISTON: I would say ... well, it's actually two of my Tibetan recordings, the one I made at Gyuto in 1972, which is an excerpt from the text of a tantra called *Sangwa Dupa.* The chordal chanting of Gyuto always moves me. And another Tibetan recording made at a monastery in the Tashi Jong Tibetan community, which is also in the Indian West Himalayas.

NOAH: Has this ever happened to you—have you been someplace, heard some music that was so wonderful, so special, that you didn't want to record it and take it away?

LEWISTON: No, that's never happened, but a couple of times I've heard music which I think—had thought—I thought I must have been dreaming and I could never find the source of it afterwards. One time I was in a monastery in the Dark of Hemis for the Festival for Padmasambhaya, which usually happens during the month of May, and as I was sleeping in my tent I heard some absolutely incredible music on the ritual instruments. But when I asked the next day, nobody knew anything about it. Then a few years ago, I was in Spiti, which is in the Indian Himalayas on the border with Tibet, and the Dalai Lama was there performing the Kalacakra initiation. And as I was sleeping one night, I heard the most beautiful folk music from Kinnaur, which is the adjoining mountain valley, and I wasn't able to find the people who'd been singing, the following day. Things like this have happened.

NOAH: Do you hope to go back?

LEWISTON: Oh, sure I'll be back in the Himalayas. That's a continuing interest.

NOAH: Anything coming up right away?

LEWISTON: No, I'm ... my personal savings are exhausted now and I want to return and work some more with my Tibetan friends in South India, so I'm waiting for some cash to flow in so I can go back and do that.

I once was asked by a friend who taught a fifth-grade class in Santa Fe to stop by and talk with the students. I had no idea what they might want to hear. I discussed the news business for ten minutes and then called for questions. "Have you ever interviewed M. C. Hammer?" they asked. "Have you ever met Arnold Schwarzenegger?" "Bonnie Raitt," I offered, and "Jodie Foster?" No, they wanted Bo Jackson!

Before the class was over I was able to make the point, or at least offer the notion, that important people aren't necessarily famous, that my heroes tend to be those who are working quietly someplace. I'd met Bill Sanchez, a Catholic priest in the village of Villanueva, sixty miles east of Santa Fe. Father Sanchez was helping workers take action against what they believed to be dangerous conditions in a fiberboard plant, the county's largest employer.

I do count Bonnie Raitt as a hero, though, as well as John Hartford, for a single reason—he's always refused to sell the rights to his song "Gentle on My Mind." You won't hear that song being used as a commercial. When I asked him why he wouldn't sell the song and how much money he's turned down, he was noncommittal. Guess it really wasn't my business.

As for John Cheever, I was simply a fan. And thrilled when he agreed to an interview. I called from Penn Station in New York to let him know which train I'd be on. I saw him waiting on the platform—it's like a movie! There's John Cheever. No, it's more like one of his stories. And he drove me to his house and we talked for an hour or so about his books and Yaddo, the writers' colony in upstate New York. "Do you want to stay for dinner?" he said. "My daughter Susan's coming." I wanted to meet Susan Cheever, but needed to get back to Washington.

Wednesday, August 23, Washington, D.C., 1989

A day of demonstrations in the Soviet bloc countries. Ann Cooper has been reporting for most of the month on the increasing sentiment for independence in Estonia, Latvia, Lithuania, and now, hundreds of thousands linked hands in a giant human chain across those countries. It was a protest against the Soviet takeover of the Baltic states fifty years ago this month. And late in the day, we got a phone call through to Estonia.

> NOAH: In the country of Estonia, Andra Vaiderman took part in the demonstrations today in Tallin, the capitol city. Vaiderman is a member of the Estonian Popular Front.

> VAIDERMAN: We were holding hands and we were singing and we were shouting slogans, and so on and so on. But these slogans were very simple, mainly one word—"freedom."

NOAH: One word, "freedom." And the songs that you were singing?

VAIDERMAN: And the songs were Estonian songs about our fatherland and how we love it and so on and so on. And we wanted to express one very important thought or idea, that all people as your very famous citizen, Thomas Jefferson, has said, that all men are born equal, but we think that all nations are equal as well. And it is not important whether these nations are small or big. They have this right to be free.

NOAH: How many people do you think in Tallin, in your town, or in Estonia disagree with the sentiments for independence? Who would be in disapproval of what happened today?

VAIDERMAN: Well, I think that this percentage is not very big, and of course mostly they are Russian-speaking people, but I want to express once again as I have said it many, many times before, that it is not the opinion of all Russian-speaking people who live in Estonia. For example, in that place where I was standing, I saw very many Russians standing around there, and they were listening and even crying. We are not demanding anything *unhuman*. We are not demanding violence, not at all. We are ready to live together with Russians in our country, but we only want that our country is free country and we can solve our problems here in Tallin or in Estonia. We don't want to have command from Moscow.

NOAH: What did your parents say to you about what happened in 1939?

VAIDERMAN: Well, they say that it was an occupation. I have known it all of my life, although in newspapers and in books it was written the other way around, but my parents have always told me how it really

happened in Tallin. My mother was in Tallin when
occupation took place, and she has told me several
times the events that took place in Tallin and other
parts of Estonia as well.

NOAH: The occupation by the Soviet troops?

VAIDERMAN: Yes.

NOAH: But you said the newspapers told the story a
different way?

VAIDERMAN: Yes, they called it "revolution." That Estonian
people had decided freely to become part of the Soviet
Union, but that's not true. Because nobody has ever
asked from Estonian people whether they want to
belong to the Soviet Union or not. Maybe now we are
going to have this possibility.

Tuesday, August 29, Washington, D.C., 1989

Stories today about efforts in Moscow to stop the independence movements in the Baltic states, peace talks in Beirut,
Cambodian peace talks collapsing in Paris, the first Cuban
American wins a seat in the U.S. House of Representatives
(Ileana Ros-Lehtinen, Florida), Leona Helmsley is found
guilty of income-tax evasion, and a Renee Montagne report
from the Bensonhurst neighborhood of Brooklyn where a
black teenager was killed last week in a confrontation with
whites. Those are the important stories, but it's possible that
much of the dinnertime conversation around the country
tonight will be about the cover of *TV Guide*.

The picture on the cover is a drawing of Oprah Winfrey.
Actually it's Oprah Winfrey's face and Ann-Margret's body.
Ann-Margret's body wearing a dress that has been seen on
television before. Oprah Winfrey is shown smiling and surrounded by money, and her new fortune is the premise of

the story inside. *Time* magazine first noticed the *TV Guide* cover. A spokeswoman for Oprah Winfrey said she would not have posed in that revealing a dress. Ann-Margret said, "I've been on the cover of *TV Guide* four times but never without my head." David Sendler of *TV Guide* tried to explain it all.

SENDLER: The story is, that we assigned this to a freelance illustrator, and we are not unaware that freelance illustrators use photographs for reference so they can get the likeness, but we had absolutely no idea that he used that photograph of Ann-Margret for inspiration and was so literal of his copying of it. We were flabbergasted when we first heard this—when a reporter for *Time* magazine called. And needless to say, we've talked to the artist about it, and we will not have a repeat of that. So it is unfortunate, but in the meantime, you know, Oprah does look pretty good, and Bob Mackie's gown got another outing, and Ann-Margret got a cover, so . . .

NOAH: *Time* magazine said that the designer, Bob Mackie, saw this cover and recognized the gown that he had designed six years ago for Ann-Margret and called Ann-Margret's husband, Roger Smith, who recalled the pose and in fact recognized the ring as Ann-Margret's ring being on Oprah Winfrey's hand. He just took it verbatim and put Oprah's head on it?

SENDLER: Right, he had that photograph in his files, and you know he was assigned the task of having Oprah sitting on this pile of money, and he had this one picture of Ann-Margret sitting in such a pose and got carried away with what he did.

NOAH: Now, you take the position that Ann-Margret should be happy because she's on the cover of *TV Guide*—

SENDLER: I don't take a strong position, I'm just teasing with you about that. No, we're not happy that it happened, but when you put it in the context of the week's events, you know, it's not going to go down in history as one of the major crises of the Western world.

NOAH: I agree with you there. You could argue, though, that both Oprah Winrey and Ann-Margret would be insulted.

SENDLER: Well, it's true, you could argue that.

NOAH: Does this kind of thing happen quite often in illustration work?

SENDLER: Not to my knowledge. You mean at *TV Guide*?

NOAH: Well, yeah, or just generally in the magazine industry, where an illustrator would take a photograph of somebody who's well known and use it as the basis for something else?

SENDLER: I know, and I wouldn't name them, but, I mean, I know there are publications that take photographs of different parts of people's bodies and put them together for different purposes and that's yet another thing—we've never done that obviously, nor would we.

NOAH: Is that done to make the bodies look better?

SENDLER: No, probably for other reasons.

NOAH: What other reasons?

SENDLER: Well, you'd have to ask them—I don't really want to get into that, but I know it happens. (*Laughs*)

NOAH: You've got me really curious because I haven't the slightest idea what you're talking about.

SENDLER: It's to put them in different clothing for different occasions to create different impressions.

NOAH: Oh, to have them perhaps appear with people they wouldn't be with or in a place they wouldn't—

SENDLER: Or in clothing they might not have been wearing, that sort of thing.

NOAH: I see. Sounds like there's a whole lot going out there.

SENDLER: Oh, well, I don't know that there's a whole lot but there's at least a little.

Monday, September 4, Washington, D.C., 1989

It's Labor Day, at home. Getting set for a three-week vacation. It turned cool yesterday morning for the first time it seems since May, and we spent most of the day canning tomato sauce. Neenah bought two half-bushels of Roma tomatoes—organic, from the Potomac Farms stand at the Arlington market. We add our own basil and some onions and it cooks down to about twenty-five pints of spaghetti sauce.

The dogs are excited. Bonny's going up to Maine with us tomorrow and they know something's up. We're taking Bonny because she's more difficult to handle. She's a young Border terrier (Border *terrier,* I usually say, not *collie;* both breeds are from the Borders region of Scotland and England). Bonny is excitable, quick to bark, and fast—she'll be two blocks away before you realize you've let go of her leash. Will is our old reliable "random breed." He sort of looks like a beagle. We found him in a shelter as a pup. He'll stay home with a good friend to look after him.

Last night I read the new book, *Katharine and E. B. White: An Affectionate Memoir*—it's by Isabel Russell, who was their personal secretary in North Brooklin, Maine, during the 1970s. I've read several books about the Whites—

this one is a bit discouraging; they were so old and infirm. But they were very kind to each other.

We'll be staying at a house on Cape Rosier, not far from Brooklin, and it pleases me to think of E. B. White driving along those roads on an errand with one of *his* dogs, Jones perhaps, the Norwich terrier, on the seat beside him.

Thursday, September 7, Maine, 1989

Blueberries! Tiny, tasty, three dollars a quart at a roadside stand and you just leave the money in a box. There's arugula in the garden here, and we have a phone number for lobster. Also, clean air, lots of sun, sailboats. Loons out on Penobscot Bay. Sleep with the windows open . . .

This could be a problem though: A classified ad in the local newspaper:

CLASSIC, EARLY 1970S MERCEDES 280. DARK GREEN. STANDARD TRANS-MISSION, ONCE OWNED BY E. B. WHITE. EXCELLENT RUNNING CONDITION. NEEDS SOME BODY WORK. 326.9423

I'm afraid if I call the number, I could end up being totally obsessed with the memory of Mr. White. Neenah and I drove down this way a couple of years ago, from Bangor to Blue Hill and Brooklin. We were looking for the Whites' old home—his dateline in *The New Yorker* was "Allen Cove." We asked around to find out which place it was; a lovely white clapboard farmhouse, with gardens and flowers behind tall roadside hedges. I know there's a boathouse there, too; I recall the Jill Krementz photograph of White sitting in front of his typewriter at a table in the boathouse. (What if somebody had that old Underwood typewriter for sale? Would I dare buy it?)

I didn't meet E. B. White. I'm not sure I wanted to really, although I would like to have heard him talk just a bit; we know his voice from the recording of *Charlotte's Web*. And I've always appreciated a letter Mr. White sent to NPR in 1979:

> I get a lot of requests to be interviewed. In years past, I acceded to some of them, though not with much enthusiasm as I don't enjoy talking or answering questions and am not good at it. A couple of years ago I decided that I had had enough of punditry and of public exposure. Now I turn down all requests. It is one of the privileges of being eighty years old.
>
> Many thanks for asking me. I'm sorry I don't feel able to fall in with your plan for an interview to be broadcast over National Public Radio.
>
> Sincerely,
> E. B. White

Sunday, September 10, Maine, 1989

In the early morning there's a wonderful golden half moon in the sky to the south. We wait for low tide and then take the canoe across the bay to the small town of Castine. Bonny goes along and jumps out once to swim for a while. Nothing fazes a terrier; we pull her back in, she shakes herself dry and resumes a position on watch in the bow. We have our lunch on the dock at Castine. Peanut butter and jelly sandwiches, shortbread cookies and pears, and watch the cadets of the Maine Maritime Academy out in the bay racing their Laser sailboats. Castine is a town of white frame houses and old trees. It's an isolated place, peninsular, it could be lonely in winter. And it's a stubborn town, enduring the invasions of the British and French, and standing against the harsh Maine coastal weather. I wander the streets, thinking about the people who settled here, perhaps even some of my relatives.

I later found a poem by Philip Booth, who now lives

amidst his family's history in Castine. It's called "Before Sleep":

> *The day put away before bed,*
> *The house almost closed before night.*
>
> *By the time I walk out over the knoll,*
> *down the steep Maine Street*
>
> *that dead-ends in the sea,*
> *the village has put out its lights.*
>
> *The winter stars are turned up over*
> *the tide, a tide so quiet the harbor*
>
> *holds stars. The planet holds.*
> *Before the village turns over in sleep,*
>
> *I stand at the edge of the tide,*
> *letting my feet feel into the hillside*
>
> *to where my dead ancestors live.*
> *Whatever I know before sleep*
>
> *surrounds me. I cannot help know.*
> *By blood or illness, gossip or hope,*
>
> *I'm relative to every last house.*
> *Before I climb home up the hill, I hold:*
>
> *I wait for myself to quiet, breathing*
> *the breath of sleepers I cannot help love.*

Wednesday, September 13, Maine, 1989

I go out for a two-mile run in the cool morning air, and when I come back in, build a fire with some birch logs; there's a cold front arriving fast.

We take some books over to donate to the Brooklin Library (there's a sign: KIDS PLEASE WIPE SHOES BEFORE ENTERING, SAND RUINS RUGS AND FLOORS) and then have breakfast at the Morning Moon Café, which opens, the waitress tells me, at 5:00 A.M. for the fishermen. I order a Cheddar omelette, homemade coffeecake. The café looks like an old one-room schoolhouse, but no, they say, it was once the post office. At the Brooklin General Store across the street there's a rack of newspapers, the *Bangor Daily News,* with clothespins attached to each paper. The clothespins have labels, names of customers: Gorski, Crosby, Loomis, Walker, Gilder, Mills.

We visit the WoodenBoat School, out on the Naskeag Road. It was once a saltwater farm, a summer house for a Boston gentleman. Now it's a sailing and boat-building school, and headquarters for a magazine, *WoodenBoat,* with a circulation of one hundred thousand. They also have great T-shirts.

Thursday, September 14, Maine, 1989

Cool with light rain. I've been reading Russell Baker's book *The Good Times,* and Annie Dillard's new book on writing. Finished Tom Clancy's *Clear and Present Danger.* You can also *hear* some good reading on Maine Public Broadcasting, for grownups and children: stories by Raymond Carver, Natalie Babbitt, Gary Paulsen. I like the idea that a statewide network can say, "Sure, let's put on 'Read to Me' at 7:30 P.M.—

it's the perfect time to have a program for kids, right when they're getting ready for bed." It seems to me this is much of what public radio should be about, and that it would be far too easy for a program director to find a more *popular* program for that time period.

There's a phone call from one of the ATC producers in Washington. They have an idea—I'll travel on Amtrak from Saint Paul, Minnesota, out to Seattle to do reports about the original Great Northern Railroad and its founder, James J. Hill. Two weeks, a field producer, a sound engineer—it's the best assignment I've ever had. But then I've never had a really bad assignment; mostly as ATC hosts we are encouraged to follow our own interests and enthusiasms.

Tonight, lobster. A late-afternoon visit with Paul Venno, as he brings his boat in. Floating wooden boxes of lobsters and crabs; he says he caught eight hundred pounds of crabs today. He gives us a paper bagful of crabs, and we buy two lobsters, with both claws—$16.25. It's pleasant to hear Paul talk about the day on the water, in his deep Maine accent. The lobsters turn out fine, steamed in an inch of water for, not fifteen minutes, I was told, but fourteen.

Sunday, September 17, Maine, 1989

Cloudy and steamy fog in the morning. The fireplace helps some. Yesterday, at an antique shop, we were told about a couple, traveling from the Midwest, who stopped in and wanted to buy one birch log to put in front of their fireplace back home.

At an auction that morning in Blue Hill, we didn't buy anything and I still regret it. We didn't know, really, how auctions work, and it was all going too fast for us and we missed some bargains, perhaps: a set of crystal for six, a Maine Central Railroad lantern, brass beds and sea chests, a goose platter (it sold for $300), and a woodworking bench. It took them most of a day to auction everything.

In the evening, with some friends, we gathered mussels at Bakeman's beach, about a bushel. It was early afternoon, the low tide exposing the large, glistening black (although these are called "blue") mussels. We cooked them in white wine and garlic and onions and olive oil, and had some great crunchy lettuce and red potatoes and bread. A bottle of Anchor Steam Ale, served at porch temperature. It's the meal I'll remember until next September.

Thursday, September 21, Maine, 1989

A quiet run in the morning's rain, about fifty-five degrees. I've had lots of coffee and listened to "Morning Edition" on Maine Public Broadcasting. We also hear "All Things Considered" every day, although I probably shouldn't listen. If you work for the program, everything you hear while you're on vacation will be either *better* than you could have done, or *worse*. Equally discouraging.

And we're listening to a community station here as well. WERU in Blue Hill Falls. It's run by volunteers, mostly, people who just come in and play what they really like: there's even a father-and-daughter program. And I heard a youngster doing a broadcast from the Blue Hill Fair, talking with an equally young exhibitor about her brown sheep.

Yesterday Neenah went to visit Helen Nearing: the Nearings, Helen and Scott (who died in 1983 at one hundred), came to this coast of Maine thirty years ago to start Forest Farm, living by their labor and their writing. Neenah wanted to meet Helen and to interview her for a radio story. She was nervous when she left and thrilled when she came back.

You can almost make friends with foxes here. A small one will walk down out of the woods and through the yard. In the afternoon it would be sunny and quiet and I'd remember it was time for the fox. John McPhee once wrote, about a similar if more dramatic moment on a lake in the north of Maine, "Stillness envelops us. It is the stillness of a moose intending to appear." On a walk with Bonny this afternoon we saw two porcupines, waddling off the road into the woods. Thank goodness Bonny was on her leash—the vets in town earn good money pulling quills from dog noses.

It can seem enchanting—this part of Maine, this time of year. The foggy mornings on the bay, the sparkling light in the afternoon, the grass almost luminous along the paths through the woods. Neenah's been reading Richard Adams's *Watership Down*, listening to the rabbits talk in her mind. You forget the signs posted along one of the roads: THIS AREA CLOSED TO ALL DIGGING OF CLAMS, MUSSELS, QUAHOGS, OYSTERS, CARNIVOROUS WHELKS OR SNAILS BECAUSE OF POLLUTION OR PARALYTIC SHELLFISH POISONING. You forget that real estate development is pushing prices out of the reach of local people. And you truly forget how tough it has been, always, to make a living on these coasts. I've read in *Down East* magazine about the granite carvers of Hurricane Island, in Penobscot Bay. In the late 1900s more than a thousand workers and their families lived on Hurricane, supplying stone for the buildings and bridges of American cities. It was dangerous work and the dust was particularly harmful: "Many of the granite cutters developed lung disease from the dust in the cutting sheds. 'When they began coughing blood, they began carving their own monuments.' "

Wednesday, September 27, Washington, D.C., 1989

Seventeen and a half hours of driving from Cape Rosier, Maine, to our house in Arlington, Virginia. We arrive at 6:00 A.M. and realize that we should have left six hours earlier than we did. It was a drowsy and dangerous, rainy and foggy drive, although it was good to hear some late-night radio.

Lots of mail, and new books, and twenty-six computer mail messages waiting at work. I'm trying to get ready for our train trip out West next week. I decide to get my Olivetti portable typewriter fixed. I found it at a yard sale for $15. The repairman says $106 to clean and recondition, but it's worth it, he says, this one's made in Italy and it's better than the newer ones from Spain or Mexico.

I have a request to do a documentary narration for a member station in Minnesota, and they've sent along the script. After I read it, I call the producer to say no. The program is about teenage suicide and the opening scene is a re-creation, using actors' voices. It's set at a high school hockey game, fans and students watching the players and making comments about a young man who later kills himself. The cheering is followed by a gunshot, echoing. I usually don't like this technique and believe it's unnecessary, especially with a subject like suicide; these stories are dramatic enough.

We've all used similar techniques, though. In the spring, Art Silverman and I produced a story about the flood that killed more than two thousand people in Johnstown, Pennsylvania, on May 31 one hundred years ago. The first line of the script read: "Let's do some imagining. Let's say that in a few minutes or so we're going to be able to experience the Johnstown Flood." Then we told the story of the events leading up to that day and the reasons for the tragedy. At the end we played the *sound* of the flood.

> NOAH: Some thought it was the visitation of God. At first
> there was a strong wind whipping past and you could
> see, up the valley, a cloud of black smoke and dust. It
> was talked of afterwards as the "death mist." And
> survivors tried to tell what it sounded like: an
> avalanche, thunder. They heard whistles blowing,
> houses being ripped apart. Screams. The Johnstown
> Flood.

Our flood effect was created for us by Ken Nordine, one of the best-known announcers in the country. He has a world-class studio on the top floor of his home in Chicago, including a lot of new digital audio computer gear. We wanted to put several different sounds together, and we wanted it to be terrifying. Most of the sounds were suggested by the eyewitness accounts. The flood had taken an hour to come down the narrow valley to Johnstown, and it carried houses and barns and horses and wagons, even burning stoves. And people. Ken used a digital sound library. He started with rain and running water; he added thunder and explosions, the whistles, screams. The flood builds to a crescendo, then fades.

This is a re-creation, to be sure. But it's a long way, in my view, from covering a news story by having people pretend the event is actually happening—the parents of the murdered woman will be shown driving down the street, parking in front of her house, just as they did on the morning they found the body. When you try to make something look real, the danger is in having the audience believe it *is* real.

It was Ken Nordine who gave me my best professional announcer's advice, a couple of years ago. He said, "Don't ever let 'em tell you that they'll add the music later." Meaning, don't agree to record what's called a "dry track," just the voice alone. If there's to be music in the final production, you have to hear it, at least in your headphones, if you have any chance of sounding comfortable with that music. He explained that producers often think you're being cranky when you ask to hear the music, but it's not their voice on the radio or TV, it's yours. And I've long thought that good announcers, actors, respond not only to the mood and tempo of the music but also to the key; it's possible that narrators change keys without being aware of it.

I have some advice of my own for new people in radio: Don't ever say anything in a studio that you don't want to hear on the air. Obviously, this relates to bad language and potentially open microphones (the ON AIR light has to burn out sometime) but also to tape-recorded interviews. One afternoon I was talking to a woman who, as a child, had been the first model for the Coppertone suntan lotion ads, showing a puppy pulling down a little girl's bathing suit. It was a pleasant conversation until someone in the control room convinced me to ask if she would be embarrassed to pose for the same ad today. "Go ahead and ask it just for fun, we won't use it on the air." The woman, justifiably, was highly offended. And I just assumed that the question and answer would be cut out of the interview. It wasn't.

This on the Associated Press wire today:

BLOOMFIELD HILLS MICH KILL THE 6TH GRAF OF THE 3RD ITEM IN AM PEOPLE AO 09180029. John Hinckley did not kill John Lennon. AP NY 15:47 EDT

I located the story in the computer. It's about a Yoko Ono art show opening in Michigan. The last sentence reads: "John Hinckley fatally shot John Lennon nine year ago in New York." (Lennon's assailant was Mark David Chapman.)

And I recently heard this on NPR, during a morning newscast after Ferdinand Marcos died, "Marcos, who ruled the Philippines for more than twenty decades..."

Monday, October 2, Minnesota, 1989

A morning flight to Minneapolis–Saint Paul. Melissa Block and I are heading west. We'll ride Amtrak's Empire Builder from Saint Paul all the way out to Seattle, collecting material along the way so that we can tell the story of James J. Hill, the man who built the Great Northern Railway—Hill was once called "the barbed-wired, shaggy-headed, one-eyed son of a bitch of western railroading."

We have special tickets that will allow us to get off the

train for a day or two as we go along. And we plan to check in
with Washington often, as interviews are still being set up
out in front of us.

Flawn Williams, our engineer from the Chicago bureau,
arrives on a later flight. We collect his equipment, all of our
bags, and start off for lunch. "How much tape did you
bring?" we ask Flawn. You want to be sure to have enough,
but you tend to use more tape if you have plenty, and that
makes for a lot more work when you get home. Weight is
also a consideration, and on this trip we'll be jumping on
and off trains. Flawn's decided to bring a DAT recorder; the
digital machine is six pounds versus thirty-five for the reel-
to-reel Nagra recorder, and the tapes are lighter and smaller,
too. He's brought thirty two-hour cassettes.

Our first interview is in the James J. Hill Reference Library. I also wanted to look through some of his papers; Hill
made copies of all his correspondence, thousands of hand-
written letters. He stayed up until three-thirty in the morning, keeping track of things, earning the confidence of older
business leaders, men with money. He was smart, ambi-
tious, honest, and in absolutely the right place at the right
time. James Hill, a Canadian, arrived in Saint Paul in 1856.
He was seventeen years old. And Saint Paul was the edge of
the frontier—steamboats couldn't travel any farther north
on the Mississippi.

> THOMAS WHITE OF THE HILL LIBRARY: Everyone in the
> nineteenth century knew what that meant. Those who
> thought about it. Many didn't. Obviously he [Hill] did,
> and this was a point of opportunity. It was a new
> territory, relatively unpopulated, it was a logical place
> to go if you wanted to make your fortune. Particularly
> if you'd come from frontier Ontario. A new frontier
> held few terrors for someone like that; they knew they
> could make it work.

Later we spend some time recording the sounds of model
trains at the headquarters of a local club. It's grand fun

watching the little trains run around a vast and detailed layout, and talking with the modelers about the old days of the Great Northern, but nothing from the modeler's club made it into the final story. When we listened to the tape, we just couldn't find the one entertaining and/or informative anecdote that we needed; the men were quite serious about their hobby. Still, I felt bad leaving them out.

Time is always the problem; even a fifteen-minute story fills up fast. I tend now to remember assignments by what I had to leave out of the final cut. The voice of a little girl at the Alaska State Fair saying, "That's the biggest pig I ever saw." A complete conversation with the parents of a young Indian woman who had committed suicide; they hadn't gone to the funeral because their daughter had become a Catholic. I still remember a sentence that was cut at the last minute from our documentary about Jonestown. I was writing about Jim Jones: "He died at the age of forty-seven, a bullet through his temple, dying anyway there in the jungle of the Orinoco Delta." I was proud of the sentence; it's only slightly overwrought.

Susan Stamberg once was discovered cleaning mayonnaise from a long piece of audio tape—someone had made a cut in one of her interviews, and Susan retrieved the tape from the garbage out behind the building. She spliced it back into the interview herself in time for air.

Sometimes these cuts can be a matter of intense disagreement between a reporter, an editor, possibly a producer. There's a joke about the way to resolve such an argument. Editor to reporter: "Which of these cuts that I'm suggesting would you quit over?" The reporter identifies some passages that he or she is prepared to defend with his job. "Fine," the editor says, "leave those and make all the others."

Quite often an ATC host will ask for some tape, after having heard the edited version of the interview on the air, within the context of the other stories. A key question may turn out to be missing, for example, and we'll try to find it on the floor of an editing booth and put it back for the next feed of the program. Of course at 9:30 P.M., after the program's gone out to the West Coast, if it's still not fixed, we just forget it and go home. But just once or twice, people have been known to make an edit in a story *after* it's been broadcast but *before* it's sent to the tape library. This could present some perplexing problems for historians of late-twentieth-century broadcasting.

Another stop in Saint Paul, the old Union Depot, at sunset.

> NOAH: The wind was rushing in from the west, on through the town and across the Mississippi River. If you go out looking for the glory that was once railroading in America, you can find just an echo here, the depot is mostly empty. In the 1920s, most everything moving west went through Saint Paul—passengers, immigrants, the express mail ... and in the pale evening light I try to imagine: the Model T Fords pulling up outside, valises and trunks being unloaded, the men wearing black, smoking cigars, women in long white dresses, the trains rumbling in below, clouds of steam and smoke and the gasp of air brakes. ...

The next morning, after visiting the Hill mansion—now a museum—on Summit Avenue (Melissa had arranged for a musician to come in and play Benjamin Carr's Flute Voluntary on the antique bellows-powered organ), we bought some sandwiches to take along on the train and reported to Burlington Northern's freight yard in Minneapolis. We had all our equipment and luggage, food and water, and we'd been told to wear jeans and heavy shoes. I'd forgotten sunglasses, though, and the sun would be bright coming into the cab as we traveled west.

The first part of our trip—up to the North Dakota state line—was in the engine of a BN freight train. Our escort was Doug Jones, a young assistant trainmaster. He's dressed like the other men, flannel shirt, baseball cap. He told me the first thing he did when he was hired was to go out and buy a watch; today's models are wristwatches, quartz, by Seiko or Pulsar, "Railroad Approved," with white faces and twenty-four-hour numbers.

Jones introduced us to the crew: the engineer, a conductor, and a brakeman. They grumbled some; they hadn't known we were coming. But mostly they didn't want Jones along, a company man who could be checking on the way they did their jobs. We had been told not to bother the crew with questions while the train was moving, but after a few miles everything was fine and they talked comfortably about their work.

NOAH: The men tell me stories about derailments and grade-crossing accidents. People every day try to make it across the track ahead of the train. A potato truck once didn't. The truck was cut in half, nobody was hurt, potatoes all over the place.

The engineer reminds the brakeman, passing towns, "Wave at the people, it's part of the job." And they tell the Lone Ranger story: somebody by the side of the tracks, wearing a black mask, *exposing himself* as the train goes by.

long train whistle

NOAH: It's dark now and a quarter moon is up, to the west, with Venus just above. The rails are gleaming ahead. They tell me it's easier to see at night, the signal lights glowing brighter, as they come up fast: red, green, yellow.

This can be a tough job, on the trains. In the winter, forty below, *not* counting the wind. And dangerous. But on a good day's run the cab of this diesel engine is right where these men want to be.

MARK JENSEN, CONDUCTOR: My dad was an engineer on the railroad, that's how I got started on it. He was forty-two years as an engineer.

NOAH: So he was with steam?

JENSEN: Yeah, and his dad before him was an engineer, too, for the Great Northern.

NOAH: There is a poem about the railroads and North Dakota. It's called "Dream Song," by Mark Vinz. It's about his grandfather, Alfred Marcus Call, who was born in 1876 and was a doctor in the town of Rugby. The poet imagines a trip on the train, a young boy and his grandfather, and he writes:

> *Yet here we are,*
> *holed up in an old Great Northern boxcar heading*
> > *west:*
>
> *Rugby, Minot, Manitou*
>
> *Again an old man whispering the names,*
> *a ghost-map of amulets*
> *in a season of difficult births:*
>
> *Williston, Cut Bank, Coeur d'Alene*
>
> *Again the last long journey,*
> > *forever conjuring our way*
> > > *toward that unfamiliar sea.*

train whistle, long, slow, fading

We ran through that afternoon and into the night, with a stop for a new crew at Staples, Minnesota, then on to Dilworth. We had a late dinner, then drove sixty miles up to Grand Forks, North Dakota, to the Holiday Inn. I could feel the vibration of the diesel engine, and the rumble, as I slept. I felt pretty good about the first day—the recordings in the engine compartment (the "front end," the train people call it) went pretty well. If Melissa had phoned back to Washington, the first question would have been, "Did you get to record in the cab?"

Wednesday, October 4, North Dakota, 1989

The train's late so we have a chance to go back into town for breakfast at Perkins'. Some people said later about these train stories that I talked too much about food, but I guess I thought of this as travel writing, and you do want to know what the food's like—especially on the train. Of course we were only on a freight train up from Minneapolis; this morning we'll be on Amtrak.

background sound of people talking inside station

NOAH: It seems like it's a different kind of waiting, for a train. The scene at the station *includes* you. It's not like at the airport, because you know which way the train's coming from, and you'll see it coming in. You listen, and watch the clock and walk outside and look down the track, and somebody spots it and you feel the vibration. And then the noise.

We interview a few passengers on the way to Minot. Mostly at Melissa's urging. She would find interesting people and wave for me to come over and talk. We meet a lovely young woman and a baby with shining blond hair—they could be from the sixties. The mother's name is Beautiful Mountain.

NOAH: Hi there. How old is he?

BEAUTIFUL MOUNTAIN: He's thirteen months. And he's getting tired of being on the train, I think.

NOAH: Where did you get on?

BEAUTIFUL MOUNTAIN: Last Tuesday. We got on in Portland, Oregon, and went to Portage, Wisconsin; it's a two-day ride. Now we're on our way home to Oregon.

NOAH: He seems to be doing great, though.

BEAUTIFUL MOUNTAIN: Off and on. (*Laughs*) We had to
make a few trips downstairs so he could holler.

NOAH: What's his name?

BEAUTIFUL MOUNTAIN: Molo Kai. *Kai,* like, is life, and *Molo*
is a spirit painting. So, it's kind of a mandala of life.

I've always had a difficult time starting a conversation
with a stranger, and I can never quite understand how I
ended up doing it for a living. Of course, the microphone
does give you an excuse, adds some courage, but I still regard an interview somehow as a very private matter. I can
remember hoping, years ago when I first started doing stories for NPR, that the person I was supposed to interview
wouldn't show up.

I'm much better now, but I still have a moment of anxiety
before starting to talk with anyone, on the radio or off. The
producers, of course, get to be very good at walking directly
up to people, smiling, as if doing a radio interview would be
just a wonderful thing. We find, generally, that the best interviews are with the people who aren't at all impressed that
someone's come from Washington to talk with them. If
someone has been thinking for weeks about what they'll say
to an NPR reporter, you then have to spend about twenty
minutes letting them get that out of their system before
you begin to hear something that sounds like real conversation.

I've had interviews fail because people didn't have anything to say, and interviews fail because people didn't say
anything *interestingly,* but I've only had one interview collapse because the person and I just weren't getting along.
James Galway, the flutist, came to the studio to talk about
his latest album and his U.S. tour. I was asking about his
home town in Ireland, and his parents and his beginnings
in music. My questions were mostly suggested by a recent

article about Galway in the Sunday *New York Times Magazine,* but for reasons I still don't understand, he became gruff and unpleasant, not wanting to talk at all. I told him it just wasn't working and apologized and left the studio. Maybe we should try again some day.

My favorite failed interview that we *broadcast* involved an elderly gentleman in the Bronx who had figured out a way to make lamps and coffeetables out of coffee grounds. The other tenants in his apartment building saved their grounds for him. He sent us a letter and some pictures of the tables and lamps. I thought it was a great idea and called him up, but when the time came for him to explain exactly *how* he managed to bind the coffee grounds together, he refused to say. But you don't understand, I urged, this is why we called you. "Why should I tell you?" he said. "This idea is worth big money." He was endearing, if not forthcoming.

Most of the time, and especially with news interviews by phone out of Washington, we know the answers to the questions we're asking. There's been, let's say, a plane crash in California. We have several accounts from the wire services, but we need a description for that evening's program. We call up a reporter on the scene, or a rescue worker, and in effect, the interviewer serves as an editor of the material, trying to elicit the information in a logical and listenable form. When the Challenger space shuttle exploded, in January 1986, no editing was needed. My father-in-law, Len Ellis, called immediately from Florida where he'd been vacationing—he watched the lift-off from a beach south of Cape Canaveral. Neenah's dad has been in radio for more than thirty years in Valparaiso, Indiana. We just started the tape recorder:

ELLIS: There we were out on the beach with a bunch of people, everybody huddling together to keep warm. That huge encompassing roar that comes around you, that's something else. After about a minute or more,

we saw what seemed to be a huge puff of smoke and
flame and then there seemed to be two vapor trails
that veered upward out of this puff. Someone alongside
of me said that just doesn't look right and I kinda was
thinking out loud, boy that looks like an
explosion—just doesn't look like something that
should have happened. And within almost a few
seconds everybody who was cheering and talking
stopped, everybody was glued to the sky. All you could
hear at that time was just the wind and the radio in
the background somebody had, and by this time the
radio said there was an explosion, and oh . . . about that
time somebody started to cry, about that time I wished
I was never on a beach watching it. Then everyone just
kind of turned and shuffled away, and within ten
minutes there was nobody there anymore.

I've been intrigued by something Larry King has said,
about his nightly work on Mutual Radio, an entirely different technique. King told a *New York Times* interviewer
that he never asks a question for which he knows the answer. He also never prepares for any interview, never reads a
book before talking with the author, saying that he wants to
be on an equal footing with the listener. He also makes two
million dollars a year.

ANNOUNCEMENT ON TRAIN P.A.: Minot, North Dakota, is the
next station stop in approximately ten minutes.

There's a good wind through the tall cottonwood trees,
still mostly green, down by the train station. They like to say
out here, "Hang on to your hat, this is North Dakota." In the
Amtrak waiting room you could put money in a small
wooden box on the wall and take a pamphlet, *The Railroad
Evangelist:* "TWO BEST WAYS TO TRAVEL: THE BIBLE WAY AND THE
RAILROAD WAY." The grain elevators are close by the tracks,

and the Cattleman's Café. Minot became a town when the Great Northern was built, and prospered for quite a while. Two retired railroaders, Bud Crilley and Bill Dollar, told us about the special fast trains that used to come through from Seattle, loaded with valuable raw silk for the mills in the East.

CRILLEY: Boy, you didn't touch a silk train in them days. What I mean by touching them, is delay them. If you did, why you didn't have a job the next day. (*Laughs*)

DOLLAR: I was a fireman on some of those trains. They stopped down at the depot, and engines and crews were changed to expedite the movement of the silk train. And armed guards would hop off the sides of the trains and watch so that no unauthorized persons would come near that silk train.

Carl Flagstad at the *Minot Daily News* shows us some old clippings from Minot's heyday. He wears a gray suit, has gray hair, and smokes Camels. Flagstad grumbled some, poking though the old issues of the *Daily News*, talking about the paper's changeover to offset printing and computers, "I like hot type, I like typewriters."

The next day we take the train over to Stanley, North Dakota. The town's name is in blue letters on the white water tower. Very late that night we stop at a ranch house (four miles back off the main road) to meet Fred and Joyce Evans, and their son Beryl. The phone's ringing as we walk in the door—it's Art Silverman, our producer in Washington. We're hours behind schedule and he's worried. I have the feeling that he's tracking us by satellite. This is actually quite unusual, to have someone paying attention back at work—normally you come back after a trip and everyone's been too busy to notice you've gone.

The Evanses have already eaten, but have coffee and

peach crisp with us, and Joyce has been keeping some lasa-
gna warm in the oven. We have a long talk about their fore-
bears, the families who came out on the railroad to farm, the
awful first winters, freezing and alone on the prairie in a
shelter dug from the sod, the wind always blowing. A lot of
them came and more left than stayed. Fred Evans is still
farming and running cattle, but now he's involved in hori-
zontal oil drilling: the drill goes straight down, and then
makes a right-angle turn to travel sideways along the oil
zone, and so a single well can cover much more territory, up
to around 640 acres. He says the money he makes from oil
mostly pays for his cattle ranching. And we're all thrilled
when Fred mentions a song—as he tells about something
that happened years ago.

> EVANS: On my grandmother's side, this'd be my mother's
> mother, her mother was a Horn. And this was kept
> pretty quiet until about thirty years ago, but they had
> a relative Tom Horn.

> NOAH: I know of Tom Horn, yes.

> EVANS: Right, the book about Tom Horn, the movie and
> the TV and all that? But it was just something—you
> didn't talk about him, period.

> NOAH: Tom Horn had been—was he a Ranger, a U.S.
> Marshal in the West?

> EVANS: Right.

> NOAH: And one time he was a hired gun for a cattle
> company, I recall that?

> EVANS: For a number of cattle companies in Wyoming,
> and you know I'm sure he did some things he
> shouldn't have done, but it really looks like he was
> framed in the end. He was hung in 1903. When he was
> hung, he had a last request. He wanted his friend to
> sing the song, "Life Is Like a Mountain Railroad." And I

think that sure sounds like the way it's supposed to
have happened, too.

Radio people are always pleased by music cues, when a
song can be an intrinsic part of the story. For a report some
years ago on teenage suicide, we used selections from Pink
Floyd's album, *The Wall*. The music speaks of loneliness and
alienation, and I'd heard about many teenagers who listened to the album incessantly. A civil rights anthem, taken
up by hundreds of voices at a demonstration, can be the
most signicant part of a story. But if you have to push to
include the music; if there's a flashing light that reads: "gratuitous music cue," the audience will sense the manipula-
tion.

Later, as we put together our story about this day, we
couldn't find a graceful way to use the song as part of the
interview. We did ask some friends to record a nice instrumental version for us—guitar and fiddle—intending to use
it as a "deadroll," the music that you'll hear fading up to end
a segment on "All Things Considered." But because of timing difficulties, only a few seconds of the song actually got
on the air. A deadroll is backtimed: the director will start a
piece of music at a point on the clock to ensure its ending at,
let's say, twenty-nine minutes and thirty seconds past the
hour. The music is playing along only in "cue" until the
director asks the audio board operator to bring it up. I always say, life is a deadroll, only we don't know how long it is
or when it started.

NOAH: We drove south from the rail line, down to the
    reservation of the Three Affiliated Tribes, the Mandan,
    the Hidatsa, and the Arikara. The radio station on the
    reservation was playing Paul McCartney's recording of
    "The Mull of Kintyre." The wind was up and there were
    whitecaps on the bright green waters of the Missouri.
    The river was dammed here in the 1950s to form a
    lake. A lake named for Sakakawea, the young Indian

woman who traveled with the Lewis and Clark
expedition. They were looking for a Northwest Passage.
They didn't find one. They did help open the land for
settlement and for the railroads.

HAZEL BLAKE, SOCIAL WORKER: When the railroad tracks
were coming, the Indians started fighting them. And
they took the land and they gave it to pioneer settlers.
When these white people came in and they saw that
that was a rich farmland, they just stayed.

NOAH: I think that's what James J. Hill said, the Indians
weren't using the land.

BLAKE: So . . . we didn't get nothing out of it.

NOAH: Which . . . are you, Mandan?

BLAKE: Yes.

NOAH: Is this story true, that the Mandan were very
hospitable to the white explorers coming up the
Missouri River, and friendly, and it was the white
people who brought smallpox and almost eliminated
the Mandan?

BLAKE: Yeah, yeah, that's what happened. They had
brought blankets or something that were infected
with smallpox. Of course in those days they didn't have
penicillin or anything to fight the flu bug or whatever
it is, and it darn near wiped them out.

Doreen Yellowbird, who works for KHMA, took us to visit
one of the Mandan tribal leaders, Carl Whitman. It was
about an hour's drive to his house, through fields of sun-
flowers blackened by early frost. Carl and his family live in a
sheltered draw, not far from the Missouri. He was healthy
and smiling, with gray hair in braids trimmed with leather.
Seventy-seven years old; twenty-three grandchildren. During much of his life he's taught high school chemistry and
physics.

We talked about the time forty years ago when the government forced the Mandan to move from their homes down by the river's edge, so the dam could be built and Lake Sakakawea created. Many of the graves were even moved, but some were not. The Mandan have felt, over the years, that their compensation wasn't fair. It's a complex issue, and it doesn't really fit into our train series. I hope to come back someday to do this story right.

We drive off and Carl and his family wave goodbye; and even though we've had a good visit, I'm always wondering at this moment, after an interview, if we're doing something that's inherently wrong. All the people I work with feel this—we run into somebody's house, take away their story, their life, put a few minutes of it on the air. Having their story told, their issue explained, helps them, it is argued. And I always agree, and start thinking about tomorrow's interviews.

Friday, October 6, Montana, 1989

NOAH: I left Stanley, North Dakota, late Friday morning. A sunny and breezy day, thirty-eight degrees after the sun was up, frost on the windshield of the car outside the motel. The Prairie Host Motel, twenty-one dollars a night. Breakfast at Joyce's Café, big plates of sausage and eggs in swirls of smoke and conversation. I took the rental car back to the Ford dealership on Main Street, and they charged me ten dollars less than the figure we'd agreed on.

We meet Mike Jacobs and his wife Suezette Bieri for breakfast. Mike's a newspaper editor in Grand Forks, back over on the other side of the state; Suezette's in graduate school there, but they're both from Stanley originally and now own a farm nearby, and they often drive home on

Thursday nights—four hours and thirty-seven minutes, one way (three Bruce Springsteen tapes and a Canned Heat)—to start a long weekend. At night on the farm, they can hear coyotes.

Yesterday we'd been told about the Whirla-Whip machine, over at the Rexall drugstore, and Mike said, sure, it would make a great story. He had written about it for the *Grand Forks Herald,* listing it as one of the state's attractions, and the local paper here criticized him for finding such a trivial thing to praise, saying, "Some people who were born in Stanley act like the Whirla-Whip at the Dakota Drugs is the most important thing in town."

So, this morning after breakfast we all go over to the drugstore for Whirla-Whips, and to tape conversations with customers and the druggist. A Whirla-Whip machine is sort of an industrial-size blender. You put in ice cream, then anything else you'd like: peanut butter, Oreo cookies, Lifesavers, even pickles (or combinations, I suppose), and the machine crunches it all up and it comes out thick and frosty, like a milkshake. Older people will tell you about their first Whirla-Whip, as a kid. This machine, the druggist tells me, is one of the last ones in the country—he buys any old Whirla-Whip he can find, keeps them down in the basement for parts. This story, which required twenty minutes and no set-up time, turns out to be the one listeners will mention when they ask about this train series.

train sounds, inside

NOAH: Later I had some lunch in the dining car—Pasta Shells with Cheese Casserole. Made fresh, they say. One of the car attendants the other night was talking about the "microwave days" of Amtrak, '81, '82.

It is said of this train, in the good old days, that the engineer would slow down at a whistle-stop up in the mountains and the telegraph operator would hand up a package of fresh-caught trout for dinner.

Everybody's got a story on the train, and plenty of time to tell it. And if you want to know why an older gentleman is singing a song to himself—just sit down beside him.

LEONARD SCHUTTE, PASSENGER, SINGING:

We'll build a little nest
someplace in the west
and let the rest of the world go by.

(Laughs)

Yeah, I like good singing, the old time songs, you know.

NOAH: Where you from?

SCHUTTE: Saint Paul. And I used to work in the railroads. I was an oil boy years ago in the old Jackson Street roundhouse, and in the coachyards. Oh, that was years ago. You see, I'm going on ninety-two now.

NOAH: Did you ever meet James J. Hill?

SCHUTTE: Oh, I used to see Jim Hill, the old Empire Builder going down ... he had them Scotch short ... you know, pants—

NOAH: Knickers.

SCHUTTE: Knickers and Scotch socks, and he'd go down to the Minnesota Club ... yeah, he was quite a railroad man, that Jim Hill.

Yes, I been around quite a bit. I guess that was my destiny, just to keep traveling and hoboeing, and then finally went to Seattle and settled down.

We all loved this man, we loved talking with him, we loved hearing the entire interview over and over again back in Washington, listening to Leonard Schutte tell his stories and sing. It broke Melissa's heart to have to edit the tape.

She sent him a copy of our train segments, and they've stayed in touch by mail—he'll send Christmas and Easter cards.

> ANNOUNCEMENT ON TRAIN P.A.: Good afternoon, ladies and gentlemen, the Empire Builder is now passing through an area that used to be known as Exeter, Montana. Shortly after the turn of the century, Exeter was the scene of a train robbery. A passenger boarded the train in Malta, walked through the coaches, climbed up over the coal tender, and forced the engineer to stop the train. This man was Kid Curry. He was riding with Butch Cassidy and the Sundance Kid at the time. Stopped the train at Exeter, blew up the express box, and escaped with sixty-eight thousand dollars in cash.

"When they get up in them mountains we'll never catch 'em." That's a line from countless western movies that I'm starting to appreciate better, as the country opens up, and you can see the Little Rockies and the Bear Paw Mountains, then later the Sweetgrass Hills to the north. The province of Alberta is only thirty miles away, and I'm reminded of some more movie dialogue. In *The Missouri Breaks,* the film written by Tom McGuane, who lives not far south of here, some cattle rustlers were riding along, getting close to the border, and one of them said, "Don't know why they had to put Canada way the hell up here."

We get off the train in Havre, a town named by a French cowboy. It's a place I'd only heard of because of its cold weather.

> NOAH: There's a sandy wind streaming through the town. Hardware stores, and convenience stores, with signs for Olympia beer, in blue neon, glowing in the weak October sunlight. The Salvation Army offers SUNDAY WORSHIP SERVICES AND TRANSIT FAMILY ASSISTANCE—hot soup and showers from one to three in the afternoon.

We have a wonderful visit with Sis Green, in her room at the Havre Eagles Manor, a retirement home. She's cooking stew for most of the morning, with tomatoes and turnips and pearl barley, for some of "her boys" at the home. She'd had a restaurant in Havre for many years, working from "before eight to after ten six days a week and washed aprons on Sunday." Then she went to work for the railroad in 1941, "when they were taking the boys to the Army," she said.

She told us about working in the Great Northern shops during the war, mixing cement, heating rivets, and it was all useful information, but my favorite part of the interview described how she came to Havre in the first place, as a young bride. And as taken as Melissa was with Leonard Schutte, I can still hear this tape in my mind.

> Sis Green: I came with my husband, we came in '26 down here. We got married September the nineteenth ... my husband had just won the rodeo in Great Falls, first in riding and second in roping in the state of Montana. So he came out and got me and we ran off and got married. I was seventeen and he was twenty-four. We told our folks we were going to go to a barn dance up in the mountains about thirty miles and we went to Fort Benton and got married.

As we're leaving Sis Green's apartment, we each get a hug and a pat and she wants to know how old I am. "Forty-seven," I tell her. "Oh, I wish I was young like you, I'd be out doin' something."

That night we watch the sun setting ahead of us—magenta light—as we ride along the Milk River.

> Noah: It's dark by the time the train starts up the grade. Hold your hand against the window and you can see the shapes of the mountains, the Rockies, all around in the dark. We're going over the Continental Divide, over what they call the Lost Marias Pass. It made the Great

Northern possible, on to the West, and now—people
pass on the trains in the night, most of them sleeping.

I notice the Amtrak conductor looking suspiciously at
Flawn's microphone, which he had mounted up on the luggage rack, with the cord running down to the recorder in his
lap. Flawn doesn't want to attract attention, and it's important that we have a quiet recording as we cross over Marias
Pass. I know I want to write about this moment, and the
music playing softly through the speakers in the ceiling
will help convey the surreal quality of the scene.

When we get off the train at Essex we're hit by a blast of
damp, cold, delightful air. Later I called a naturalist at Glacier National Park to find out what trees would have the
most scent: spruce and balsam. But I think I failed in writing about that moment, stepping off the train and breathing the night air. Nature can indeed be stubborn about description—once we landed on Mount McKinley, in Alaska.
Landed on a glacier at seven thousand feet in a ski-equipped
red Cessna 185. We had flown over "ancient rivers of ice and
snow, the surface often treacherous now in late summer,
with pools of intense blue water. . . . The last hundred feet," I
wrote, "was all white, all around. It was like landing on top of
clouds." But I couldn't describe the infinite sense of space, or
the clarity of the sky.

Sunday, October 8, Montana, 1989

Clear skies at sunrise, forty degrees. There could have been
some rain during the night—I was sleeping pretty well, with
the window open and an extra blanket, and the sound of a
diesel locomotive idling on a side track right out in front of
the Isaak Walton Inn. The engine is a "helper," waiting for
trains making the climb up the grade and over the pass, just
to the east.

The inn was originally built by the Great Northern, for train crews and visitors to Glacier National Park. The land for the park, and the railroad as well, was bought from the Indians, the Blackfeet and the Flathead. The Great Northern got busy selling Glacier as an exotic yet safe place to visit. Blackfeet were hired to pose for postcards in native dress. The captions read: "Us Indians will be glad to see you at Glacier Park. We shake hands."

The Isaak Walton Inn is now known for cross-country skiing—240 inches of snow every winter—and as a place to watch trains. A large group of railfans had come for the weekend, most of them from Canada. They carried radios so they could listen in on Burlington Northern communications, and they spent the days running around taking pictures—we'd see three or four of them up on a hillside waiting for a particular engine to come around a curve—and their nights showing slides and talking trains.

RAILFAN TALKING ABOUT HIS SLIDE ON SCREEN: U.P. runs a lot of cabooses down there in that area.

slides changing in projector

This is near Caldwell. He took off that stretch. I was also taking video of this and I had to drive eighty to try to catch him, after he'd gone past. He was running a good seventy miles an hour across there.
That's all that's on this tray.

applause, from the other railfans

diesel horn, outside

NOAH: From the dining-room windows you can see the main line of the Burlington Northern running along out in front. And when a train comes by and the railfans are eating supper, and talking, it's like one of those E. F. Hutton commercials. All the conversation stops, all the heads turn toward the windows. They're

watching for certain locomotives, or individual freight
cars they haven't seen before.

It was time for us to take a day off, and we spent most of it
in a rental car, one hundred and twenty miles, driving up
through the mountains in Glacier National Park. I'd read
that the Going-to-the-Sun-Highway was one of the most
spectacular drives in the country, and it really is. The peaks
are above ten thousand feet, higher than you can see by
looking up through the windshield. And we did some walking, in Avalanche Gorge and along the trail to St. Mary's
Falls. There was a short, pragmatic discussion before we left:
should we take a tape recorder, even if we were officially not
working? For many years I would say, yes, absolutely, always take a recorder, you never know what you'll find. But
now it's easy to agree with Flawn and Melissa that if you do
it, you're not really taking a day off, that the experience is
changed (actually, we found a creek with wonderfully me-
lodic water, and Flawn came back later with two digital recorders). I have the same sort of feeling about taking along a
camera on a radio story; if there's a camera available, you
start looking instead of hearing.

> TOM WITTINGER, U.S. FOREST SERVICE (*excited*): Oh, there it
> is, it's a grizzly. See him—there in the bottom? Pretty
> good-sized grizzly.
>
> NOAH: I see him. He's just sitting there like a big oversized
> dog looking at us. What would be the weight of that
> bear, could you tell?
>
> WITTINGER: Well, it's hard to say but he's probably a four
> hundred-, five hundred-pound bear. Which is typical
> for an adult male, would be large for an adult female.

Our encounter with the grizzly was actually uneventful—
we were safe in a car and the bear had lots to eat. During the
last winter here at Marias Pass three freight trains went off

the track, one hundred and four cars went over the side, all filled with corn. In the spring the grizzlies and the black bears came out of their dens and down the mountain and found the corn. Some grizzlies have been hit by trains; two have died that way. An electric fence isn't helping much. I heard a scary story about this a few days later out in Washington State. An Amtrak conductor who used to be a brakeman on the run over Marias told me that often at night the train would have to stop because of reports of rail damage in the pass, and he'd have to get out and walk along the tracks in the dark with his flashlight and two-way radio, wondering about the bears. This same conductor also told me about the caskets that are regularly shipped by rail, and the ad he heard about once in a mortician's magazine: "Timely Departures for Your Dearly Departed."

We had time to wash some clothes at the inn, and a chance for several good meals. Great soups and apple pie. They've got a good season's worth of huckleberries in the freezer, and one morning we had perfect whole wheat pancakes. You start thinking that you could stay in a place like Essex, maybe help do the cooking, go fishing in the summer, skiing in the winter.

But surely the train whistles would make you restless. It's an enchanting sound, the echo slapping off the mountains and rolling down the valley. We recorded the whistles several times, usually at night. We'd call up the Burlington dispatcher to find out when a train was due, and Flawn would go off with his microphones and recorders to try to catch the first, faint sound.

train whistle, far away

NOAH: My train, going west, was right on time . . .

whistle, getting louder

. . . with white strobe lights flashing on the engine. And golden rectangles of light from the coach cars moving through the dark. And the whistle resounding in the valley.

Also, while we were waiting for the train, we taped some music from the old jukebox, a High Fidelity Wurlitzer, in the basement of the inn. A lovely, scratchy version of "Sentimental Journey" that we used at the end of the series.

Wednesday, October 11, Seattle, 1989

As we check into our motel in Wenatchee, The Chieftain, we ask about a fax message we were expecting from Washington. I had wanted a copy of a *New York Times* article about Alar. Alar, we would learn, is a bad word in apple country.

Yes, it came, I was told. "And you know," the woman behind the desk says, handing me the faxed copy of the article—she had noticed the subject—"there's more Alar in mushrooms than apples." We also are told several times that people in town are upset with Meryl Streep, because of her testimony before Congress concerning Alar.

It is high apple time in the Columbia River Valley. Granny Smiths and Scarlets and Red and Golden Delicious, and the Fuji apples from Japan. I had apple juice for breakfast and toasted apple bread. Out in the orchards you could pick your own for ten cents a pound, if you bring a box. Seasoned applewood (it makes a splendid, aromatic fire) is only thirty-five dollars a cord, you haul. At home, applewood is surely a hundred dollars more. The scary job in the valley is flying, spraying the orchards. Last week a helicopter hit a sprinkler pole; the pilot died.

From any place in the country—Baltimore's Fells Point Market, for example—a phone call to Wenatchee in the morning will cause a container load of apples to be on a freight train by evening. We decided to visit an apple-packing house, a few miles outside of Wenatchee; we just walked

in and asked for a tour and an interview and, we're told,
"Sure, why not? I'll show you around. Who'd you say you
were with again?" Back East, more than likely, the door
would have been shut and only opened after several phone
calls and a letter.

apples rolling down production line, machinery sounds

BOB ACRES, BEEBE ORCHARDS: After we've gone through the
    pre-sorting operation, the fruit's brought out of
    common storage by variable sizes that we require for
    packing. We put it into a dump tank, which is a water
    solution that the apples are floated through up to the
    time that they receive a second bath, then they're
    dried very quickly. Goes through a very quick waxing
    process, then goes through an extended long drying
    tunnel to get very quickly sorted; we put on the logo
    stickers, then into the boxes, and onto the pallet stack.

NOAH: And then it goes—?

ACRES: Then it goes back into cold storage until such time
    you either sell the fruit—or it's already sold and it's
    shipped out immediately.

Time to get back on the train, to cross the Cascade range,
going down to the coast, and Seattle. This is a daytime trip;
the one night sitting up on the train, leaving Montana, had
been about enough for me. The sleeper cars were full—we
should have booked a compartment months in advance, but
I thought it would be interesting. The night passed, and the
mountains, as a dream.

inside train sounds, quiet

NOAH: As we left Essex, I had two seats to myself. A
    pillow, but not a blanket. Some people, I noticed, had
    brought quilts from home. I kept the light on for a
    time. I was reading. I don't think I slept . . . although

Idaho went past in the night, then the lights of
Spokane. It was 4:00 A.M., the sign on the bank in
Spokane said, and I tried to make sense of my watch
and I guess we lost an hour going into Pacific time and
that's a whole 'nother hour to be on the train and I
can't get back to sleep ... if I was home I could go
downstairs and have a bowl of cereal ... and the train
keeps stopping and people get on and I'm spread out
over the two seats, but later I feel guilty about it and
there's a big metal thing in the middle of the two seats
anyway. And I realize the best sleep on the train is
sitting up in the single seat next to the window with a
pillow ... and the train rocks through the night and
soon it's almost daylight, you're almost there—and it
wasn't so bad.

The Great Northern Line going on to the West from Wenatchee passes through the New Cascade Tunnel; it's more
than seven miles long. The tunnel was grandly opened in
1929, when the first train went through, and Melissa discovered that the event had been broadcast on NBC Radio.

> *whistle*

STUDIO ANNOUNCER: The Oriental Limited has arrived now
at the West Portal of the tunnel. We now turn you over
to Graham MacNamee at Scenic, Washington.

MACNAMEE (*scratchy and distant, with static*): Ladies
and gentlemen, we are now at the West Portal of the
Cascade Tunnel. We got onto the train, jumped
through a few cars, and got out onto the [inaudible] of
the engine, and it certainly was a lovely sight coming
through that tunnel. We expected to find a great deal
of excitement and so forth among the guests in the
thirty-five cars, but there was nothing of the sort, it
was just a quiet little ride through a very nice tunnel.
We're not sure whether this is the first time a tunnel

has ever had itself broadcast or not, but we think
possibly it is. The passengers' reaction was a complete
disappointment. They didn't react at all. They just sat
there as though they were out having lunch
someplace.

train chuffing, and music in train rhythm, fading

In Seattle we wait around the Amtrak station for more
than an hour, hoping to record an end-of-the-journey greet-
ing. Dick and Ellen Bates had ridden the train out from
their home in Walker, Minnesota, and their daughter was
expected to come and meet them. We only need ten seconds
of tape, "Hi Mom, hi Dad." Scenes like this are essential when
you're putting a story together; you need them for transi-
tions. The time goes by, we have a pleasant chat with the
Bateses, but everyone's tired and soon getting bored—and
no daughter. So we all get into taxicabs and leave.

We're staying in a pleasant bed-and-breakfast, over an
X-rated movie theater, in the Pike Place Market section of
Seattle. And we have a few hours to walk around the market
and stop in some nearby bookstores. The next day I visit
both the local public radio stations, KUOW and KPLU. The
stations would probably be a bit put out if they found out
later that we were in town and hadn't stopped by. I'm guess-
ing about that, perhaps out of guilt—I've been through
Seattle twice before, traveling for NPR, without even taking
the time to call.

Melissa has made an appointment with a local historian,
to help us complete the story of James J. Hill's railroad. In
1893, Seattle was *not* the end of the line: Hill was still looking west, to China, Japan, India. We tape our interview while
looking out over downtown Seattle.

MURRAY MORGAN, HISTORIAN: His vision of Oriental trade
did a lot toward shaping the growth of the city. Almost
anything you look at around here, if you look down

below from up where we're standing and see the
railroad tracks, that's Hill's work. You look farther
down to the right and you'll see the wheat towers for
exporting wheat, that was one of Hill's big ideas.
Shipyards out there, Hill built the first two American
ships to go into the trans-Pacific hauling trade, the
Dakota and the *Minnesota*. They didn't work, it
simply was uneconomic. And Hill said it was terrible
that we had the best transportation system in the
world, could produce more than we could consume; we
take it to the ports and it had to go on foreign ships
and they would charge us for doing our work for us.

We go down to the waterfront and find out that James Hill
was right. Several foreign ships are offloading at the piers.
About a dozen huge tall cranes are positioned to lift the
containers from the ships to the docks. Hitachi cranes,
bright orange, with a sign that says: PORT OF SEATTLE. A ship
called the *Kwang Yang* stands at Pier 46. More than two
hundred blue and green and maroon containers will be
taken off, each one settled down onto the flatbed trailer of a
truck. No one seems to know what's in the boxes: radios,
televisions, running shoes—everything. The *Kwang Yang*
will return to Korea with a new load of containers, but, I'm
told, 40, 45 percent will be empty. And that—you could
say—is the balance of trade.

We stop recording for our train stories at about nine o'-
clock on Friday evening. On a ferry, coming into dock at
Seattle. We'd been riding back and forth on the ferries, interviewing passengers, taping the blasts of the foghorn from
several perspectives—we even took one trip across in the
wheelhouse of the ferry with the captain.

At last we stop recording because we realize the story is
over. And Melissa—who's been talking with everyone who
looked like they'd be a good story—has found a charming
young couple, Richard and Laura, who are in love with the
ferry as well as each other.

RICHARD: We were courting and I decided it was time to ask Laura for her hand in marriage and so I figured no better place to do it than on the ferry.

NOAH: Now, where were you on the ferry?

RICHARD: Actually we were out on the very front, on the bow area. And when I took the box out of my pocket, the ring had come loose ... she opens the box and the ring falls out and rolls across the ferry deck, and it was caught just before it went over the edge.

LAURA: It was very romantic. We just have a terrific time, every time we ride it's real romantic for us. That made it real special.

ferry horn, distant

NOAH: I decided to ride back on the top deck of the ferry. It's open to the wind. It was past sunset on Friday evening. The clouds above Puget Sound now lit from above, by moonlight. The air was wet and clean. And the city a mile or so across the water was light against the darkness. Towers of light, whites and blues and green. I realized I was looking to the east for the first time in two weeks of traveling.

An hour later, the equipment stored away in our rooms, we almost fall asleep in a restaurant, waiting for our food. It's great fish, but Flawn has to lift his head off the table so the waiter can serve it. The next morning I wake up early, to have coffee at a café in the market, and read the papers and the magazines I'd been missing. From the airplane leaving that morning, we can see Mt. Rainier, then Mt. Hood to the south and Mt. Baker. Melissa has all of our tapes close by in a separate bag; it was hand-checked through the airport metal detector (they say it won't hurt but why chance it). These cassettes, at this moment, are quite valuable. They contain all the expense and work and worry of the trip. We've recorded thirty-eight hours of tape. Less than one hour will be used on the air.

Sunday, October 15, Washington, D.C., 1989

Back home yesterday. Time to watch some of the World Series, and go through two weeks' worth of *The Washington Post* and *The New York Times*. Jo Miglino has called from Florida, she's an old friend and colleague, an NPR reporter now based in Tallahassee. She's also our music adviser. "Go get the new Linda [Ronstadt]." And then she has a second message on the answering machine, "Aaron Neville, Rosemary Butler." Jo's always right, so we go to the record store and also pick up a Nadia Salerno-Sonnenberg CD, Brahms, with the Minnesota Orchestra, and an old Kate Wolf album, recorded in someone's living room in California. I've been wanting to do a story about Kate Wolf—she died about six years ago. I didn't meet her, didn't see her sing, but I've become more and more involved with her music.

I go into work for a while. Melissa is in a studio with Linda Mack, our technical director, dubbing some of the digital tape to analog so she can start editing. It sounds good.

And a movie in a theater! After a quick dinner at home we go out to see *Sea of Love,* with Ellen Barkin and Al Pacino. There's a credit at the end for "voices." I've never seen that before and don't know exactly what it means.

Tuesday, October 17, Washington, D.C., 1989

I'm at home watching the World Series when the earthquake hits San Francisco. It looks terrible at first, less so as the evening goes on. Robert has the beeper this week. They call him in to do a couple of interviews for the West Coast feed of "All Things Considered." The earthquake was at 8:04 EDT and our last feed of the program is 8:00–9:30 EDT. Linda usually takes the beeper home; of the three ATC hosts, she lives the closest. It's a Motorola paging system: a phone call to the beeper number produces a loud chirping, or you can set it to "squirm"—a silent vibration in case you're in a movie or at a concert. It's more often the case, though, that we're simply phoned at home to come back for updating.

There has been talk at NPR of installing high-quality phone lines to our houses, so that we could update the program more easily. A couple of years ago they set up a line to Cokie Roberts's house, so she could talk with Bob Edwards on "Morning Edition" without having to come all the way downtown—Cokie was tending to work eighteen-hour days. She sounded great from her house, you couldn't tell she wasn't in the studio—until the morning her dog, a good-hearted basset named Abner, started barking during her report. There's also now a line to Nina Totenberg's house, and when ABC's "Prime Time Live" ran their story about Cokie and Nina and Linda Wertheimer, after the Anita Hill–Clarence Thomas hearings, we all got to see both Cokie and Nina in their bathrobes, talking on the radio. In March 1992, Nina attained official celebrity status, coming out from behind the curtain to sit and talk with Jay Leno on the "Tonight" show. She was a real star, bright and funny; you even forgot that Warren Beatty was sitting there right next to her. Leno asked about the ongoing Senate investigation, ef forts to find out how Nina and Timothy Phelps of *Newsday* learned about Anita Hill's allegations about Clarence Thomas. Nina described her worst-case scenario: "The United States Senate votes to cite me for contempt. I then go to the courts to rescue me in the name of the First Amendment, and I end up in front of Justice Thomas in the Supreme Court." And she explained that no law actually requires a Justice to disqualify himself in such a situation.

I recall the Sunday morning in October when I first heard

about Anita Hill's accusations of sexual harassment. I was in the bathroom shaving, listening to Liane Hansen and "Weekend Edition." Nina began telling the story, and it was clear from her deliberate pacing and careful choice of words that a big story was opening up. Soon we were all watching Professor Hill and Judge Thomas on television, and talking about harassment in every workplace in America. After Thomas's confirmation, though, Nina Totenberg became the story. Hundreds of interview requests from the media, and one subpoena from the Senate's special counsel, Peter Fleming. Nina refused to reveal the source of her information, saying she wouldn't mind going to jail over the matter. NPR also refused to cooperate, stating: "The First Amendment protects the right of the press to gather news and to find out about the workings of our government." The Senate Rules Committee, after a time, agreed. The chairman, Senator Wendell Ford, said to pursue the matter further "could have a chilling effect on the media and could close a door where more doors need opening."

Nina handled most of this with great poise—she knew she was simply a good reporter who had worked very hard on an important story, following up on something the Senate had failed to investigate—plus she usually finds something to laugh about every day. (Washington provides lots of humor opportunity. Years ago Nina wrote a magazine article about "The Ten Dumbest Members of Congress." One of them, Bill Scott of Virginia—who's no longer serving—immediately called a news conference to deny it. Hardly anyone had read the *New Times* article, but millions around the country saw this man arguing that he shouldn't be on the list.)

Nina did lose her temper once, though, and started yelling at Senator Alan Simpson. They'd appeared on "Nightline" together, Simpson accusing Nina of "bias" in her reporting of the Anita Hill story and saying that Hill's name should not have been revealed. After the program Simpson followed Nina out to the street, waving what he said was a journalistic code of ethics. Simpson said later that Nina "whirled on me" and called him several choice names, concluding with, "You are an evil man." A few months afterwards Nina and Senator Simpson had made peace; he was even her guest at the Radio and Television Correspondents Dinner, held every year in Washington.

The Senate might have had a better chance asking Nina to sing. She's quite good—her father is concert violinist Roman Totenberg—and she loves to perform. Scott Simon once needed someone to sing the rock classic "Stairway to Heaven" for a "Weekend Edition" feature. Nina obliged, even though she'd never heard the song before.

Several people I've worked with admit to having "radio dreams" from time to time, nightmares of frustration that usually involve a deadline. In my dream I'll be in Georgetown, ten blocks down M Street from NPR; I'll hear the ATC theme music, the program is starting and I can't get to the studio. This sort of thing is so common that someone actually put together a feature about radio dreams. Among my favorites: "I dreamed the station was such a low-budget operation that they broadcast from the front seat of a '62 Buick. The turntables were mounted in the dashboard and I realized there weren't any records there." Or: "I've messed up and there's no news prepared. I'm panicked. I think for the first time I'll read straight wire copy." Or: "I'm on the air and all of a sudden I get violently ill and there's no one to relieve me, and here I am just convulsing. And then I wake up." And: "I dreamed once there was a nuclear war and realized that the only skill I had was cutting tape and it was a skill that was entirely unnecessary."

There's another category—the *waking* nightmares of radio. As a teenage disc jockey, a telephone conversation with a girlfriend while a record was playing—and the microphone was open. Signing on the station in the morning without having turned on the transmitter. A few years ago at KUNM in Albuquerque there was an actual fight in the control room with the mike open the whole time. There had been an ongoing argument at KUNM. Some of the staff and volunteers wanted less national programming from NPR and other services, and more locally produced programs, reflecting New Mexico's diverse ethnic culture. The conflict became known as the "Radio Wars," and the issue was often discussed on the radio. The on-air fight was simply an extension of the argument.

But here's the worst one: working for a station (my first job in public radio) with so few listeners that when lightning knocked the transmitter off the air for an hour—nobody called.

At the end of tonight's "All Things Considered," a nice conversation with Annie Dillard about her new book, *The Writing Life.* She won a Pulitzer Prize for *Pilgrim at Tinker Creek,* an account of time spent on an island in Puget Sound. Other titles include *An American Childhood* and *Holy the Firm.* She is proud and happy to be a writer, but sometimes believes being a painter would be more immediately satisfying.

DILLARD: In painting you get to move your arms. All of your senses are called into play, you get to stand up. You get to fool around with colors. You get to feel the texture of the colors and smell them. Writing you do in a state of sensory deprivation ... to which you gradually become accustomed. I used to be so deprived that for my big pleasure of the day, I would change the color of pen I was using. It was very exciting.

NOAH: Are you working with a word processor now?

DILLARD: That's right. And on the computer now, it's just like painting. You literally cover over the passage you were working on. It is obliterated from above. I think a little piece of silicon actually paints over those terrible words.

NOAH: You describe a writer friend in Washington State who (*laughs*), who found himself so blocked that he

started writing with momentum. Would you describe
what he would do?

DILLARD: He was writing a novel. He wrote a sentence or
two of the novel, and then he'd leave the house and go
shopping or undertake some errand, and then he'd
rush in the door again, recopy all that he'd written to
that point, and then in a surge of momentum stammer
out a couple more sentences before he was paralyzed
again by consciousness of what he was doing and
would grind to a halt.

NOAH: He would type out the whole thing again and hope
to get a new sentence on the end of it?

DILLARD: All of it.

NOAH: My goodness.

DILLARD: Chapter after chapter after chapter—he figured
the more he typed, the greater his momentum would
be, and he could write more sentences then at the end.

NOAH: How was the book?

DILLARD: The book was wonderful.

NOAH: Why do you think he did it? You know Joan
Didion's line about writing is that the time has come to
go "in there," she said. You know, in this sort of dread
place.

DILLARD: Yeah, that's right. You keep it in a place like a
lion in a cage and then you go in with your little
armchair held out in front of you and shout: "Simba!"

NOAH: It is such a painstaking thing and indeed
painful—do you ever wonder why you do it for a
living?

DILLARD: It's not really so bad. I don't mean to stress that
at all. In fact, there are many things about it I enjoy

very much and I've said so in my book. But why do I do
it? I do it to praise God. I do it because . . . some painter
was asked what was the relation between his life and
his art and he said, "Life obliges me to do some things,
so I paint." Life obliges us to do something. I write
books.

NOAH: You write near the end of the book [*The Writing
Life*] quite a bit about a stunt flyer in Washington
State who flew out of Bellingham where you were
living, by the name of Dave Rahm, and you went to see
him at an air show and then eventually flew with him,
but would you read just a bit of the description of his
flying performance?

DILLARD: I went to an air show in Washington State.
(Reading) "For the end of the day . . . the air show
director had scheduled a program entitled 'DAVE RAHM.'
The leaflet said Rahm was a geologist who taught at
Western Washington University. He had flown for
King Hussein in Jordan. A tall man in the crowd told
me Hussein had seen Rahm fly on a visit the King
made to the United States; he had invited him to
Jordan to perform at ceremonies. Hussein was a pilot
too. Hussein thought he was the greatest thing in the
world.

Idly, paying scant attention, I saw a medium-sized
rugged man dressed in brown leather, all begoggled,
climb in a black biplane's open cockpit. The plane was
a Bücker Jungman built in the thirties. I saw a tall
dark-haired woman seize a propeller tip at the plane's
nose and yank it down until the engine caught. He was
off; he climbed high over the airport in his biplane,
very high until he was barely visible as a mote, and
then seemed to fall down the air, diving headlong, and
streaming beauty in spirals behind him.

The black plane dropped spinning, and flattened out
spinning the other way; it began to carve the air into

forms that built wildly and musically on each other and never ended. Reluctantly, I started paying attention. Rahm drew high above the world an inexhaustibly glorious line; it piled over our heads in loops and arabesques. It was like a Saul Steinberg fantasy; the plane was the pen. Like Steinberg's contracting and billowing pen line, the line Rahm spun moved to form new, punning shapes from the edges of the old."

NOAH: You wrote once that you could never have loved him. What sort of person was he and why could you have never loved him? What was the distance?

DILLARD: I have no idea what sort of person he was, and I thought it was necessary, a woman writing so ecstatically about a man, to eliminate from the reader's mind any thought of romance at once. Maybe I protested too much. I don't think so. I have no idea what sort of man he was. He seemed to be a little technical guy who was interested in geology and flying airplanes. He flipped buttons, he seemed bored, he looked like G. I. Joe. Nothing fazed him. I like a man to be *supremely* fazed.

NOAH: Did he have an idea of what he did as art?

DILLARD: I don't know.

NOAH: This is near the end of your book and your book ... starts by saying that writing is a line of words, a fiber-optic line of words that "fingers your own heart" and "feels for cracks in the firmament." There is a relationship between the line that Dave Rahm made in the sky for you with writing?

DILLARD: Sure. That's the controlling metaphor of the whole book. That it's an epistemological line that the artist pushes out by a fingertip, by the tip of a pen, by the cockpit of a plane, or the prow of a rowboat, pushes

out into the abyss of the unknowing, if I may. Behind
you, you shed coherence, understanding, maybe even
beauty, behind you, you shed knowing; ahead of you is
just bare nothing, and you try to push through it a
word at a time. It's very interesting. I love writing.

Wednesday, October 18, Washington, D.C., 1989

Ten stories tonight on the earthquake, including reaction in
Japan, people there offering to help in the rebuilding. We've
sent several reporters, engineers, and producers to San
Francisco, and the coverage is excellent. My morning staff
meeting earthquake joke is this: If Billy Martin had still
been running the Oakland "A's," he would have demanded a
forfeit from the Giants.

I learn, finally, and simply by just looking it up in the
dictionary, that "temblor" is synonymous with "earthquake" and is not "tremblor."

And I've been reminded of the ending of Thornton
Wilder's *The Bridge of San Luis Rey.* We get a copy from the
library and I put together a short essay to go along with our
other stories.

> NOAH: Someone said this morning about the Bay Bridge
> in San Francisco that every time you go across the
> bridge in a car, you always have a moment's
> thought—could this be the day for an earthquake?
> And it brings to mind an expression from a novel by
> Thornton Wilder, the saying, "I may see you Tuesday,
> unless the bridge falls."
>
> Mr. Wilder's book starts this way: "On Friday noon,
> July the twentieth, 1714, the finest bridge in all Peru
> broke and precipitated five travellers into the gulf
> below. This bridge was on the high-road between Lima
> and Cuzco.... It had been woven of osier by the Incas

more than a century before and visitors to the city were always led out to see it. It was a mere ladder of thin slats swung out over the gorge, with handrails of dried vine...."

Wilder goes on, "The moment a Peruvian heard of the accident he signed himself and made a mental calculation as to how recently he had crossed by it and how soon he had intended crossing by it again."

And it happened then, in the story, that a Franciscan monk named Brother Juniper set out to determine why those five people died. He thought, "Either we live by accident and die by accident, or we live by plan and die by plan." He resolved to inquire into the secret lives of those five persons, and therein lies the novel, *The Bridge of San Luis Rey.*

In the end, though, even Brother Juniper was unhappy with what he could find out. Wilder writes: "He thought he saw in the same accident the wicked visited by destruction, and the good called early to Heaven." Also, "There are a hundred ways of wondering at circumstance."

The Bridge of San Luis Rey concludes with these sentences: "But soon we shall die and all memory of those five will have left the earth, and we ourselves shall be loved for a while and forgotten. But the love will have been enough.... There is a land of the living and a land of the dead and the bridge is love, the only survival, the only meaning."

Monday, October 23, Washington, D.C., 1989

I go out for a walk after dinner; I've left my bicycle up at the Metro stop. It's a cool, clear night, smelling of woodsmoke. Halloween is coming up Tuesday. Neenah's going away, so maybe I'll try to keep the house dark and stay in the kitchen

that night; it's just too much trying to control the dogs
when the kids come to ring the doorbell for trick or treat. I
guess I'll quickly become known in the neighborhood as
that weird guy in the dark house.

On Saturday we drove into the country, out in Virginia,
for an apple festival. Brunswick stew, cheeseburgers, hot
fresh cider, apple butter cooking in large copper kettles: we
bought a pumpkin pie, and a half-gallon of honey for four
dollars, and a bushel each of Grimes Golden and York Apples, to make applesauce.

Monday, October 30, Washington, D.C., 1989

Finishing the train stories this week. The last page is difficult. I wrote a draft last night and called Neenah (who's in
Chicago doing some radio stories) and read it to her over the
phone.

Sunday night I went to hear some music at the Birchmere, a club across the river in Alexandria, Virginia. John
Gorka, Bill Morrissey, Cliff Eberhardt, and Sara Hickman.
They all have songs on Windham Hill's first folk release,
entitled *Legacy*. The evening has a strange, cold feeling.
Windham Hill has put together this tour to publicize the
album, but no one seems to be having much fun. Maybe it's
too much of a competitive situation; each singer comes out
to do about fifteen minutes.

There's a *Washington Post* Sunday magazine cover story,
"NPR Considered: From Radical Radio to Washington Institution." I have a lot of trouble even with the premise. NPR
was never a radical news organization, nor is it now a Washington institution. The author, Marc Fisher, fails to offer examples of either extreme, although he's close when he says,
about the beginnings of "All Things Considered" in 1971, "
. . . the idea was to capture the energy and idealism of campus radio stations brimming with new voices and alternative ideas."

Bill Siemering, the program's originator, has said he wanted to fight against the arrogance of the commercial networks, and that a news program should be talking *to* the people of the country, rather than *about* them, but that he wasn't motivated by ideology. He simply wanted the finest possible program, not alternative but competitive, and that's the reason for the five o'clock start, ninety minutes ahead of the TV evening news. The program also had a friendly, conversational style, and that *was* radical. (We're happy with our name, even if it's an easy target for disgruntled listeners who believe we consider very few things indeed. It's hard to find a good name for a program; for ours we thank George Gescy, NPR's first operations manager.)

And some of the inspiration came from Canada: "As It Happens," on the CBC, predates "All Things Considered" by several years, although it's always been a telephone-only program, no news reports, no feature stories. Barbara Frum, a long-time "As It Happens" host, remembers that the CBC borrowed the idea of a phone-out interview show from a popular radio station in West Germany.

I often think of Bill Siemering on those days when we're not paying enough attention to the country; when we end up just talking with scholars and scientists and pollsters. And I think about a church newsletter I brought back from a trip to New Mexico. It's from Our Lady of Guadalupe, in the small town of Peña Blanca. Father Donnan Herbe had written:

A word from your pastor . . .

This past week Fulgencia Baca was suddenly called by God to meet with him. The funeral Mass and burial took place yesterday. She was the wife of Sigfredo and bore him 10 children, eight of whom are still living.

A number of people have not picked up their tickets for the raffle. We ask you to do so today as we need all the help we can get to take care of our bills.

Holy Communion will be brought to the sick at Peña Blanca and at San Felipe on Friday. . . .

Last week Martin Rosetta and Arvada Garcia were married

at Santo Domingo and Anthony Gurule married Rosamaria
Sandoval at Peña Blanca. May God bless them all!

                                                        Fr. Donnan

The *Washington Post* article also brings up the issue of
"dedicated" funding. NPR continues to accept underwriting
grants from companies and organizations that provide
money for specific subject areas. UNICEF has given money, for
example, to pay for coverage of relief efforts in Africa. I've
made a trip to Tokyo, with money from the United States-
Japan Foundation, and to Europe with help from the German Marshall Fund of the United States, but I've never
talked with any funding organization; and usually—when a
project is approved—the reporters don't know or care where
the money's coming from.

NPR's policy has indeed been questioned. Richard Salant,
the former head of CBS News, resigned from the NPR board
over this matter. (Also, according to Marc Fisher in the *Post,*
Salant once got upset when he heard about plans for "product testing" of an NPR program. "In my shop, if you called
news 'product,' you had to wash your mouth out with soap,"
he said.) Later, Dennis Haarsager of KWSU, Pullman, Washington, asked in a letter to the NPR board of directors: "Why
on earth does NPR News have to compromise the appear-
ance of its independence, the essence of any news organization?" Haarsager complained about accepting grants from
"organizations like the National Education Association and
the Natural Resources Defense Council, whose primary purpose is to influence public policy." "Dump these guys," he
continued, and concluded, "Bill [the] stations for the lost
revenue."

It's only Haarsager's conjecture that the stations would,
or could, come up with the extra money. The stations are
having tough budget times these days; although direct listener funding is increasing admirably around the country,
many states and universities and communities are having
to cut way back in their support. NPR believes the listeners

understand the necessity for these corporate and foundation grants and trust that journalistic integrity won't be
compromised. It's often pointed out that no real connection
exists between the funder and the story, and that NPR "only
seeks grants for things we want to do, projects we have initi-
ated, stories that might otherwise be beyond our means and
capabilities. The issue is not whether we will cover a story
but how well we can cover it."

Some funding offers are discouraged, though. Just after
the oil spill in Prince William Sound, the Exxon Corporation
sent $32,000 to the Alaska Public Radio Network. APRN
had been trying to raise some extra money to pay for its
coverage of the Exxon oil spill. Exxon had been an under-
writer for APRN in the past, and wanted to help out. The
network at first was going to take the money. "It doesn't
mean that we won't report anything negative about them,"
an APRN official said; but on second thought, and after a
weekend of publicity, the offer was turned down. And NPR
recently refused a grant that could have helped pay for a
much-needed Tokyo bureau—the money was coming almost directly from the government of Japan.

Wednesday, November 1, Washington, D.C., 1989

Nixon's in China. With the news from Beijing, Richard
Nixon talking even with Deng Xiaoping, China's leader—
apparently talking with the blessing of the Bush administration—it was an irresistible notion to call the composer
John Adams. His opera, *Nixon in China,* tells the story of
the President's visit there in 1972. Adams talked with us
from KSJN in Saint Paul, about Nixon's performance so far
on this trip.

ADAMS: Nixon pulled no punches in speaking his mind
about what he considered—I believe he used the word

"oppression"—and although I'm no apologist for Nixon, I had to compare his remarks with our more recent ex-President, Mr. Reagan, who's pocketing two million dollars to be the guest of a large Japanese corporation at virtually the same time.

NOAH: I also noticed in *Newsweek* magazine, they have this little section that's called the "Conventional Wisdom Watch," Richard Nixon this week has an *up* arrow and it says: "Rehab nearly complete, even docudramas make him look sympathetic."

ADAMS: Yes, well, there was a wonderful article in *The New York Times* the other day by Leonard Garment, who, describing his horror at seeing himself portrayed in this most recent docudrama, that his wife almost fell off the chair in laughter but he himself didn't think it was very funny. I do not consider *Nixon in China* in any way a docudrama, or a docu-opera. I'd say I view my treatment of Nixon somewhat as Shakespeare may have viewed his treatment of Julius Caesar. He represents the American arrogance and sort of smugness of power suddenly run up against an inscrutable mask.

NOAH: Do you know if Richard Nixon has ever seen the work?

ADAMS: Well, I can only speculate from what I know of him and what I imagine of him. I doubt that he would leave any stone unturned, and I imagine he probably saw the PBS telecast and beyond that, I frankly don't care.

NOAH: Has there been a telecast of the videotape in China?

ADAMS: I don't believe there has been. There certainly—when you talk about prescience—it's certainly a tremendous irony that the events in China that have unfolded in the last several months are, I think, portrayed in the opera. The final scene of the second act, where Madame Mao comes out and takes over in her rather hysterical authority and punishes the young people . . . is a scene of utter mayhem, and when I watched on television the events in Tiananmen Square, I was staggered by its closeness to what we had staged in the opera.

Monday, November 6, Idaho, 1989

It's "Boy-see," and not "Boy-zee," I learn quickly, and will write it down, and say it often and try to remember. We've come—a producer, and an engineer and myself—to Idaho for almost two weeks, to do some stories and to broadcast from KBSU for five days as part of "All Things Considered." It's great fun to work from an actual radio station: I've been on before from KUT, Austin, Texas; Alaska Public Radio, Anchorage; WOI, Ames, Iowa; WBGO, Newark, New Jersey; and I started in public radio at a member station—WBKY in Lexington, Kentucky. Many of the NPR voices were first heard on the local stations: Lynn Neary and Brian Naylor worked together at WOSU, Columbus, Ohio; John Ydstie came from KCCM, Moorhead, Minnesota; Elizabeth Arnold from KTOO, Juneau, Alaska. Susan Stamberg began as a producer at WAMU, in Washington, D.C.—she always tells us her big break came when they needed someone to go on the air and read the weather. Also we have lots of technicians, and editors and producers with experience at the member stations. NPR doesn't really pay enough to be able to encourage someone with a family to move to Washington, but over the years lots of people have been willing to throw everything they own in the car and head out for the big city. When I came to NPR in 1975, I was only planning to be in Washington for two years—get some network experience and then find a job in a strong public radio market, Chapel Hill, North Carolina, or Ann Arbor, Michigan. I realized one day—after about ten years—that I'd forgotten to leave.

When "All Things Considered" came along, I'd already given up on radio as a career. I had worked in commercial radio in the 1960s—as a rock 'n' roll DJ, as a program director, salesman, station manager. It was just an ordinary, tough sort of business and I wasn't having much fun, so I left after five years. Lots of jobs later, in 1972, I found myself doing construction work in the daytime and working as a part-time announcer for the University of Kentucky's WBKY. I would sign off the station at 2:00 A.M. and wake up at 6:00 to get in my truck and leave for the job site. I listened to "All Things Considered" on the way home and public radio seemed to be an honorable calling; maybe I could find a place.

WBKY was a small station, five full-time people, a $65,000 budget, but the door was wide open. People were encouraged to play with radio. "A documentary series? A bluegrass music show?" "Sure. Why not?" I was on the full-time staff by 1974, with a daily air shift that included running the control board during "All Things Considered." I was separated from the NPR people in Washington by just an instant in time.

A year later I saw a job announcement: ATC Production Assistant, writing and tape-editing experience necessary. I sent a letter, we talked on the phone. And at the end of August, at age thirty-three, I drove across Memorial Bridge into downtown Washington to find NPR and to see if I could fool them long enough so that I could learn something. "All Things Considered" had been on the air for four years then; the people I met were happy, tired, talented, distracted: Susan Stamberg and Bob Edwards were the co-hosts, David Creagh the director, Jim Russell the producer, Smokey Baer was the other production assistant, and Claire Etheridge answered the phones and did the paperwork. Linda Wertheimer was a reporter, and Bob Zelnick, and Nina Toten-

berg. Soon to arrive: Cokie Roberts, Neal Conan, Robert Krul-
wich, Robert Siegel.

We put the program on the air every day and Susan would
say, "The good news is we get to do it again tomorrow. The
bad news is we have to do it again tomorrow." I found a
garage apartment in Georgetown and would go there every
evening to listen to the program we had just finished—I
didn't listen with pride, I was always afraid I'd hear some
terrible mistake that I'd made.

On the flight out today there's a good chance to read all
the papers—we stopped in Denver—especially the entertainment sections. The new CBS program with Connie
Chung is using re-creation techniques. The Reverend Law
rence Jenco, responding to a question about a segment on
the Mideast hostages, said: "You mean an actor is playing
Terry Anderson? You mean an actor is playing me? They
didn't tell me that." And the show's executive producer, Andrew Lack, is quoted as saying, "I don't talk about my work."
I saw this particular program, and even though I don't like
re-creations, I thought the hostage segment was really well
done.

ABC-TV was receiving congratulations for its coverage of
the New York Marathon. I'd watched it on Sunday and was
pleased by the use of live music—Bill Conti, wearing headphones, watching a monitor, was conducting the Juilliard
Symphony—written especially for the race. They even backtimed the last piece of music to end as the winning runner—Juma Ikaanga—crossed the finish line.

The music was producer Geoffrey Mason's idea, I read in
USA Today. Most years we don't manage to come up with an
idea for "All Things Considered" about the New York Marathon, or even the Boston, which is run on Monday. My all-
time favorite marathon story came in *The New York Times*
the day after the 1991 Boston race. Just a paragraph: "Running in his 60th Boston marathon, Johnny Kelley, an 83-
year-old former Olympian, finished in 5:43:54. As he crossed

the line, he collided with his wife, Laura, who was waiting for him, and they fell. Neither was hurt, and he pronounced himself ready to run his 61st."

In Boise, we have dinner at Jyl Hoyt's house; she's KBSU's program director. A couple of friends and neighbors join us, and it's helpful for story ideas and background.

Wednesday, November 8, Idaho, 1989

5:45 A.M. The school lunch menus are shown on television. We've heard coyotes barking in the night. Breakfast is early at Julie and Dorothy Domowitz's house; Julie, who's had coffee and has already been outside to smoke his first ciga- rette, is cooking bacon and eggs. The eggs come from Dicey Davis, over on the other side of the canyon. Seventy cents a dozen; she delivers. They tell us that ice cream is sold here from refrigerated trucks that come by—the good-sized su- permarkets being a melting distance away. The Domowitzes have been kind enough to put us up; he's a retired principal and coach. They have kids away at school and work and three empty bedrooms. One of their daughters works with us at NPR, and it was her idea that we do a story about the Peruvian sheepherders who work for the nearby ranches.

The phone rings and then soon Ricardo Beraun, a fore- man for Little House Creek Ranch, is out front with his red Ford flatbed truck. Bales of green alfalfa are on the back, and an English sheepdog is on top of the bales. Ricardo is off to visit the herders' camps—the sheep are being brought in for the winter—and we follow in the car, down through the canyon, across a river, and up onto the high grasslands. The sun comes over the horizon on our left at 7:29. Ricardo waves from his truck, pointing out the antelope, perhaps a hundred of them running with easy grace, flowing to the south along the hillside.

Farther along the road we find Ulysses, one of the herders,

moving a flock of sheep down to the ranch. We wait while
Ricardo and his dog help direct the sheep through a gate
into the next field. Ulysses could be in a movie. He's wearing
a red plaid wool parka with a hood, and a tan corduroy
jacket over that, and sunglasses. His horse, he says, is called
"Negro"—"The Black."

At the main holding corral, the sheep are being culled—
some of the old ewes will be sold this winter. All these sheep
are Ramboulet-Columbia, light gray and brown with white
faces, and with wooly ridges on their sides—they've just
been shorn.

loud "baaah's," sheep moving, and bells

NOAH: It's cold if you're only standing around. We spend
the morning drinking coffee from a thermos, watching
the herders at work—they move with a confident
athleticism, sorting the sheep. And there was another
movie scene. A cowboy on a fast horse, going after
some runaway sheep but mostly riding for the fun of
it, his dog out in front and to the left, circles of dust
rising behind, and the *sound* came from all the
Saturday matinées—the speedy "clippety-clops" of the
hooves echoing in the clear mountain air.

Most of this work used to be done by men from the
Basque region of Spain; now the herders are from Mexico
and Chile and Peru. The sheepherder's wagon is about the
size of a camping trailer. Inside, a bed with gray woolen
blankets, a wood-burning stove, fold-down table, cupboards.
This is home for most of the year. Two dogs—they sleep
under the wagon—one horse, and about a thousand sheep to
watch over. Ricardo brings supplies up from the ranch, groceries, occasionally some mail. Also dog food, and alfalfa for
the horse.

The sheepherders work on three-year contracts, often
leaving families behind. Ricardo Beraun, the ranch fore-

man, came here from Peru fifteen years ago, decided to stay. He supervises four herders, all Peruvian.

NOAH: Is it a good salary to be a sheepherder?

BERAUN: Well, in comparison to the money we make over there in Peru, yes. A sheepherder is six hundred and fifty dollars a month.

NOAH: And does that include the groceries?

BERAUN: No, the groceries separate.

NOAH: Is there a lot of competition for these jobs, in Peru? To come to Idaho. A lot of people want to do it?

BERAUN: Yes, well especially right now with the situation there, those terrorists.

On late-night television, back in Boise, they're showing a John Wayne movie, part of what the station calls "Ten Days of the Duke." And as I'm going off to sleep a pioneer woman—a "Texican," she calls herself—is out on her porch in the evening talking to Wayne about the death of her only son: "Some day this country's going to be a fine good place to be. Maybe it needs our bones in the ground before that time can come."

Thursday, November 9, Idaho, 1989

Asa Sopia for lunch. It's a Basque soup: cabbage, potatoes, garlic. It's been cooking while we interviewed Domingo Aguirre in the kitchen of his ranch. His brother Felipe comes in to eat. Henry, a retired ranch hand, fixes their lunch every day. He's also made deer's heart in tomato sauce, and the three older men watch carefully to see if we'll eat any of it. We take careful bites, nodding, "It's rich." On the wall there's a picture of a cattle dog named "DEKE—A LEGEND, 1957–1975." A long working life; Deke was Domingo's favorite dog.

Domingo Aguirre is sixty-eight and strong and smiling with the pride of fifty years of sheep and cattle ranching and raising a family.

AGUIRRE: The Basque sheepherders used to tell me, *"Domingo, Domingo, isena da biarra eta segiru ainLxe—biarrien segiru."* And in English, "Domingo—the name, it means work."

NOAH: Now, do you know specifically why your father came, and in what year?

AGUIRRE: He came here in 1905, the reason was that the work was not there in Spain and they wanted to come to the New World of the United States. We get people from Spain, they walk right through that door—you could put them in the mountains, you'd never lose one. They're natural, they're very natural in the mountains. In the thirties we had the Civil War in Spain. And Franco, you might say, opposed to the Basque pretty much. And the Basque areas. And Franco asked Hitler to send his troops. So they sent the Stukas, the best fighter-bombers they had, the eighty-eights, the best cannon they had, and they attacked the Basque. The Basque fought at night, and I remember still reading inserts in the *Life* magazine at that time, the German officers said, "If I had a detachment of those Basque, I'd whip the world." Natural mountain people.

NOAH: Is it unusual for sons and daughters of Basque immigrants to speak Basque so well; do a lot of them stay away from the language?

AGUIRRE: No, I think in our case, we were always around the Basque men. And then my aunt and my mother, they made sure, they made certain we spoke Basque.

And they kept that heritage in us very strong. They
would take us, my oldest brother and I, to the Basque
boardinghouses; Mountain Home had a lot of Basque
boardinghouses, both sides of the track at that time.
There was an accordion player—his picture's right up
there on the wall—they call him Arrieta, Sono Larishe.
Arrieta was where he was from and *sono larishe* is a
music maker. They didn't know his name—I didn't
know his name, until the year that he was going to die.
He had cancer. And his name was John. And I don't
think anyone knew that his name was John, it was
always "Arrieta."

There was two brothers, big handsome men, strong,
physical men. And I remember those men dancing in
this one boardinghouse one time, they danced with
American Basque girls, or I think some might have
been American girls. But they were so strong,
eventually they'd be picking this girl up and her
skirts'd be going up and the next thing you know I saw
this girl slap this man in the face (*laughs*) and he put
her down and continued dancing. They come from the
mountains, the girls would dance with them, they'd
play this music, and they'd be there in the wee
hours—they were the happiest people in the world.
You would think there was not a worry in the world.

Domingo Aguirre's voice is soft, telling the stories. He
pours more red wine, and plays tapes of Basque songs. "Do
You Hear the Drums, Fernando?" But we should leave. It's a
long drive into the mountains to Silver City—we're off to
visit a ghost town.

We turn off Route 78 onto a gravel road, into a space that's
just inches of white on the map. It's 2:50 in the afternoon,
and we're listening to Stephen Jay Gould, talking about his
new book with Terry Gross, on "Fresh Air." But soon I turn
the radio off: it's going to be a serious drive. The road is
corrugated with small hard ruts and it's risky to go much

over thirty, sometimes ten miles an hour is too fast. It's a long grind up several thousand feet—the road runs straight out to the mountains and then up.

There was a sign back down by the highway warning that this road was impassable after November 1. And after about fifteen miles, I realized that this is indeed November; I was thinking it was October. The road winds up through some canyons and across narrow passes. The views are splendid and scary. And soon there's snow on the road, we're close to seven thousand feet high. Our engineer, Jason Stelluto, has his eyes closed. I'm driving; he's riding in the back, and I think it seems more dangerous than it is. Melissa grins and says, as she always does, "Let's go for it." But it is a lonely road and it would get pretty cold if we got stuck.

Then I notice there's a white four-wheel drive van behind us. And as it follows us around a curve, I can read: "NEWS 7." This is the station that's been requesting an interview all week—is it possible they're following us? Doing a story about us doing a story? I slow down and the white van goes on around.

When we get to the top—Silver City—the town's caretaker is sitting by the side of the road, talking with the News 7 folks, a young woman who's shooting video and a man dressed in a suit and tie—he's the reporter. They've driven up to do a feature story about the ghost town and the coming of winter. And they have also figured out who we are, and ask if they can tape us as we wander around. Well, why not?

bird sounds, water dripping

NOAH: The melting snow drips from the roof of an old wooden building onto the sandy street. The town of Silver City is mostly still here. About forty stores and houses, some cemeteries. There's a sign on the old hotel: PUBLIC EARTH CLOSET. Silver City was a mining town, beginning in the 1860s. Millions in gold and silver. Lots of people stayed on well after the good years, but almost everybody was gone by the mid-1950s. These days some visitors come in the summertime, and a few stores are open, but after the cold weather starts, there's only a watchman and his family living here. Del Etchinson was born in Silver City and he's used to being snowed in. Snowed in for most of the winter.

ETCHINSON: Ah, it varies. Sometimes six months, sometimes four.

NOAH: What do you do in a real emergency?

ETCHINSON (*laughs*): Haven't had one yet. If I ever have one, I'll let you know. Know that Life Flight? Out of Boise? They come in here if we need anything, we've got radios.

NOAH: Helicopters?

ETCHINSON: Yeah. It takes about thirty minutes to get here. We've had snowmobilers get hurt, and they come in and pick them up.

NOAH: They call it a ghost town—do you ever sense the presence of the older people here, the people who were here?

ETCHINSON: No, you hear stories about ghosts wandering around here at night. I never seen anybody up here that was that vindictive or had any grudge against anybody. They was okay, they was good people. Most of them I knew, they wouldn't bother me anyway. (*Laughs*)

There's not much daylight left. The caretaker says, "Going back down that way? Got chains? Better not." He points out a back way, an easier road, down over the mountains into Oregon. It sounds a long way off, and it's a slow, gravel road at first, but then it's a wonderful, fast drive, through Oregon's Jordan Valley at sunset, and north back to Idaho, and Boise. And on the radio, we heard the first stories from East Berlin. And Linda talking with Dan Schorr. The Wall was coming down. How could that be?

Friday, November 10, Idaho, 1989

You should know better than to get supper in a place called Lardo's, even if you're in a nice friendly town like McCall. I probably just ordered the wrong thing; it seemed like a popular place. Somebody told us that Peruvian men had gotten in trouble in Lardo's in the past. Single women, it's said, in such a place in Peru, would be prostitutes.

And earlier, on the way up? When we stopped at that roadhouse for lunch and went inside and saw a full-sized dummy, dressed like an Indian, with long black braids, sitting at the bar? Shouldn't we have been a little apprehensive about the food?

But other than you'll-be-sorry cheeseburgers, it's a fun day. Bill Abbott, an old friend and former colleague, has come along as a producer, and he'll be around through this next week, as we broadcast from Boise. Bill's working in Hollywood, helping with sound production on *Talk Radio, Glory*, other films—experience that comes in handy today. We had to leave town without a good ending. The ending is the *essential* part of a radio story: a print story can always be cut from the bottom, it's the lead that's critical in print. So, on the drive back, Bill and I devised a cinematic structure, to build some tension. We could see it in our minds like a movie. The narrative, the information in the story, would be intercut with the felling of a 130-feet-tall spruce tree, in the woods outside McCall. We would *begin* with a voice saying, "Wow, that's a nice tree," and *end* as the tree hits the ground.

We had been to visit David Simmonds. He makes a living cutting wood for violins and guitars, cellos. The Engelmann spruce grows nearby, tall and straight, and the wood is valued by instrument makers; it's light and responsive. The Stradivarius violins have tops made from spruce cut in the Black Forest three centuries ago.

outside sounds, some panting

NOAH: This is the one you saw from down at the road?

SIMMONDS: Yeah. I'm going to take this tree.

NOAH: Now my vision of this from here on out is limited to what I've seen in cartoons . . . (*laughs*) and it always goes wrong in the cartoons.

SIMMONDS: Well, this is quite dangerous. The best place to be is close to the tree where as it falls—it will be moving very slowly—you can walk faster than it will be moving.

saw starts up, rips into tree

saw stops

SIMMONDS: I should be able to put this down with wedges from here. Somebody keep an eye up and yell if limbs start to fall (*panting*). They're called "widow makers."

inside shop, electric motor noise

NOAH: Simmonds has a twelve-foot-high band saw in his shop, a power planer, big chunks of spruce all over, shavings, sawdust. He cuts the wood into thin sections about two feet long, to send to the instrument makers. Idaho spruce now goes to Germany, to Japan, to the Martin Guitar Company, the Gibson Company, and many independent luthiers. The spruce tree David Simmons is cutting today is three hundred years old and died not too long ago. He says if he takes fifteen to

twenty trees a year, he can be a player in the world
market for instrument wood.

hammering again

SIMMONDS: When this starts to go, I'm going to take off
toward the creek (*out of breath*). You may want to join
me.

light taps

SIMMONDS: Here it goes.

*creaking, cracking, straining . . . then crash of tree onto
ground*

It was a thrilling moment when the spruce tree came
down. The sound that Jason recorded was wonderful, the
splintering and cracking and crashing, and there was a
heightened *silence* afterwards, and in the air—an explosion
of evergreen scent. Later, down by the road, you could smell
it coming down through the trees like a river.

Wednesday, November 15, Idaho, 1989

We have another breakfast at the Dutch Oven in Boise. It's
the most *stubborn* restaurant I've ever seen. Tom Sweeney
owns the Dutch Oven, and runs it, and has for thirty years
now. He has also decided what you'll have for breakfast:
sourdough hotcakes, sausage, homemade fruit salad, cranberry juice, and coffee or tea. Four dollars. It's great food. If
you want something else, don't come in the door. Plus he's
fun to talk with.

At KBSU it was a fast day of editing tape, and cutting time
out of stories, writing and recording copy to be assembled in
Washington. And after the program's off the air, it's time to
tape our last interview in Boise; we set up a sixteen-millime-

ter projector to watch a Nell Shipman movie. She began acting in 1912. She is absolutely captivating on the screen, with dark hair, a smiling, open sensuality, and flashing eyes.

projector sound

NOAH: How did they get their eyes to look that way in these old black and white silent films?

TOM TRUSKY: Well, they do have ocher and mascara and things like that to highlight—she had incredible wide eyes, huge eyes, very luminous, very expressive.

Tom Trusky, who teaches at Boise State, has edited a book of Nell Shipman's writings, *The Silent Screen & My Talking Heart,* and has managed to find many of her old movies. Last week six Shipman films were shown at the Museum of Modern Art in New York.

Nell Shipman had a short, troubled career making silent movies, adventure stories about women who are splendidly victorious over desperate circumstances. She would be the producer, director, writer, and star, working at her own studio at Priest Lake in northern Idaho. We were watching her in the role of Dreena, a writer who lives out in the wilderness.

projector sound continues

TRUSKY: Here's the dog team; one of the dogs realizes, though, that they've left their mistress, and he escapes his harness and he's going back to rescue them.

NOAH: All her dogs and animals were trained. She has bears that untie knots, dogs that carry messages. She's always saved by her animals in her films. One of her themes is that animals are kinder and more humane than many humans.

(TO TRUSKY): Did she actually appear naked in a movie in the twenties?

TRUSKY: Actually, in the teens, yeah, she's frolicking in a pool of water and an evil villain comes creeping up with rapacious intent, but naturally Nell has one of her guardians there, a big bear named Brownie.

NOAH: Now in an article you wrote about Nell Shipman, you said that her dogsled trip over miles of snow and ice—*this is real life*—"to rescue her *gangrenous, delirious lover/co-director* made national headlines." (*Laughs*) Can you give us that story in a brief way?

TRUSKY: Her lover was a man named Bert Van Tuyle, who'd worked with her on a film, her first major film, called *Back to God's Country,* in Canada. The leading man on that died, by the way, from the weather. He got pneumonia and died while they were shooting it. Bert Van Tuyle suffered frostbite. Later they come to Idaho, they're in the middle of the worst winter on record to that time. The frostbite returns with a vengeance. His feet go gangrenous, he goes insane, he won't accept any help, he rushes down Priest Lake on snow and ice; Nell takes after him with a dogsled to catch up with him and save him . . . Well, the freaky thing about that is that the story in *Back to God's Country* is precisely that—it's fiction made in 1919, but in 1924 suddenly it's life. And she does rescue Bert. She takes him down, and they finally get down to the end of the lake, put him in a car, they get him to a train, they take him to Spokane and his toes are amputated. Then they return to make these two-reel films, even after that they're so obsessed with making films.

Friday, November 17, Idaho, 1989

Everybody's fighting for air time today, discussions back and forth between producers about what stories can be how

long. We grudgingly manage to edit our last report from
Idaho—about David Simmonds and the spruce tree—down
to five minutes fifty seconds.

A three-way conversation is set up for "All Things Considered": Linda's in Washington, Robert's in West Berlin, and I
join in from Boise. It's taped in advance because of satellite
availability (the term "pre-taped" always seemed strange to
me, or worse, "pre-taped before a live audience"). The three of
us talk for about ten minutes. It feels a bit awkward; our
time in Idaho sounds inconsequential compared to the
news from Europe, but Washington says it's going to sound
fine. We say goodnight from Boise, and pack up our equipment. Jason's got several cases of microphones, recorders,
and mixers to get to the airport tomorrow.

I walk back to the motel, about three miles along the
river. It's already dark and chilly; I have my radio with me
and I'm listening to the program we've just finished, it's now
being broadcast on KBSU. Robert has a nice story from East
Berlin about the lack of medical supplies. Our tree story
wasn't too short after all.

It's always hard for me to listen to my own work. It's not
that I'll be overly critical of the editing or writing, it's simply that I don't like to hear my own voice. Sometimes in
Washington I'll get in a taxi after an especially stressful day
and find that the driver's listening to "All Things Considered." I have to ride all the way home with my hands over
my ears when I know my voice is coming on.

I find that many in radio don't feel comfortable listening
to themselves; it has to do, I believe, with the way we hear
our voices coming through the bones of the head, as compared to the way we sound on tape. I've taken part in several
NPR workshops around the country; a few of us from Washington will get together with reporters from member stations, and freelancers. We'll spend three days in an airport
hotel in Atlanta or Chicago, talking about radio news, techniques of recording, writing, delivery—and I'll always ask,
"How many of you are happy with the way you sound?" No

hands go up. Possibly one. And I simply suggest—if you're working on the air and someone brings you a paycheck every Friday, then who cares?

Some radio people try to change their voice, a strained, affected effort to get closer to the way they think they should sound. I knew an announcer once who was asked by NBC to come to New York for an audition. He spent a day reading newscasts, commercial copy, doing a weather report, warming up a game show audience. NBC said, you're pushing too much, trying to make your voice sound lower, but we think you're good and we'll give you a job if you just use your natural voice. He turned it down because he didn't think he could make the change, and soon left broadcasting altogether.

From time to time I'll get calls asking if I'd be willing to do commercials. Voice-overs only, my name wouldn't be used, nor my picture. A San Francisco ad agency wants to know if I'd read for an Isuzu campaign. They've faxed the scripts; the spots are low-key, pleasant. I have to call back and say no. Our union contract would allow us to do commercials, but I've always felt it could hurt our credibility as journalists. Maybe not. Martin Sheen does Toyota ads, Michael Douglas does Infiniti, Demi Moore Keds—does anyone think Gene Hackman is less believable as an actor because you hear him on television doing voice-overs for United Airlines? Does anyone even know that's his voice? There's big money involved in this sort of work—six-figure fees, I've read.

Later we join some folks from KBSU for dinner, and to thank them for helping out. We've been in their way all this week, but they still managed to put on a successful membership campaign. I did get a chance to join in with the on-air fundraising, and to answer some of the pledge calls. The NPR hosts and reporters try to do as much fundraising as they can. Stations will ask if Bob Edwards, of "Morning Edition," can come and help for a couple of days, or Robert will go, or Linda, Cokie Roberts, Scott Simon, Liane Hansen, many others.

What I enjoy most is taking on-air calls from listeners—
questions about what's going on back in Washington, complaints, or compliments, about NPR's news judgment. It's
not quite as much fun making speeches to groups of underwriters, usually business people, but these events mean a lot
to a station. And it can be delightful, or frustrating, to be at
the absolute center of attention. A few years ago in San
Diego during a KPBS fundraising campaign, about seventy-
five couples bought tickets for a Saturday morning cruise
on a paddlewheel excursion boat. "A boat ride with NPR's
Noah Adams," the promo announcements said. As soon as
we left the dock, I realized that all these people were already
quite familiar with San Diego Harbor, and they'd probably
been on this boat before—I was the attraction, and I'd better
get busy meeting everyone. This isn't really hard; to keep
from talking about myself all the time, I've learned to ask
questions: How long have you been listening to KPBS, did
you move to San Diego from someplace else? Even, what
local stories aren't being covered nationally? At one point,
though, I got a little overwhelmed, and escaped below decks
to the men's bathroom. I was standing there at the urinal,
when the man next to me said, "Have you seen him yet?"

Mostly, though, we are treated as ordinary people, more as
colleagues of our listeners, and everyone's happy at the
chance for a visit. I often think of individual listeners when
our program is on the air, and it's easy to recall a cold, sunny
afternoon in Vermont, seven years ago. A local teacher wel-
comed us into the kitchen of his farmhouse. We met his
nine-year-old son, who had a learning disability—the father
and son spent a great deal of time together during the day.
The young boy took me over to a table by the window.
"Here's where we sit when 'All Things Considered' is on.
Here's where my dad sits, here's where I sit. And there's the
radio, right over there."

Sunday, November 19, Washington, D.C., 1989

This morning we drive over to Takoma Park, in Maryland. Neenah wants to meet Ward Sinclair, who left *The Washington Post* a couple of years ago and now has a "truckpatch" farm up in Pennsylvania. He writes a weekly column for the *Post* from there, datelined "Dott, Pa." Sinclair sells his produce every Sunday at the Takoma Park Farmers Market. But we're an hour early, and after two weeks of eating out I don't want to have breakfast in a restaurant, so we decide to come back another Sunday.

We stop by NPR to pick up my mail—magazines, review copies of books. I did a lot of reading on the plane yesterday: *Esquire, Vanity Fair, Premiere, BusinessWeek,* and a wonderful piece in the *Atlantic* about Wes Jackson and the Land Institute in Kansas. I've had a vague, incorrect idea of what it is he's doing out there. He wants to create a "domestic prarie" that could be harvested. I should write a proposal to go out to Salina, Kansas, and do a story about Wes and Dana Jackson, and especially about the interns who work at the Institute.

Thursday, November 23, Washington, D.C., 1989

I'm up at 4:00 A.M. to take the NPR turkey out of the refrigerator—Julia Child, in her latest cookbook, wants the turkey to be at room temperature, seventy degrees to start. So I wake up again at seven to put it in the oven. Before breakfast I go out for a nice run in the snow, and then around noon, Neenah and I take the turkey and dressing downtown to the people working today on "All Things Considered." We also take Bonny, sneaking her past the building guard, just a small quiet dog in a bag, and she has a great time running around our newsroom, accepting bits of food from at least twenty-five people. It's a potluck dinner; others have made mashed potatoes and salads and pies—it's a nice tradition, especially for the younger, newer members of the staff.

In 1975, when I came to Washington, I had one of my saddest Thanksgivings ever. I just spent the day at work and went home to an empty apartment. The next year, a colleague and I went to a nearby hotel after the program for an even lonelier Thanksgiving meal. Then I began going to Susan Stamberg's house in the evening—great leftover food and a warm, friendly house. And several years ago, our producer Chris Koch brought in a turkey for those who had to work. The next year, everyone brought food, and now it's a feast. Chris left to work in television, and I now have the honor of cooking the turkey.

On Thanksgiving Eve, 1991, our foreign desk received a message from Mike Shuster, stationed in Moscow. Mike's a fine cook, and a resourceful shopper. He'd been on a reporting trip to the Ukraine:

> I bought a turkey in the Kiev market! Had a refrig in my hotel room. It was okay until yesterday. But the delay at the Kiev airport was horrendous. I was supposed to get back to Moscow Tuesday around noon. I got back today (Wednesday) around noon. So I had to start looking for places to put the turkey. First an airport café had a refrig. But then it got late, they closed and I thought we'd at least fly last night. So I took the turkey out of the frig. Then they told us no flight until this morning. So I fumed and fumed and then realized I had to do something about keeping the turkey cold. Could find no other frig. Finally in the middle of the night, I wrapped it up and hid it in a bush outside, assuming it would not be there in the morning. But nobody saw me and it was still there today. Now it's safe and still fresh, and in my refrig. Such is life in the USSR. Mike.

A couple of weeks after this, NPR, after long effort, opened a direct line to Moscow—just a regular NPR extension, dial four numbers and Mike's on the phone. This was announced just the day after Russia, Ukraine, and Byelorussia decided to form a new commonwealth, based in Minsk. John Keator, who watches after telephones and broadcast lines for NPR, had assigned 2227 as the Moscow number—or dial CCCP, initials that, as John's memo put it, "seem to have wound up in the dustbin of history."

NPR also has a potluck lunch in late February, to mark Black History Month, along with music and poetry and remembrances. Our Christmas parties, I've found, usually turn out to be somewhat cold and depressing. But we had great fun with a company picnic in June of 1990—an extravaganza to celebrate NPR's twentieth anniversary.

You never know who's listening on holidays. You can have the feeling that most of the regular audience is missing, out of place. And you wonder about those who *are* listening, if indeed they are lonely. On Thanksgiving several years ago, I was asked to write an essay to welcome James Brady home from the hospital. The White House Press Secretary had been wounded in the assassination attempt on President Reagan earlier that year. I said I'd be glad to try, but everything I wrote sounded discouraged. I mentioned Brady, but then went on to write about the number of homeless people on the streets of the cities. Our editor kept asking me to take sentences and even words out of the essay, until in the end, as it ran, it was meaningless. I remember being mad at myself that night, and I finally understood that you can't write that sort of commentary to order—if you have something to say, it comes easily, sometimes urgently, but it's tough to sit down to write someone else's idea, especially if it's a serious theme.

Sunday, November 26, Washington, D.C., 1989

Woke up hot and dry with slight laryngitis. So I try for a quiet day. Read the papers, watch the news shows. A change of government in Czechoslovakia (I've been jealous this week of the reporters who've gone there and have been with the hundreds of thousands demonstrating in Wenceslas Square in Prague), Hungary will have free elections for the first time in forty years, Gorbachev meets with the Pope. I'm happy to work with an editor, Brooke Gladstone, who dislikes the word "historic." It's overused, even in normal times. Brooke will usually take it out of copy, or change it to "unprecedented," which few things really are, but it's an improvement over "historic." Robert Siegel enjoys spotting the inappropriate use of "literally." Most of the time, he says, when people use "literally" they actually mean "figuratively." I've noticed it a lot since he pointed it out—after Magic Johnson's announcement of his positive HIV status, someone wrote that it was a national tragedy because Magic, playing basketball on TV, has "literally" been in millions of American living rooms.

Wednesday, November 29, Washington, D.C., 1989

Erythromycin and Tylenol 3 with codeine and lots of water and time in bed. A terrible sore throat and fever. I sound like I should be in a horror movie.

It's a good reading time, though: a biography of Rod Serling, a new book about Georgia O'Keeffe, Bill McKibben's *The End of Nature*. Paul Schurke's book about his trans-Siberian expedition. Also some movies we've brought home:

Manon of the Springs (great), *How the West Was Won* (terrible), and *Miss Firecracker* (pretty good).

Thursday, December 7, Washington, D.C., 1989

Margaret West, one of our two desk assistants, tells me today she's leaving. We only ask people to do this job for two years, and she's well past that. It's tough and mostly thankless, being on the phone all day, finding people for interviews, often talking them into going into a studio somewhere. You can spend hours trying to get through to a place like Soviet Armenia, and then not find anyone who speaks English. Margaret has a husband, two teenage boys, a British law degree, and now some valuable experience, and I hope she doesn't continue to work so hard.

A discussion at our morning meeting about David Duke, the former Klan leader, now a Louisiana state legislator. He's planning to run for the U.S. Senate. The opinion is offered that you shouldn't legitimize him by covering his campaign. Others argue that you can't keep people out of the news because you find their morals disgusting. I wonder, when this comes up, about discussions that must have taken place in newsrooms in the fifties during the McCarthy time. Did some at CBS, for example, believe it was wrong to have Edward R. Murrow devote a entire program to Joseph McCarthy?

I interviewed the songwriter Sammy Cahn, about his colleague, Sammy Fein, who died yesterday at eighty-seven. Fein wrote "I'll Be Seeing You," and "Love Is a Many-Splendored Thing." Sammy Cahn had worked with Fein on songs for the Disney film *Peter Pan,* and said to me about that experience, "Two men working in a room with a piano is like making love, and the songs are the babies."

Sunday, December 10, Washington, D.C., 1989

Princess excalibur, early yellow, single late cream delight, and others—Neenah's been planting tulips for the spring in the yard of the house we're moving to in Maryland. She made it in time: seven inches of snow arrived on Friday. We stayed in and cooked and read and listened to music—Tom Harrell's albums; he's a trumpet player I'll be interviewing soon.

My voice is pretty much back to normal, although it tires easily. Most of the high range has returned. It's hard to sound lively and interested without the high notes.

We heard a lovely story on Scott Simon's Saturday morning program "Weekend Edition." Alex Chadwick has just returned from Czechoslovakia and he wrote about a young woman, Nàtasa Dudinska—his interpreter, actually—and the importance of Czech students in the nonviolent revolution in Prague. It was part of the story I hadn't heard about, and Alex described it wonderfully—I could *see* the look in Dudinska's eyes, exhausted, exhilarated, as she began to realize the significance of what she and the other students had done.

Tuesday, December 12, Washington, D.C., 1989

I have an interview with John Mack, a psychiatrist at Harvard Medical School, about my post–Cold War notion that nations do somehow *need* enemies. He mostly agrees with the premise and theorizes that the threat to the environment should be the new focus of antagonism. And when I ask him why not get the politicians and psychiatrists together with the Disney people to create a new monster movie along those lines, he said he's already been told about a movie treatment that deals with a monster threatening the environment.

A pretty good in-house argument today about Santa Claus. A young girl, a first-grader in Wisconsin, was sent home from school because she told her classmates Santa Claus doesn't exist. It was thought I could interview her mother, but I said, "Wait, this has come up before. I don't think we should do it." A child, listening, could be hearing for the very first time that someone has doubts about Santa Claus, and for me, these stories usually aren't important enough to take that risk. Brooke Gladstone, the editor, and Ellen Weiss, our new executive producer, totally disagree with me. Jill Crawford, our desk assistant, is on my side. And Cokie Roberts, passing by on her way into a studio, says, "Of course you shouldn't do it." And we don't. Cokie's the mom here.

Many of us came to NPR from small public radio stations (some from Pacifica Radio), a group of liberal, idealistic, stations around the country; others from newspapers—mostly all alternative, low-budget, eclectic backgrounds. Cokie (full name: Mary Martha Corinne Morrison Claiborne Boggs Roberts) arrived as an experienced reporter; she'd worked in print and broadcast in New York, Greece, California, Washington. Her husband was writing for *The New York Times*; her father had been in Congress, then her mother. She's a grownup, responsible friend and colleague, and she provides hope that it is possible to have a career in public broadcasting and a family and a home. Susan Stamberg is another example: twenty years on the job, twenty years in the same house, a happy marriage, a twenty-year-old son.

Wednesday, December 13, Washington, D.C., 1989

A story tonight about a proposed new skyscraper in Chicago, downtown on the corner of Madison and Wells, three blocks from the Sears Tower, which is one hundred ten stories high. And after the report from Chicago, I spoke with the architect of the new building, Cesar Pelli. He explained that the Miglin-Beitler skyscraper, as it would be known, will be fifteen stories taller than the Sears Tower, and engineered to sway by only two feet at the top. Studies have shown that when tall buildings sway more than three feet, the workers get sick and want to go home.

> NOAH: Mr. Pelli, are you quite comfortable at a height of almost two thousand feet ... a building that high?

> PELLI: Yes, why not? (*Laughs*) It only feels scary as an idea. Once you are on top of the Empire State, for example, or in the Windows on the World [at the World Trade Center], you feel perfectly comfortable up there.

> NOAH: Is there a limit as to how high a skyscraper could be built?

> PELLI: With today's technologies, the limit would be very high. The most difficult technical problem is elevators.

> NOAH: The elevators are the most important factor?

> PELLI: As the buildings get taller, you need to increase the number of elevators, and the volume that the elevators start occupying in a very tall building starts to be out of all proportion to the space available for usable offices.

> NOAH: Am I recalling this correctly, did Frank Lloyd Wright at one time at least make up a drawing of a very high skyscraper for Chicago?

PELLI: That is correct, he proposed a building that he
called The Illinois, which was a mile high.

NOAH: Did people scoff at that?

PELLI: Well, no, because it was presented by an incredible
architect who was also a great showman and a
beautiful design; but it was never a real proposal, it
was never worked out as a real building.

NOAH: If that Frank Lloyd Wright building, a mile high,
were built, you would have no qualms about being the
first to go up to the observation tower?

PELLI: Not at all. It would be marvelous if it was built.
That was a very beautiful design.

My questions for Cesar Pelli come from a fascination with
high places: the Sears Tower, the World Trade Center buildings, the CN Tower in Toronto—and the exquisite terror I
can feel, looking down over the side.

Also, another dog story tonight, an interview about a
bomb-sniffing dog in Memphis, named Magoo, who was re-
united with his former human partner in the police department. I think the ATC producers and editors got together
one day and said, let's only let Noah do three of these dog
stories a year. A surprising number come across the wires,
almost one a day.

My favorite lately: MANITOWOC WIS AP "A retired police dog
returned his nose to service long enough to help find a missing blind and deaf three-year-old." Angela Bolle, who has
Down's syndrome, wandered into the woods. About one
hundred volunteers and two other dogs couldn't find her.
"As daylight faded," the story says, "searchers summoned
Duke, an eight-year-old German shepherd that retired two
years ago because of waning stamina." Duke found the girl
quickly. "He likes kids a lot," the deputy sheriff said. Of
course, every news organization in the country was calling
Manitowoc to get some part of this story on the air or into

print, but the sheriff's office said no, let's don't bother. We're
busy, it's over.

Thursday, December 14, New York, 1989

An early train trip to New York. Peter Breslow, one of our
producers, and I have three stories to do in two days. I have
an interview scheduled with Tom Harrell, a jazz trumpet
player who is schizophrenic; Peter has always wanted to do a
story about piano movers in Manhattan; and we'll do a
Christmas feature about some Juilliard students who play
in hospitals and nursing homes. Usually at NPR, when you
propose traveling someplace for a story (spending some
money), they'll say, that's fine, but what else can you do
while you're there (two more stories)?

Gary Fink, an engineer from NPR's New York bureau, is
set up and ready to record at Roosevelt Hospital when we
arrive. The three young Juilliard students play Haydn, Beethoven, some Christmas carols, and talk earnestly to a small
group of older patients, who suffer from alcoholism, Alz-
heimer's disease, organic-brain syndrome. Many seem to
enjoy the music, others appear somewhere else in thought.
One man, as the trio is playing, starts talking loudly about
Carnegie Hall and Christ in New Jersey.

After lunch at a deli (I usually order turkey on white,
with mayonnaise, thus proving, I've been told, that I'm from
Kentucky), we take a taxi up to West 84th Street. I learned
about Tom Harrell from a friend of mine, Jim Anderson,
who works in New York as a freelance engineer, specializing
in acoustic jazz. He'd recorded one of Harrell's albums, *Sail
Away,* and sent me a copy. It wasn't my favorite kind of jazz,
but I could tell Tom Harrell was a superb and technically
brilliant player. And I was haunted by his eyes in the picture on the album cover, and intrigued by the description—
on the liner notes—of his schizophrenia. When I was put-

ting this story together later, I first referred to this as a "disease." I recorded the narration, went out for a walk and a sandwich, and realized that I was uncomfortable about the word; came back, checked with an expert on the phone, and changed it to "disorder."

It wasn't at all clear if this interview was going to work, but Peter had talked with Tom Harrell and said that although he was very hesitant and slow on the phone, he seemed friendly and wanted to cooperate. He even said he was honored by the request for an interview. I was worried too about whether he would be willing to talk about his condition. Schizophrenia had been mentioned on an album cover, and in a couple of reviews, but as far as I could tell, Tom hadn't discussed it. A feature article about Tom in *Down Beat* magazine, which included an extensive interview, didn't refer to schizophrenia at all.

We ring the bell. A long wait, a small dog barking inside. Then Harrell opens the door, laughing about the dog that lives in the first-floor apartment, "Moppet," he says. And he leads us slowly—he was almost shuffling—up to his apartment. He's been asleep most of the day; he mentioned he'd just gotten up, and has made dinner for himself. He sits at a green card table and eats as we talk: a small steak, some cheese and bread, club soda. His head is usually down, and shaking a bit. He looks up at me only briefly, and I don't catch the color of his eyes. We talk on through the late afternoon in his apartment, with the airplanes coming in, it seems, close by over Manhattan. Harrell mentions that he learned from John Cage to be aware of everyday sounds, and that the airplanes sometimes remind him of trombones.

I'd asked Peter to make some notes during the interview; a description of the apartment: the furniture, book titles, records—I wanted to pay absolute attention to the conversation. Jim Anderson had told me not to underestimate Tom, that he processes information very quickly, and that it's a mistake to talk down to him, or to talk slowly.

Tom's comments are often elliptical, with long, long

pauses. As we edited this tape later, minutes of silence went onto the floor. Sometimes, thinking he was lost, I would try to help, suggesting a response or asking another question. But then I began to trust the silence, waiting for a line of thought to find its end. The wait was always worthwhile, especially as he explained how his playing relates to chord structure, and his feelings about the beauty of music.

fast trumpet run, music for about fifty seconds, then fades

music continues softly

HARRELL: Sometimes I'm not as . . . the music is . . . is a tangible thing and sometimes I'm not as connected to the music as I'd like to be, but sometimes when I've spent a lot of work on writing, for example, like for the, for the last album, I felt this incredible energy, and I felt in touch with something that was really . . . that really . . . is intriguing. I guess I'm not sure if I'm an innovator, but I, I . . . I want to try to use the talent that I have, and I . . .

NOAH: It can take some time for Tom Harrell to complete a thought, in conversation at least. He seems painfully shy. He is a paranoid schizophrenic, the diagnosis was made when he was in his late teens. But he was going to be a jazz trumpet player. He left home in California and went on the road with the Woody Herman band. He came to New York to play with Horace Silver, then the Phil Woods Quintet. Woods called him the best trumpet player in town, the best *musician* he ever met. And over the last few years, Tom Harrell's music has been more his own. He's doing a lot of writing, playing with his own quintet, playing often, he says, outside the literal notes of the chord.

HARRELL: I want to be . . . I want to be able to play in each chord, to find the beauty of each chord, and by finding

certain notes that bring out the, the beauty of the
chord, but I also want to play melodies that ... that
flow through the chords, and also maybe don't always
... aren't limited to the notes in the chord, but
sometimes that has a lot of beauty.

NOAH: I've asked a lot of musicians this. Do you ever hear
music in your mind that you can't play?

HARRELL: Oh, yeah, a lot. That's frustrating. But ... I think
that's one of my main motivations is to try—the fact
that I can't do it—I can't always play what I hear. I
mean, it's not just a technical thing. I mean, sometimes
the reason I can't play what I hear is because I'm—my
chops aren't at the level I want them to be, but
sometimes I hear things that are maybe less specific,
but I hear a sound in my head. Sometimes I don't hear
specific notes, but I hear a quality of sound that I want
to ... translate into notes. But I remember Charlie
Parker said something when he first started playing
the upper intervals of the chord on the bridge of
"Cherokee," that he, he could play this thing that he
had been hearing and I think from what he said, it
sounded like he'd been hearing something, but he
hadn't been able to play it until that moment.

I had been apprehensive about asking the first question re-
lating to schizophrenia, but it came up quite naturally. Tom
talked with us honestly, sometimes struggling with the ob-
vious difficulty of his situation, but still with great hope.

HARRELL: I think of myself and all musicians as a vehicle
for music, and part of the preparation or the condition
that you have to be in is to be receptive to ... to the
music that's inside. Also it's good to be relaxed
physically and I think it's possible to really bring a lot
of energy....

music faintly in background, as if on radio

NOAH: When, when you had to start taking medication, what did that do to your playing?

HARRELL: Well, it really helped me, because I guess I had a lot of paranoia that prevented me from ... I wasn't able to compose very much. And I wasn't working on new ideas as much, and then when I started taking the medication that I take now, the, the Stelazine, it would cut down on the paranoia a lot and I was able to ... also I was able to interact with people, although the medication does sometimes, it seems like it lowers my energy level, but I guess there's a new kind of medication now for the same symptoms that I want to try to work with that wouldn't have as many side effects.

NOAH: Does the Stelazine affect ... your playing physically at all?

HARRELL: Well, sometimes I think it does, also since I've stopped drinking, I've been taking Cogentin, which is supposed to alleviate the side effects of the Stelazine, but the medication makes me, sometimes has a tendency to make me drowsy or a little less alert, but I ... sometimes I take caffeine to counteract the side effects of the medication.

NOAH: Music then, Tom, has got to be absolutely important in your life.

HARRELL: Yes, yes ... right, I ... it's a way to ... it gives my life meaning, I mean I've sort of—sometimes I lose hope regarding social interaction, sometimes my paranoia is ... I can never draw the line between paranoia and reality sometimes, and I never know exactly what people mean by certain things. But music—it does come from people, but people are vehicles for the music and ... it seems like music has

got so many levels, I mean, you can approach it from
your feelings or you can approach it with your head,
with your brain, or you can approach it
mathematically or philosophically.

NOAH: Are you saying in a way that sometimes it's
difficult for you to trust people, but you can always
trust . . . the music is always honest?

HARRELL: Right. I think there's something that connects
people, and music is part of that, I mean, I think if I . . .
every time I play, I feel if I'm a good vehicle, then I'll be
rewarded . . . by being able to experience beauty.

Before we leave I ask Tom to play some scales for us, one of
the Clark exercises that he said he uses to warm up. He picks
up his Conn Constellation trumpet, puts in a mute, tries the
scales, and misses a few of the notes. He's embarrassed, saying his chops aren't in good shape. Later, listening to one of
his songs—a fast, complex solo—it's difficult to believe this
was the same person playing.

We go on down to Greenwich Village to interview some
musicians who have played with Tom and know him well.
Then to end the day, a Cuban-Chinese dinner, and a visit to
the jazz section at Tower Records. I'm staying at the Gram-
ercy Park. I'd planned to spend the night with friends over
in Brooklyn; had called to get directions on the subway, but
I'd had a premonition for a day or so about going into Brooklyn late at night.

Friday, December 15, New York, 1989

I like to ride with a good driver in New York City. They're
fast and aggressive, they never hesitate, but they're not
mean—no one's going to get into a fight at a blocked inter-
section. And, in his black GMC Jimmy, Mike Narcisco gives

us—in a solid Queens accent—a piano mover's tour. The world of Dun-Rite Movers Incorporated—thirty-five years in the business—is mostly just a few blocks of midtown Manhattan, close by the Steinway and Baldwin showrooms and the concert halls, recording studios. A Steinway artist may be playing at Carnegie Hall and would like to practice in a hotel room—that's *four* moves. Dun-Rite moves fifty pianos a day.

> MIKE NARCISCO (*talking into car phone*): Butch, it's Michael, how are you? Is Henry there yet, Henry and Ted? Oh, they're not there yet? Okay, I'll be by in a little while. Good enough.
>
> *beep, phone hanging up*
>
> NARCISCO: They haven't got to Steinway, they had to make a few more pickups. One thing about pianos, people think they're like flowers. You know, "We're here with the piano"? This is, for logistics, the city is probably the worst place, you can't get nothing done and no one cooperates.
>
> NOAH: Mike Narcisco cruises the city, directing a fleet of Dun-Rite vans. And he wants us to see a move in progress.
>
> NARCISCO: I would imagine that the only place that would probably compete with New York has to be Vienna. I guess Vienna's a big concert town. Haven't been to Vienna.

We find one of Mike's crews and ride in the van for a while: one piano into the Hilton for a music presenters convention, another one over to ABC for "Good Morning, America." A Steinway model D concert grand is nine feet long, weighs a thousand pounds; the men handle it easily. It's tilted, the legs removed, the piano rides on a dolly, standing sideways. We're getting some interesting tape, but Peter had hoped for one of the more dramatic moves—a hoist, the piano swaying in the wind high above the street. We had also hoped to hear some stories about famous musicians. Leonard Bernstein, for example.

NARCISCO: Bernstein was a funny guy, he lived in the Dakota, on Central Park West. That is the cruelest service entrance—you from the city, Noah?

When Peter started putting this story together, back in Washington, he decided to include audio of some scenes from the old Laurel and Hardy movie, *The Music Box*, taking advantage of the humorous tension that's inherent in the business of moving pianos around. One scene in particular was a perfect fit.

scratchy film music

WOMAN'S VOICE: I think it's adorable, I'll take it.

PIANO SALESMAN: I'm glad you like it. You see, it's our latest model.

WOMAN: Can you deliver it right away?

SALESMAN: Right away, madam.

WOMAN: You see, it's my husband's birthday, and I want to surprise him.

movie sound fades out

NOAH, TO MIKE NARCISCO: Do you ever surprise anybody, does that happen?

NARCISCO: Oh yes, yes sir, plenty of times. In fact, when we did Robert De Niro's piano—was in the Village—what it was, it was his girlfriend or wife at the time, I don't know, she didn't want anyone to call up the house. So what happened was, the men, they had to call Steinway, which then gave the number, because

Robert De Niro didn't want anyone to know, of course,
where he lived—but it was a surprise for him.

As Mike Narcisco drops us off at the NPR bureau, I ask
him about something we heard: the Julliard students mentioned yesterday that Dun-Rite had dropped one of the Juilliard pianos, doing some damage. Mike seemed hurt and certainly surprised—he'd told me that his company had never
dropped a piano. Scratched, yes, but not broken. I was almost sorry I asked.

movie sound

Stan and Ollie moving a piano: Heave, ho . . . heave, ho.
Ollie, I can't make it.

OLLIE: Don't weaken now, we only got a couple of more
steps. Now pull together—

piano falls down flight of steps, clanking and smashing

One of the best radio pieces I ever heard was simply an
"imagining"—with sound effects—of someone dropping a
grand piano down the steps inside the Washington Monu-
ment. This was years ago, and I can still hear the dissonant
clattering all the way down from step to step . . . to final step.

We left New York on the three o'clock train; snow was
coming, they said, as well as President Bush, to land by helicopter in Central Park for a talk at the Waldorf-Astoria. The
city was on gridlock alert.

Tuesday, December 19, Washington, D.C., 1989

Tonight an interview with Mark Helprin about his new children's book, *Swan Lake.* Helprin talked with me by satellite
uplink from KUOW in Seattle, but he didn't want us to say

which city he was in or even what part of the country. I didn't bother to mention that I've already read that he's moved with his family to Seattle. Later, when Helprin's novel *Soldier of the Great War* was published, he came to Washington and we could talk face to face. We taped a twenty-minute interview, and as we were leaving the studio, Helprin asked how much of it I would use. About seven minutes, I said. How do you do that? I edit the tape. How do you edit tape? So we went into my office for a demonstration. He's the only author ever to be shown how to cut audio tape; he's the only one who's ever asked.

Mark Helprin isn't as tall as he appears to be in photographs (I take a short person's notice of these matters). But I wasn't surprised, authors want to be have a certain stature, an appealing, intelligent look to their book-jacket photos. I've only met one writer who turned out to be *more* attractive in person. That was Gretel Ehrlich; she doesn't look at all like an older, wind-burned, Wyoming rancher.

Swan Lake, with illustrations by Chris Van Allsburg, is already a Christmas best seller. Helprin wanted to write a classic, a book that could sell year after year—and that meant a children's book. His story, he says, is both a prequel and a sequel to the *Swan Lake* ballet.

HELPRIN: The ballet was not really written. It was mounted the way a Hollywood movie is from an idea that Tchaikovsky and his confidant and friend, stage manager, whoever he was, a fellow named Begachev, had when they were sailing down the Rhine, about the time of the American Civil War. One of them came to the other and said, let's exploit this. Because it was in the period of decadence, or German Romanticism, and the imagery was there—and they did. They went back to Petersburg and put it into a ballet. However, there was no real story, and it shows. In the ballet, the evil magician Von Rothbart has no motivation whatsoever—he's simply an evil magician Von

Rothbart. And what I did was, in regard to the
motivation for Von Rothbart's evil, I made it a quest
for power.

  music from Swan Lake

NOAH: The emperor's palace: 17,500 gilded rooms,
  candelabra that looked like flaming trees, a training
  academy for truffle-sniffing pigs—a wonderful place for
  a story, involving the Damavand horsemen, who guard
  the empire, an infant princess, saved by a scullery
  maid, a young prince in danger, and the marvelous
  notions of storybooks: "It must be fun to be a squirrel,
  but think of music and mathematics and chocolate
  cake."
    Helprin's book is full of marvelous images, especially
  his description of the emperor, who didn't at all look
  like an emperor.

HELPRIN (*reading*): "They brought me to a white-bearded
  bald old fellow who was lying on a worn Turkoman
  carpet in front of a half-dead fire. He had a book beside
  him, a catalogue of his railroad bridges, and he held a
  pen between his toes. He used his magnificent, sleepy,
  burgundy-and-gold-colored hunting dogs—dozens of
  them, Antoles, Purgamanians, Zywynies, Bosteroles,
  and Voolenhausers—as pillows and rugs. Even if he
  rested his elbow on one's head, it only wrinkled up its
  eyes and continued its dream of fetching birds from
  the reeds. It was an odd and tranquil scene. And you
  could hear strains of a waltz coming from deep within
  the palace."

NOAH: What sort of way did you work with Chris Van
  Allsburg to see—to get an idea of what his pictures
  were going to be like?

HELPRIN: See, I had written it beforehand. I wrote it and it
  was completed, and then we had to choose an

illustrator. And I said I would like Chris Van Allsburg
to illustrate it, if you possibly can. Actually it was
Polar Express that was my introduction to his work.
And I was told that he didn't illustrate anything
except his own work, his own writing. And I said, well,
let's ask him, why not? And evidently he knew me, and
he was willing to do it.

NOAH: Do the pictures look like what you had in your
mind, though, when you were writing it?

HELPRIN: No. They don't, which is good, because it gives
the book a different dimension. He said that he didn't
want to illustrate, in every case, all my strongest
images, because those didn't need to be illustrated. So
he picked some of the ones that I wouldn't have
imagined anyone would illustrate. Such as the
truffle-sniffing pigs.

NOAH: But you're happy with it.

HELPRIN: Oh, yes. No question about it. As far as I'm
concerned, he's the best illustrator now working.

Wednesday, December 20, Washington, D.C., 1989

Moving day—we're up before six to pack the last boxes. Neenah and the movers will handle everything; I leave a house
in Virginia and will go home tonight to Maryland.

It's the morning after the invasion of Panama. There's
talk at the office about who should try to go down there—
apparently we're not getting anything from the White
House pool reports—and, for a change, I'm glad I don't speak
Spanish.

There have been killings over the weekend in Romania, as
a result of anti-government protests in the city of Timisoara,
and I interview a Romanian expert about "systematization,"

Ceausescu's so-called modernization program. It's one of the reasons why Romanians are unhappy with the Ceausescu regime. I also talk with one of our producers about the chances of going there should Ceausescu ever fall. About four years ago I had proposed a trip to Romania—when children and old people were reportedly dying of cold and exposure in the apartment buildings, even the hospitals. Ceausescu was cutting back on heat and electricity so he could pay off the country's foreign debts.

I take my old favorite Red Line Metro train home (we lived in this house for a year before going off to Minnesota—the landlord remained a friend and called us when it became vacant again). Neenah has finished the move; she's tired but happy, and we go out to a neighborhood Cajun restaurant for red beans and rice.

Thursday, December 21, Washington, D.C., 1989

Panama is still a frustrating story, we can't find any reporters who have been on the streets—it's very dangerous. NPR has one reporter, John Burnett, in Costa Rica, waiting to get into Panama, and Tom Gjelten's also on the way. ABC managed to get a plane in, but they didn't have much real news, and on "Prime Time Live" Sam Donaldson did what I thought was a jingoistic interview with an Army public relations officer, full of platitudes about America's military might.

In Romania, Nicolae Ceausescu, making a speech, was booed and jeered, and he stopped talking. Then the Romanian state television switched to classical music.

A plan is quickly put together that would send me to Romania, along with Andrei Codrescu, and a producer. Andrei—one of the commentators on our program—was born in Romania, and hasn't been back since he left there more than twenty years ago. I'm happy that he wants to go; it should really help to travel with someone who knows the country. Andrei's a poet, teaches English at Louisiana State University, lives in New Orleans, and sends along his commentaries every other week or so. We're trying to abolish this word "commentator," on the basis that it doesn't mean anything. The people who do it are more interested in writing than they are in commentating on anything: Daniel Pinkwater, who lives in the Hudson River Valley and writes children's books; Bailey White, a second-grade teacher in Georgia (from her voice most people would judge Bailey White to be an older woman, but she's only forty); Donald McCaig, a writer and sheep farmer in Virginia's Allegheny Mountains; John McIlwraith, of Los Angeles, who reads his work in a robust Scottish accent; Carmen Delzell, Texas-born, street-smart—she's a lovely writer, often sad, always honest.

We pay $125 for each commentary we use (and we get about twenty-five unsolicited manuscripts a week). The recordings are often done at NPR stations; McCaig, for example, will wait until he has two or three pieces written and needs to go into town anyway, and then will drive down to WVTF in Roanoke. It's too much work for the money, but the writers want this audience, want the chance to read their own words to listeners in San Juan, and Harrisburg, and Portland and Anchorage.

A preliminary budget for the Romania trip is quickly approved—$2,500, to cover our air fare and expenses. The foreign desk also starts trying to line up one of their reporters to go, as Andrei and I wouldn't be covering the breaking news and would be working mostly for "All Things Considered." Our foreign editor, Cadi Simon, also wants to make sure a more experienced correspondent is in place. She's asked me, "Can you handle a two-show file?" Meaning, can you report this story for both "Morning Edition" and "All Things Considered"?

Friday, December 22, Washington, D.C., 1989

Ceausescu is gone—I couldn't believe it! "Morning Edition" is doing interviews about the new leaders of Romania and reporting that Nicolae and Elena have fled the presidential palace. I find my passport in a file drawer; I'll need some visa pictures. We could go through Hungary, or possibly Yugoslavia. At NPR we ask the finance department for some cash—$4,000 (now being more realistic about the costs), but no luck. They promise a check by Tuesday.

An ATC desk assistant manages to get a phone line into Bucharest, and I interview Agie Kuperman at the American Embassy. She's very excited and describes Ceausescu's leaving the palace and the people celebrating. All the rest of the day we try calling her back but can't get through. And later it develops that there was a great deal of fighting in Bucharest, involving Ceausescu's security forces. I feel bad that I hadn't asked Kuperman about this possibility. ABC-TV has dramatic tape of bodies being dug up in Timisoara, saying that even children had been shot by government troops, shot as they were being held by their parents. Kuperman had told us that perhaps thirty-five hundred people were killed in the Timisoara protests. Cadi Simon comes by my office to say that John Hockenberry, who's stationed in Jerusalem, will be leaving Sunday for Romania—he'll fly to Belgrade first. John's an excellent reporter, fast, with lots of energy, and he's fun to work with. Michael Sullivan, ATC's daily producer, is also being sent from Washington, along with engineer Rich Rarey.

For today's program we finally get some good interviews about Panama, first-hand accounts. And I call Havre, Montana, where it's been forty-three degrees below zero. I talk with Lee Grant, whom we met while doing the train series, and he tells me about a couple—"foreigners [out-of-staters],"

he called them—who froze to death after they left their car
and tried to walk a mile and a half. At forty-three below, he
said, ice crystals and plumes of car exhaust hang in the air.

In the studio while the program is on the air, Robert and I
talk about Romania. He believes there's going to be a blood-
bath there, in retribution.

After supper I call my mother, in Ohio, to tell her we won't
be able to visit them over the weekend, and suggest that she
and Randy, my stepfather, could drive up here for Christmas.

ABC's "Nightline" has two reporters in Bucharest; lots of
fighting, and now it's clear it's between the army and the
security forces—the *Securitate*. Andrei Codrescu was on
from New Orleans, talking with Ted Koppel about the "revolution" in Romania, as it's beginning to be called.

I try to get some sleep, but the name "Ceausescu" keeps
going through my head. For one thing, it's going to be difficult to pronounce it correctly. "Chow-*shess*-coo," not "Chow-
chess-coo."

Saturday, December 23, Washington, D.C., 1989

New York Times headline: CEAUSESCU FLEES A REVOLT IN RU-
MANIA BUT DIVIDED SECURITY FORCES FIGHT ON.

David Binder, who has been reporting on Eastern Europe
for decades, wrote the story from Washington, with dis-
patches from Romania (several months later the *Times*
dropped Rumania and changed over to Romania). Binder's
story says the *Securitate* is perhaps more powerful than
the army. The estimate of dead in Timisoara is as high as
forty-five hundred. And the *Times* has this quotation: "Not
even Hitler killed his own children and here they used automatic machine gun bursts to shoot them down."

On NPR News I hear that hundreds were killed in Bucharest Friday night. Security police were using the subway,

popping up and shooting people; the *Securitate* were taking off their uniforms and going into hospitals and killing. Also rumors of Syrian and Libyan troops coming to help Ceausescu. I call Michael Sullivan; he wants to leave for Romania as soon as possible.

After a late breakfast, Neenah and I go over to the farmers' market in Bethesda for Cheddar cheese and freshly squeezed grapefruit juice, then downtown to try to find some books about Romania. Nothing, but I do buy a *Frommer's Eastern Europe & Yugoslavia on $25 a Day.*

In the afternoon we hear on the radio that the Inter-Continental Hotel in Bucharest is closed because of sniper fire. Then I go into NPR to read the wire stories on my computer:

—Ceausescu and wife arrested by the army

—Five thousand may have died in Bucharest

—Red Cross driver killed

—Five hundred injured at airport trying to get out

Then, later, from the BBC: security police massacred an entire village one mile from the airport. Numbers go up to twelve thousand dead in Timisoara.

There's a call on the answering machine at home, Andrei wants to wait a few days. And my mother phoned—they're coming Sunday, Christmas Eve.

I talk again with Michael; he wants to go to a border country and wait there until things settle down. He's put together two thousand dollars in cash. I asked if he'd heard about the Spanish journalist crushed by a tank in Bucharest. He had. And I was thinking—this is crazy, to go there now. In Czechoslovakia, as the government fell, there was only one death reported, a student who had been beaten. Romania's in a civil war—someone has to say, "Wait, I'm afraid, I don't want to go."

Monday, December 25, Washington, D.C., 1989

The announcer on Bucharest Radio, reporting on the executions of Nicolae and Elena Ceausescu, says, "Oh, what wonderful news. The anti-Christ died on Christmas Day."

I'm not working today, but I stop in at NPR to say goodbye to Michael, who's leaving tonight—he and Rich have a flight into Yugoslavia, and they'll try to drive from Belgrade to Bucharest. Andrei and I now plan to leave Wednesday and go to Hungary—Budapest; it's a place I've always wanted to see. Andrei says he knows people there, and we can do some stories while we're waiting, perhaps talk with refugees who've crossed the border from Romania.

Our Christmas dinner at home is wonderful—turkey and mashed potatoes and gravy. There's a tree and candles and music and lots of extra attention for the dogs. The news reports from Romania, though, on television from time to time, are terrifying. Scenes of people being shot in the streets, and wild rumors: the water supply's been poisoned, patients have been killed in hospitals.

We listen to "All Things Considered" and I'm relieved to hear John Hockenberry, safe in Bucharest, talking with Robert Siegel. John's just arrived, overland from Belgrade. Said his car was searched more than two dozen times; he'd heard lots of gunfire, both from sniper rifles and .50-caliber machine guns, but apparently he got through fine, and even described the scene around the Inter-Continental hotel as hellish, but somewhat festive. This is the first Christmas Romanians have been free to celebrate in forty-two years. The next day at NPR, Cadi tells me that John had promised to wait at the Romanian border until she told him it was safe to go in. He crossed anyway, and then called to say, "Yeah, you were right, it wasn't safe. Tell those other guys they'd better wait." He could have used the help, but really did feel it was unsafe.

Wednesday, December 27, Washington, D.C., 1989

At 3:25 P.M. Neenah drives Andrei and me to Dulles Airport. My mother has fixed turkey and ham sandwiches for both of us, along with an apple and cranberry juice, and candy. We have paper sacks with our names written on them. We've also brought plenty of groceries along: condensed milk, chocolate bars, and Knorr dried soup—Andrei says everyone in Romania wants the Knorr brand of soup—and several cartons of cigarettes, Kent 100's, and Marlboros. John Hockenberry told us you can get a lot done in Bucharest for a pack of Marlboros—he bribed his way through roadblocks by passing them out. We've also been told to bring lots of U.S. one-dollar bills.

ABC's "Nightline" asked if they might use Andrei as a commentator in Romania. A quick deal was made—Andrei can do some work for ABC if we can have some of their satellite time.

I'm worried about Michael and Rich. They were driving across the border from Yugoslavia today. Just before the plane leaves at six-fifty, I call in to the ATC desk; it's now past midnight in Romania and still no word. Then we're off on Pan Am Flight 60, seven hours to Frankfurt, a 747, full, mostly with very young out-of-uniform servicemen going back to Germany after the holidays, some of them drinking Michelob, and Bacardi and Coke, and talking through the night.

I read some newspapers and learn that Nicu Ceausescu, Nicolae and Elena's son, is said to be "fond of Scotch and rape," and that Nicu's forces in Sibiu, Andrei's home town, opened fire with machine guns in the town square. Other *Securitate* are said to be undetectable during the day. They mix with crowds like "wolves in lamb's clothing," and at night they come out and kill. After supper, before sleeping for a while, I read a nicely written *Sports Illustrated* account of Greg LeMond's victory in the Tour de France bicycle race last summer.

Friday, December 29, Hungary, 1989

Lots of news from Romania: we can get CNN in our Budapest hotel room, and the *International Herald-Tribune* downstairs. The first skepticism appears about the number of dead in Romania: higher estimates have put the total at 60,000, even 80,000, with 130,000 wounded. Months later, it's believed that about a thousand people died, and that the high numbers had been disinformation from the National Salvation Front.

Those suspicions, that leaders of the Front had grabbed power in a bloody charade, continued to intensify. William McPherson, a journalist who spent most of two years in Romania after the Ceausescu downfall, put it best in *The Washington Post* in November 1991, saying that the fundamental question—was there indeed a revolution?—remains unanswered. He writes: ". . . if the new power is not an emanation of the people's genuine struggle to be free of Communism and of the dictator they despised, but springs instead from a violent fight between factions of the discredited former regime, then it has no real legitimacy." McPherson cites several examples of lawlessness. He says the *Securitate* is still operating, now under a new name, and that "In Romania every few weeks a critic of the regime—a journalist, a doctor, a scholar—is beaten or otherwise threatened by mysterious strangers. Most of them say very little about it for the record."

A Romanian-born professor in Chicago was killed in May 1991. Ioan Petru Culianu had been a critic of Romania's new leadership. And indeed, Andrei Codrescu was the victim of

what perhaps was a disinformation campaign. A week after
Professor Culianu was shot, I received a call at home from
someone at the Voice of America. "Did you know Andrei
committed suicide?" "What?" I asked. "How do you know
this?" I had just seen Andrei in New Orleans and knew that
he was probably now in Brazil, on assignment for a magazine. "Well, we heard it from someone in New York who
heard it from someone in San Francisco."

I refused to give his home number. "Don't you dare try to
call his wife until you have some real information." The
phone calls went back and forth—the Voice of America said
yes, this person who had called me does some work for them
from time to time, and he was planning a story about Andrei's new book on Romania. It wasn't until the next day
that we could locate Andrei in Brazil. He wasn't surprised,
said it was a standard Romanian intelligence trick. Andrei
managed—at least on "All Things Considered"—to avoid
saying that the "reports of my death have been greatly exag-
gerated."

Downstairs in the hotel lobby I do some asking around,
trying to find a way to cross the border into Romania. No
one's going. It might be possible to go in by car, as part of a
Red Cross supply convoy. Still no flights to Bucharest—yesterday at the Frankfurt airport I asked Lufthansa to check
and the agent's screen warned "not to overfly" Romania. We
could take a train, but I can't find out if they're running.
When I talk with Washington, I learn that Michael and Rich
arrived Thursday morning in Bucharest, riding from Sofia,
Bulgaria, in the back of a panel truck they rented with a
cameraman from International Television News, London.

In the evening, Andrei and I go to an old synagogue—
there are many Jews in Budapest who have come from Romania, from Transylvania. Andrei wants to write about the
Passover service and the persecution of Jews under Ceausescu, and I need to record some of the singing to use with
his story. We sit close to the front; I have the tape recorder

and microphone in a shoulder bag. The young boy who is singing during the service notices the recorder's red light—he's standing in front of us, and he looks back over his shoulder—but it's not a problem.

In just this same situation, some years ago in East Kentucky, I *did* have a problem. We were working on a story in Letcher County and had been invited to the Sunday morning service of an Old Regular Baptist church. We sat in the back row of pews and I was taping the singing and the testimonials, as unobtrusively as I could. One of the church elders noticed and said, "I don't feel like saying what's in my heart this morning because there's a tape recorder going." The entire congregation turned to look at us. Later the man explained that once, in Detroit in a record store, he'd seen an album of Old Regular Baptist singing. "I think that's wrong," he said. "The Gospel happens here, in this church, this morning. You can't take it away." I agreed with him, and felt like saying, "Amen."

In Budapest, on the way back to the hotel, Andrei and I stop at a café for a *czernok*, cherry brandy, and make a decision. We will try to leave tomorrow night by train.

As I'm going off to sleep, Michael calls from Bucharest. He sounds healthy and happy; it's past midnight and they've just finished sending a story to Washington. Can we bring something from Hungary? Yes—champagne, good champagne for New Year's Eve.

Saturday, December 30, Hungary, 1989

An early trip to the West train station pays off, and I buy two tickets to Bucharest, leaving at 6:00 P.M. No one knows if you need a Romanian visa at the border. We take a cab out to the embassy but can't raise anyone. Later I go to the headquarters of the Hungarian Red Cross to do some interviews, thinking I might put together a story about the relief efforts. And after lunch we find a wonderful sound to use: children playing in the streets, blowing New Year's noise-makers. The folks at Radio Hungary kindly—on a Saturday with no notice—open one of their studios for me, and even book a high-quality phone line to Washington, so I can feed my story to "All Things Considered."

street sounds, trucks being loaded

NOAH: In a large old building in downtown Budapest, there is an intense effort to help the people of Romania. Relief supplies are coming here from Finland, Denmark, Switzerland, all over Europe and elsewhere. Supplies to be sent on to Romania by the Hungarian Red Cross.

RELIEF WORKER SPEAKING HUNGARIAN, INTERPRETED: Medicines, bandages, syringes, food, clothing and books.

NOAH: What sort of books?

RELIEF WORKER: Literature for the children yet in Romania.

The books written in Hungarian are significant: they had been banned during the Ceausescu years. The part of Romania called Transylvania once belonged to Hungary; now even the village names have been changed, by decree, to Romanian ones. And I was told that hundreds of people—most of them émigrés who fled Romania in recent years—have been giving blood at the Red Cross in Budapest. The supplies are sent by truck convoy. It's dangerous, a volunteer driver was killed last week. But a social worker, just returned this morning, said her convoy had been escorted by the Romanian Army.

CZUJAK ELONA, SOCIAL WORKER, INTERPRETED: We were guarded by the soldiers. We stayed in a hotel and the people we took the food to were very, very happy. They cried, they laughed.

While I was working at Radio Hungary, I met one of their reporters who had been in Romania. Joe Oros played some tape for me that he made on Friday night in Bucharest, from his hotel window. A recording of the shooting and the screaming, and of his description of the scene. His tape is terrifying—and you don't need to know Hungarian to tell that innocent people are dying

The radio listener hears an emotion that can't be approached in print. In the fall of 1991, a young American freelance reporter, Kurt Schork, called our foreign desk with the story of a massacre in northern Iraq—an eyewitness account. The town was Sulaymaniyah. At least sixty Iraqi soldiers had surrendered to the Kurdish rebels known as Pesh Mergas, and then were shot at point-blank range. On "All Things Considered" that evening, Kurt Schork told Robert Siegel about joining up with the Pesh Merga as they captured some buildings. We heard his tape of rattling gunfire and grenade explosions, then Schork describing what came next; he was simply talking into his tape recorder as a way of making notes:

gunfire

SCHORK: The prisoners are yelling *"Allah hoo Akhbar"* . . .

more shots

SCHORK: . . . they're firing at them. Oh, no! He's shooting at them. He's killed, shot point-blank by the Pesh Merga. Six of them (*shooting continues*). That was an execution, they were on their knees with their hands up (*shots increase*). It's going on—they're still shooting.

shooting and yelling, fades

This reporter—as a witness—was in a dangerous situation, in a treacherous part of the world. No journalists were killed during the actual fighting between the Allied forces and Iraq (quite possibly because so few were allowed to get anywhere near the action). Gad Gross, a photographer working for *Newsweek,* was killed by Iraqi troops who were fighting against the Kurds, near Kirkuk. Two members of a BBC Television crew died in northern Iraq; a Turkish guide admitted killing them in a dispute over his fees. A third member of the BBC crew remains missing. NPR's Deborah Wang, and John Hockenberry, spent a great deal of time in the mountains along the border between Iraq and Turkey, sending out stories about the refugee camps and the simmering conflicts between the Iraqis and the Kurds.

In Budapest, I'm waiting at the train station. Andrei had gone to the hotel to pick up the bags, and then to buy some food and water, as well as the champagne—there would be nothing on the train, not even coffee, and it was an eighteen-hour trip. I had told him: "Andrei, the West train station, meet me at five o'clock. The West train station, five o'clock." I have the tickets, he has everything else.

Five-thirty goes past, then five-forty-five. I start running up and down the platform, looking for him. Five-fifty, five-fifty-three. Everyone's on board. I don't think he's in trouble, he's probably sitting in a bar someplace trying to figure out if he should go. It's been twenty-four years since he left Romania and he's told me his name used to be on a list at the border, as someone not friendly to the country. I climb up on the last car. The train leaves on time. Without Andrei. I've made a big mistake—I've lost the talent. I've never heard of this happening to a producer before.

Sunday, December 31, Romania, 1989

Just past midnight the train starts moving again. It was almost a two-hour wait at the border. We stayed on the train. A dirty mist swirled in the darkness outside, a few yellow lamps burned, troops stood guard. Some workmen came on board to try and fix the heat. The passengers were tense, but a young Romanian woman asked me, in perfect English, "Where are you from?" She smiled, and I started to explain, but then the police came in. "The drug dog," she said, indicating the small German shepherd. The border guards under Ceausescu were said to be involved in drug smuggling, working for the secret police. We went back to our compartments to wait to have our papers checked. "United States?" the guard asked. "Yes," I said. "Russian," my seatmate said. "Hungarian?" the guards guessed about the two others, a woman traveling with an older man. *"Da,"* came the answer.

I paid for a visa—thirty dollars—to enter Romania. And they made us change some money, twenty dollars for *lei* at the official rate. As a journalist I knew this was a wonderful moment, but I just couldn't find the energy or the courage to bring out my tape recorder and microphone. I pretended to myself that I wasn't working.

My seatmate is thirty-five possibly, perhaps, with graying blond hair, stylishly cut. He's wearing a dark blue sweater with a *New York Times* logo in white stitching. "American?" I had asked him as the train left the station in Budapest. "Half." He laughed. "My wife is Celestine Bohlen of *The New York Times.*" He is Vladimir Lebedev. He tells me he distributes documentary films and has joint venture projects with some U.S. companies. He has flown from Moscow, plans to stay only overnight in Bucharest, then eighteen hours back to Budapest, and on to New York. All this just to see his wife. He'd been late for the train, too, and so we shared the only food I'd been able to buy, at just the last minute—two salami sandwiches and a large bottle of cherry soda.

Celestine Bohlen meets us at the train station in Bucharest and we take the subway over to the Inter-Continental Hotel. The streets, the trains, are full of people—it's New Year's Eve. There are piles of dirty snow around the hotel, many of the big first-floor windows are boarded up. You can see where bullets—lots of them—had struck the buildings around University Square.

Bohlen was one of the first Western reporters to enter Romania. Vladimir said they were together in Budapest that week; she decided to go after hearing about the killings on Friday night. The Hungarian cab drivers she talked with refused to take her, but finally she was able to hire a driver and they left on Saturday, traveling over the mountains through Transylvania, driving on into a night that was wild with rumor; people in the villages warning them to hide. Another *New York Times* reporter, John Tagliabue, was wounded the next day by sniper fire; he was traveling with some other journalists. I asked Vladimir, did the *Times* ask Celestine to go in on Saturday? No, they just told her to use her own judgment.

I find Michael Sullivan at the Inter-Continental and demand some coffee and we go into a restaurant for lunch. "Where's Andrei?" Michael notices. I tell a brief version of the story, but soon, Andrei appears, smiling; he even has someone carrying his bags, and my luggage as well. "The West train station?" he says, "No, you told me the East train station." You can't blame a poet for this, I thought. "But, who cares—I had a great time," he says. While my train ride was cold and hungry and tense, Andrei's was a celebration with Romanian expatriates returning in triumph with baskets of food and wine. But of course, he has no tape either, because I had the equipment.

John Hockenberry comes into the hotel restaurant to say

hello; he's going off to try to find gasoline for the rental car. He seems happy, exhilarated even, working on this story. Michael tells me about watching John—who uses a wheelchair—churning through the deep mud of a Bucharest cemetery, covering a memorial service. There are stories far more dramatic: one frantic day in Iran he talked his way onto a helicopter to get a better view of the Ayatollah Khomeini's funeral; he had to leave his wheelchair behind.

John was injured in a car accident in 1976 and has been in a wheelchair for all of his radio career. Colleagues in the Middle East press corps admire his aggressiveness and courage; listeners only know that he's a first-rate reporter. (At the beginning of the war in the Persian Gulf, John was on the air with us from Israel at the time of the first Iraqui Scud attacks. The sirens were screaming; everyone in the Tel Aviv Hilton was ordered into the basement. But John's wheelchair wouldn't fit through the door of the bomb shelter. He came back upstairs and called us from the now-empty press room).

Here in Romania, after a week of trying to figure out what's really going on, John's losing patience with the National Salvation Front. He even yelled at some of the leaders during a news conference, Michael says, because they were so evasive.

There's a noisy crowd at the registration desk, but Rich Rarey manages to get us a room—he has a Gold American Express card, and an ample supply of Kents.

Late in the evening, we go out to do some taping. It's New Year's Eve, and we'd heard about a memorial service, but nobody's on the streets. There is enough starkness in the scene, however, to give us some material. In my story I wrote about the shrine at University Square, a simple cross and some evergreen branches, red carnations, daisies on the snow, and dozens of thin yellow flickering candles. Perhaps hundreds of people died in the Square; they had come to celebrate and had been shot.

I described some British teenagers who came up to the

shrine while we were waiting there. They'd been drinking, and one of them did something that was so callous that I couldn't mention it in the story—I thought it would have been misdirecting. He lit a cigarette from one of the candles. I'm sorry now that I just didn't simply tell what happened.

outside street sounds, muffled

NOAH: New Year's Eve, just before midnight. Hardly any cars going by, not many people around. Only a few windows lit and some street lamps, a soft orange glow. The sidewalks were covered with snow and ice and far off through the cold mist you could see the faint white outline of the presidential palace, a vast presence that dominated Bucharest and all of Romania.

Some young people with British accents came to the shrine just at midnight to sing and take pictures of themselves. Fifty yards away a white Mercedes was abandoned, stuck in the snow, with its headlights shining. The sign on the windshield says TV NEWS. Some police cars went past and there were ten or so soldiers with automatic rifles patrolling the Square. At an entrance to the Metro, the subway, one of the officers took time to talk:

Young man, in Romanian, fading

NOAH: He told me that in quiet times New Year's Eve is a great celebration and we should come back next year. And yes, he explained about this night—it does seem too quiet, as if something is waiting to happen.

People in the city have been fearing another attack by the "terrorists," the members of the security force who remain loyal to Ceausescu. This officer, who was in the *Securitate,* is now on the side of the new government. He told me that some in his uniform did terrible things. He said he was not in University Square the night of the shootings. He was on duty some distance away.

Soldier continues in Romanian

NOAH: He said yes . . . a friend [was killed], a bullet in the head.

Monday, January 1, Romania, 1990

It's expensive to call back to the United States from your hotel room—up to seventy-five dollars a minute (you overhear phone stories in the elevator: an NBC Radio reporter had a $1,200 call, one CNN call to Atlanta was $1,800). So we try to use the telecommunications center that's been set up on the second floor. Four telex machines running, reporters writing stories from their notes as fast as they can type. And seven phone booths, with two operators—women who have volunteered—booking calls. Someone brings their supper by, on plates from the restaurant. It's okay to offer a pack of cigarettes, but only as thanks, you'll still have to wait, possibly up to an hour.

The reporters walk around in fast, tight circles as their deadlines approach, hours earlier in the West. Then . . . "London? It's ringing, number four." "Barcelona? Number two." "Belgium? Number five." "Washington? Number six." The reporters are directed to the numbered booths, where they start dictating or recording their stories loudly, precisely. If you're willing to eavesdrop, you could learn what Michael Dobbs has written for tomorrow's *Washington Post*.

My turn at last. "Maryland? Sorry." If you're trying to call home and talk to your wife, the operators will smile sympathetically if just the answering machine picks up.

ABC "Nightline" now wants to take Andrei to Sibiu, his hometown, up through the mountains in Transylvania. Michael Sullivan, our boss on this trip, says no—that's NPR's story. So "Nightline" plans to go ahead with a segment set in Bucharest. The ABC producer gives Andrei a room of his own in the hotel, and assigns him a car and driver. That's helpful to us—we'll use ABC's car—but they take up a lot more of Andrei's time than we'd anticipated.

Deborah Amos, an NPR reporter who's based in London, shows up in the Inter-Continental lobby, just in by way of Bulgaria. She had called me last week from Prague, where she was covering the Havel inauguration, and said she was being sent on to Bucharest to help out—John Hockenberry's due to leave Tuesday. It's great to see Deborah again, and to watch her—she had hired a driver/interpreter before she even walked into the hotel. She has ten story ideas already and thirty or so Bucharest phone numbers in her thick maroon-leather Filofax. In the States, whenever I talk to groups of NPR listeners, I can always expect the question, especially from young women, "Tell us about Deborah Amos." What they mean, of course, is, "How do you get to *be* Deborah Amos?"

The answer involves talent and a bit of happenstance but mostly determination. Deborah came to NPR from Florida, with a journalism degree and some television experience. She began as a director for "All Things Considered," then started producing documentaries and working with reporters in the field. An assignment to Beirut—to help cover the civil war there—convinced her to change jobs. She said after watching the carnage of Beirut and the appalling violence, she had to learn more about the Middle East and how things had gotten to that point in Lebanon. She moved to Amman, Jordan, to work as a reporter, and has been running ever since—Afghanistan, the Soviet Union, China. Deborah's close to forty, small, with dark hair. One part of her smile is friendly, the other part is always asking a question.

For another part of our New Year's Day story we visit one of Andrei's old friends, Adrian Montsiu and his wife Betty, who live with their daughter and his mother in a small apartment in Bucharest. There's a color television set, lots of books: Shakespeare, Molière, Dickens. Plates of food are set out, homemade wine, chocolate cake.

Montsiu had encouraged Andrei to be a writer, many

years ago. We talk about the revolution and the new hopes for artistic freedom, but when I start asking about the past, especially about the Communist Party, Montsiu stops smiling. I ask again, understanding what the answer must be, were you a Party member? He doesn't need the translation. I can tell from Andrei's eyes that we should stop. Montsiu is an official with Romanian state television; you'd have to be in the Party to get that job.

We need to rush back to the hotel to start putting the story together, and I feel bad about pushing for an answer, and worse about having to leave so abruptly. I've asked Andrei, who stayed behind, to try to explain this to his friends, but I'm afraid our reasons aren't really good enough. We finish producing our story and send it on to NPR by 11:00 P.M., more than an hour before it absolutely has to be there. It's quite a luxury being seven hours out in front of your deadline: five o'clock—air time—in Washington is midnight here.

I had a feeling about how this New Year's story should close. I'd been trying to figure out if you could trace the downfall of the Ceausescus to one moment, even to one person, and that's the way I wrote it, hoping I wouldn't be proven wrong in the days ahead.

NOAH: The New Year has now come to Eastern Europe, to Romania. On University Square, the moment of midnight slipped by without much notice. For the people of Romania, though, it is possible that a new time truly began on the afternoon of Thursday, December 22.

Thousands of workers and young people had dutifully assembled to listen to a speech by Nicolae Ceausescu. The crowd was supposed to applaud and wave flags, but started booing instead. It could have been a spontaneous demonstration. It could have been planned by students, but perhaps it was just one voice at first, a single voice in protest.

Ceausescu left the balcony ... and Romania was a
new country.

Tuesday, January 2, Romania, 1990

The National Salvation Front, led by the new president, Ion
Iliescu, has declared an extra New Year's holiday and it's
difficult for us to get new stories started. No government
announcements on television, no news conferences in the
hotel. A translator, Mariana Ullen, has been stopping by the
hotel in the mornings to read the newspapers to John and
Michael, but the papers haven't published since Friday. She
comes up to our room today though for coffee, and talks
about problems at the school where she teaches. After the
revolution, many of the students and teachers built a bon-
fire, burning Ceausescu pictures and propaganda (it was pretended in Romania that Elena Ceausescu was a scientist,
and textbooks were published in her name). But Mariana
fears that many on the faculty will remain committed to
the old regime.

She says that she and her students had often been required to do "loyalty work"—on Sundays they would go to a
Metro station and spend hours picking up used tickets. She
also tells us about the theater in Bucharest. In winter the
actors would have to wear heavy coats on stage, and the
audience would wear their coats and hats as well, and sit
with their feet tucked up underneath them, trying to stay
through to the end of the play—if they left early, the actors
wouldn't be paid.

I go out for a walk around five o'clock, just before sunset. I
wander along, stopping to record the screeches of the electric streetcars as they go around the corners. But I'm using a
short shotgun microphone, mounted on a pistol grip, and
people are looking at me warily. A few dogs are out, and
some kids, sliding on the very icy streets. The shop windows
don't offer much: some groceries, but also used vacuum

cleaners and electrical parts. On the way back I pass by the shrine in the Square. Not many people there, but plenty of candles are burning.

It's probably still not safe to be out much after dark, so we usually order something from room service for dinner: Goulash, pepper steak, french fries, a Moldavian stew, and if someone's changed money at the black market rates, Russian caviar. Aside from the caviar (I don't like caviar, but I'm told this is quite good), the food is quickly boring.

I heard a reporter today asking a colleague if he had anything to read. A Philip Marlowe, the other one said. And I realized that a paperback book, in your own language, and not *about* the country you're covering at the moment, can be extremely valuable. It's an escape, it helps bring sleep. Deborah has brought me her copy of Josef Škvorecký's *The Bass Saxophone* and at night I'm quickly back in the 1960s, in Czechoslovakia.

Wednesday, January 3, Romania, 1990

A good night's sleep, the first in a couple of weeks. Rich and Michael were up late, though, filing Andrei's first story, using time on the NBC satellite circuit. We're paying fifty dollars a minute and that's big money for NPR, but mostly NBC's just doing us a favor. ABC had promised us some satellite time in return for borrowing Andrei, but it never seems to work out when we call. Promises are easier made in Washington than kept in Bucharest. The hotel's breakfast room is half-empty. International Television News had a charter flight out—$1,700 to Heathrow; they filled the plane, I heard. And CNN has a charter today to Frankfurt—the sign by the elevators reads: "$1,000, wheels up 12:00–2:00 P.M.ish." A reporter says, "When the shooting stops it's time to go, otherwise you'll have to stay around and do the economic stories."

We have a lucky encounter in a park with a young girl

and her grandfather. The scene works nicely as part of our story today.

streetcar bells

NOAH: There was for several days a civil war fought in Bucharest and you can still see tanks and a lot of soldiers, but you can walk into one of the many large parks in the city and be away for a time.

traffic fades, birds sing

A light snow is starting to fall. The dark branches arch over the walkways. An older man and a small child, a girl about two years old, wearing a red snowsuit, have brought bread to feed the pigeons.

child's voice, asking questions in Romanian, the man explaining, then an explosion of fluttering wings

NOAH: The pigeons fly away. The grandfather, Victor, walks along the path with us, pulling Addie on a sled. We come to a circle of trees, and a circle of statues. Some statues of old men, dignified, even with several inches of snow on their heads. These are, quite obviously, heroes from Romania's past.

VICTOR, READING NAMES: Eminescu, Eminescu. Poet, national.
Odobescu, Odobescu.

NOAH: Poet?

VICTOR: Scritor.

NOAH: Writer.

VICTOR: Maiorescu ... politician. I. L. Caragiale, 1852–1912. Scritor, satiric.

NOAH: Satirical writer.

VICTOR: Da.

child's voice, laughing

NOAH: Goodbye, Addie.

ADDIE, PERFECTLY IN ENGLISH, SWEETLY: Goodbye.

Victor laughs, and says goodbye

And then we're off to the television station with Andrei—he's to go on the air and read some messages to Romania from writers in America. The area still looks like a battle zone. It is said the army defended the station against the *Securitate.* There was fighting here as late as last Friday, December 30. Houses on the nearby streets are burned out. The station itself—two stories, turquoise and light blue tiles—appears to have been under heavy fire. This is Romania's main television center, and it was taken over immediately by the National Salvation Front. We keep asking, why didn't the Securitate cut the electricity, why didn't they blow up the transmitter?

To get inside we go through passport checks, metal detectors, and our bags are searched, but some of the soldiers are eating apples and watching an old movie on one of the monitors. The state television, since the takeover, has been showing old movies like *Animal Farm,* Daffy Duck cartoons, and rock'n'roll videos, pirated from the international satellites. In the studio the staff people tell us stories of fear and of heroism. And they give us NSF armbands—the same ones we've seen the TV commentators wearing—with yellow and red and green stripes.

Then it's across town to Radio Bucharest, where we have to show our passports just to get on the same street. We've stumbled into a real story here. We didn't really know anything about the radio service, but we get excited as we learn about what happened on the day Ceausescu fell. Radio Bucharest, for the moment and with the help of the army, belongs to a committee of young people: a composer, an electronics engineer, students in architecture, metallurgy—

they had seen the Ceausescus' helicopter lifting off from the
palace, and they met in the street outside Radio Bucharest,
demanding to be let in. But then came five days of fighting,
attacks from the pro-Ceausescu forces. Many of the committee have been sleeping in the offices every night. The gunfire, mostly from snipers, continued for a week. At one point,
they say, the *Securitate* called up on the phone: We have
two thousand men on the way; you'd better give up. It was a
bluff.

NOAH: The committee running Radio Bucharest will have
a lot of decisions to make, and very quickly. For
example, who gets to be on Romania's free radio? Dan
Cristescu says that as of yet, none of what he called
"serious" political parties has asked for air time. They
would get on the air, he says. But he's already turned
down one other request.

CRISTESCU (ELECTRONICS ENGINEER): Yesterday, a woman
asked me if she could form a party who could protect
pigs and chicks against sacrifice, you understand?
Such a party, you understand, it couldn't be serious.
Democracy, democracy all right, but letting anybody
enter here and spoke stupidities, it is too much.

NOAH: Radio Bucharest continues to broadcast worldwide
in more than a dozen languages. But in the past, in the
Ceausescu years, broadcasting not much real
information.

ENGLISH-LANGUAGE ANNOUNCER MARIAN BISTRICEANU: The
news, with Ceausescu. A political commentary, with
Ceausescu. And a feature or a spot about Ceausescu.
Some music, praising Ceausescu. And then, you name
it, we had it, about Ceausescu.

Thursday, January 4, Romania, 1990

A sunny, snowy day. We're soon to leave for Sibiu, taking Andrei home, but first some interviews at the Town Hall about Ceausescu's plan to raze the villages in the countryside and move people into apartments in the cities. The new government has said the plan would be immediately suspended. So I'm amazed that Bucharest's chief architect, and the city historian, still seem to think *sistematizare* is a good idea. Paul Focsa, the architect, did admit there were some problems, but refused to repudiate the concept.

> NOAH (*unfolding map*): I want to ask you about this map of Bucharest. The areas in yellow show complete reconstruction, a lot of single-family homes being torn down, is that accurate? And much of this was done in order just to build wide boulevards for the glorification of Ceausescu?

Correct, he says. And the projects that have been started at great expense should now be finished, it makes no sense to abandon them.

The city historian, Ion Paunete, is also talking with us, and I asked Professor Paunete if Romania was not in danger of losing its past, its heritage, if so many villages are being destroyed.

> *Paunete explains, in Romanian*

> NOAH: He says we owe our existence to the peasant. Our salvation was always the extraordinary resistance of Romanian peasants, but "We are not a peasant people anymore."

The historian and the architect are Party members and
long-time bureaucrats, and it is a fair question to Dan Prede-
scu, the new city manager. Will Paul Focsa, for example, be
able to keep his job?

> PREDESCU: He's a good specialist. He's a good man. He's a
> good Romanian people and he will stay here. That's
> true.

And I'm amused by a discussion of temperatures. The city
manager (a biologist, with no government experience) tells
us proudly that the heat's now been turned up in many of
the buildings around Bucharest. Under Ceausescu, he says,
the normal setting was ten degrees. That would be Celsius.
What is that in Fahrenheit? And suddenly a conference ta-
bleful of bureaucrats starts scribbling on scraps of paper,
everyone trying to remember the conversion formula. (Just
more proof for my conviction—one I share with NPR's
Cokie Roberts—that life doesn't really go much beyond junior high school.)

We leave at about ten to drive up through the mountains
to Sibiu. Four of us in a sixteen-passenger blue Mercedes
diesel bus. Five hundred dollars for two days, and that includes the driver, Dumitru, who is silent, stalwart. It's fun at
first, like going off to play an away game, but the roads are
soon ice-covered and it's a long day's drive to Sibiu.

Andrei tells me about the villages and stories about the
mountains. The people would hide inside the haystacks,
when the Turks came. The Turks burned the haystacks.
We're in Transylvania—the country of Vlad the Impaler—
Dracula's castle is not far away. It is said Nicolae Ceausescu
had great respect for Vlad. And I've seen, spray-painted in
red on buildings in Bucharest, the word VAMPIRUL. One of the
surely apocryphal stories about Ceausescu has it that he
once was cured of a terrible illness by transfusions of blood
from strong healthy young men from the countryside,
young men who were then put to death.

I was taking some notes along the way, just images, colors. And I kept remembering one scene especially, from the day's trip. Later, back in Bucharest, I filed an essay for Saturday's "All Things Considered."

NOAH: We stopped for lunch on Thursday in the small town of Valea Ursului, the "Valley of the Bear." This is about sixty-five miles north of the city of Bucharest. The road from here goes on up into the Carpathian Mountains and Transylvania. The houses along the roadside are small, light green and blue stucco with laundry hanging frozen on the clotheslines. In every village we've seen children out sleddiing.

The restaurant is cold inside; a tile floor, worn tablecloths, some Christmas decorations still up, garlands of silver and gold tinsel. Some Romanian champagne is for sale and jars of pickled green tomatoes. Most everyone in the restaurant is watching television. They're wearing their hats and coats and eating lunch and talking, and watching television. The waitress comes to bring us—*ciorbă*. It's a hot, clear peppery soup with cabbage and chunks of pork. And we have grilled ham and french fries. She brings mineral water, and steaming cups of sweetened tea called *ceai*.

Then there's a change in the voices in the restaurant. Ever since the first day of the revolution in Romania, the National Salvation Front has been controlling the television, and they stay on the air with interviews and news reports, movies, and cartoons. But now the pictures on the screen are of bodies. Some people killed on the streets of Bucharest two weeks ago. The bodies of young people, mostly, lying on their back with their clothes on and their eyes open.

We hear a voice on the television off-screen, speaking with authority and with anger, reading the names, and after each name the word *Deces*—as an epithet. It means "Deceased." No one in the room is talking now. They sit and stand, watching the television.

Then the final picture, the bodies of a mother and a small child. In the child's hand someone has placed a burning candle.

The segment is over and everyone looks away. The waitress comes to get our money. She's crying still, but she smiles goodbye.

Andrei's excited as we come into Sibiu's main square. We find rooms in a charming old hotel, now renovated, and go out into the streets to talk with people. They describe how the *Securitate* opened fire from the windows, in the buildings surrounding the square. The small attic windows, with rounded overhangs above, looking like eyebrows, are known as "the eyes of Sibiu." Andrei wants to show us his old high school, and the newsstand where he bought the magazine containing his first published poem. We have a fine meal in the hotel restaurant that night, and watch the townspeople who have come to dance—there's a four-piece band playing, mostly rock, some American country music. Andrei realizes that the attractive young women on the dance floor could be the daughters of his classmates.

I sleep with an open window, and it is frosty, silent, in Sibiu.

Friday, January 5, Romania, 1990

clacking, mechanical sound

NOAH: At a sentry station on an army base, a Romanian soldier is loading bullets into the clip of his automatic rifle. He has a hatful of cartridges beside him on the cot. He is young and smiling. His side won the sudden civil war.

In the town, an eight-year-old boy tells us about the fighting he saw, three days of it. He watched from the window of his house.

BOY (*excitedly, with sound effects of the bullets flying*): Ce să văd?! Numai gloante treceau pe linga geam! Bum—Bum!! Asa treceau. Si eu nu om mai putut dormi. Erau numai explozii! Continu!

We're on the streets early in Sibiu, just seeing what we can find out. Why not try to interview some *Securitate* who have been taken prisoner? It's a good idea and it might have worked, but then it cost us a few hours of standing around in the cold outside the army headquarters. We'd heard about prisoners. We heard they were being kept in an empty swimming pool. We saw wives, perhaps mothers, bringing baskets of food to the army compound gates. Finally an officer told us it might be possible to let us in if we had a member of the National Salvation Front with us—we hadn't thought of contacting the local NSF. But it was time to go; we still had to drive far out into the country to visit Andrei's great-aunt, and then try to get back to Bucharest to file a story for tonight.

Andrei located his aunt, and her husband. He went upstairs to their apartment, with only Rich along, to record the reunion. Andrei said his aunt didn't recognize him, she probably wouldn't recognize anyone from her past: she was in the kitchen, standing at the stove, warming her hands over a pan of milk. Her husband, a retired army officer, was pleased to see Andrei. The visit was over soon. Andre left them food and money, and promised to return. He came back to our bus with tears in his eyes. They were a proud old couple, he said, living on hardly anything, in a cold apartment.

The Sibiu airport seems ominous as we pass by on the way back. A lot of troops around, and helicopters. The country-side grows darker as we drive on toward Bucharest, climbing over the mountains. Large flocks of sheep are moving along the roadsides, escorted by dogs, followed by the shepherds; they're wearing huge sheepskin coats, they look like haystacks walking, their breath frosting in the cold evening air.

Our driver, Dumitru, finally finds some diesel fuel for the bus; hardly any stations are open, and at one of them we are waved away from gas pumps by a man with a rifle. It gets colder, darker. And then we start having engine trouble. Dumitru has to downshift to keep the motor running, driving in third, then second, and, at last, first. Then he stops. Then the motor dies. It's below zero outside—I already had my sleeping bag wrapped around me. We're a long way from Bucharest. No cars or trucks are passing; no lights nearby, no houses. I had thought before that a band of *Securitate* men, hiding out in the country, would sure like to have this nice Mercedes bus.

Dumitru takes the cover off the engine. He doesn't have a flashlight or tools or gloves. I have never known the driver of any vehicle that has broken down to get it running again. But Dumitru cleans the ice out of the fuel filter, bangs the engine cover shut, turns the key, the bus starts, we cheer, and he drives on into the city.

By the time we get through to the ATC desk, it's too late to finish putting together Andrei's homecoming story. And Washington decides they want us to bring it back with us, rather than worry about feeding from here (they want this story in full fidelity, and even the satellite circuits from Romania have been sounding bad).

They need *something* from Romania for tonight's program, though, so I'm asked to tape a short interview with Robert Siegel, talking about our two days traveling up into Transylvania. When we talk with one of our own reporters, it's referred to as a "two-way." Reporters will often ask to be on the program as a two-way: you can present information in a more conversational way, speculate just a bit, and it saves you the time needed to write a full report. Sometimes there's a list of questions, discussed in advance—spontaneity's nice, but it's quite unfair to totally surprise your colleague in the field.

Once I was talking with an NPR reporter about one of NASA's space shuttle flights. Some of the heat-reflecting tiles had fallen off the shuttle and Mission Control in Houston planned to have some ground-based telescopes take a look on the next pass over the United States. Our reporter was on live from the Johnson Space Center, and I asked, "What kind of telescopes are those, that can see that kind of damage, that far up in space?"

There was silence—well into the "dead air" zone—and then the reporter said, "Really *good* telescopes, Noah."

They were running out of studio time in Washington— our two-way from Romania had to be started immediately: Robert said, "Wait, what should I ask you?" I said, "Ask about the new government trying to reassure people and if it seems dangerous in the countryside." Then Robert read the news of the day from Romania, mentioned that I was there, and we were off: or I thought we were. The producer in Washington interrupts, asking for more energy, more push in my voice. I almost have to yell before I can sound normal on the radio, above the noise of the overseas phone line. Take two.

> NOAH: Robert, we went a day's drive north of Bucharest up into the mountains of Transylvania, to the town of Sibiu. We wanted to go up there because there was a lot of fighting in Sibiu. It started even before the fighting in the capital, Bucharest. The estimates are in Sibiu about a hundred people have died in five days of fighting. The people there, Robert, seem very proud of their victory, their revolution, there's a joy and an empowerment that you can sense in talking with them. We went to dinner at a restaurant last night and they were very happy and dancing, even though at the same time there as a soldier with an automatic rifle in

the kitchen standing guard. I did notice a contrast
with the people of Bucharest, though. In the
countryside the people seem to be a lot more cautious
... the people in Sibiu were saying things like, they
wanted to wait and see exactly what the National
Salvation Front puts forth; one man told me the real
struggle had just begun for control of Romania, and a
woman said that if free elections are not held in April,
they'll have to fight again.

ROBERT: Noah, given all that suspicion and doubt out in
the countryside, what is the government doing to
reassure people?

NOAH: Well, quite a few things. They're on television
practically all the time talking to the people; more food
has been made available. There was a story in the Sibiu
newspaper today, a request for the people to come to
the banks and get new paper money. We'd heard this
story before about the people of Romania being
insulted by the Ceausescu government's attitude
toward money. The money is very, very old and the
people refer to it as "toilet paper." It's about that
quality. So they're going to get fresh money. Also, the
city manager of Bucharest tells us that more
electricity and gas have been turned on so people have
a lot more heat and the houses and buildings are
warmed up, and that's a very important matter
because it's been as low as forty degrees for many
winters *inside* in apartment buildings and public
buildings in Bucharest, and as you can imagine the
issue of heating has been a revolutionary matter here.
Those are some of the things, and I think the people
now with the revolution are going to be in a mood to
demand a whole lot more from this government or
whatever government might follow.

ROBERT: You're not describing fighting or any gunfire. Is
the security situation now pretty well calmed down?

NOAH: In Bucharest it's quiet but there's a lot of army activity up in the countryside at Sibiu, lots of troops at the airport, they had troop transport helicopters there, as well as attack helicopters. The local militia are out guarding the railroad bridges. I guess they're concerned about sabotage. And there are army checkpoints on the highway, but no reports of fighting anywhere that we've heard, and indeed a lot of people were out after dark this evening. We saw a peasant woman, for example, walking along the highway carrying a bundle in one hand and a lantern in the other hand. I don't think the people are all that concerned now about the troops that were loyal to Ceausescu. But apparently the army is still quite concerned, and perhaps they know something that the people don't.

ROBERT: Thanks, Noah, take care.

Sunday, January 7, Romania, 1990

The story is slowing down. We talked yesterday about how to get out; still no planes leaving Bucharest. Drive south to Sofia? We don't have visas for Bulgaria. Drive west to Belgrade? Yugoslavia would be friendlier. Take the train north to Hungary? That's eighteen hours again. We decide to believe a Lufthansa prediction that they would be flying Monday.

We cover a demonstration, a march through the streets near University Square, finally hiring a cab to follow the procession so we can stay warm, and it's discouraging to realize that we're just waiting for something drastic to happen, perhaps even some violence, to provide a few seconds of good tape for a story.

Andrei meets us in the hotel lobby; he's heard church bells ringing, the first in decades, someone said. Michael and

Rich run outside to a cab. "Bells!" Michael yells to the driver,
and pulls out some dollars. An hour later they're back with
a great recording of the bells of the Mitropolia Cathedral.

Later in the afternoon we have a glass of wine and cookies,
standing around an apartment at Otopeni, a community
near the airport. Before the revolution, I was told, it would
have been less dangerous for these people to get close to an
atomic bomb than to be seen talking to an American. Several proud, stubborn people explain the difficulties of their
lives. They live in apartment buildings, four stories high,
concrete block and stucco, badly built and now in ill repair.
The dark stairwells have the cold, damp smell of unfinished
concrete. They've been here since the Ceausescu regime destroyed their village nearby.

> YOUNG ROMANIAN, SPEAKING ENGLISH: It's amazing, it's a
> terror, it's a national terror, this demolition.
> Sometimes in one single afternoon the house was
> crushed and the people are moved in the other place.

> NOAH: They lived in Damian. It was an old village, the
> name means "of thousands of years." Bulldozers came
> in, the houses were torn down, the shops, the farmland
> ripped away, the graves dug up and the coffins moved
> to Otopeni.

> *Another former villager speaks in Romanian*

> NOAH: This man works at the airport nearby, and he says
> that one day Nicolae Ceausescu was flying in, saw the
> village from the plane—told his people to tear it down.
> He didn't want foreign visitors to see the old houses
> and barns.

> *Another man speaks in Romanian*

> NOAH: It was an ecological catastrophe of great
> proportions, and children in the apartment buildings,
> this man tells me, will never hear the sound of a
> chicken or a pig.

Woman's voice, protesting

NOAH: A woman says they often now have to wear their coats in the kitchen while cooking. The cooking is by propane gas, and if they run out, two weeks can go by before they can get more.

But, isn't it a good place for young people? I ask. They can come in from the country and get jobs in town and live in the apartments?

Yes, she says, it is good for her. She does have a job, but she also has a child and sometimes finds the conditions impossible.

Then it's a fast wild ride back downtown, four of us in two cabs, and an argument over the fare. The men who wait outside the big hotels in Bucharest, to be taxi drivers and to change money (whatever else you might need) will do okay under anyone's system of government.

We have a room-service meal and try to get some work done on the *sistematizare* story. Last night, Andrei took me to the Capsa Café, a few blocks away. It was chilly and dim, and out-of-towners were eating there. Once, Andrei said, the Capsa was a grand literary salon, where Romania's writers and poets would come to hold court. If you were growing up in Romania, hoping to to be a writer, you would dream of dining here. I had *sarmale*, the cabbage rolls, with ground beef and pork, that I know from my wife's Croatian heritage.

Monday, January 8, Germany, 1990

After most of a morning's negotiation, we have four tickets to Frankfurt. We pack up, say goodbye to Deborah, who will stay for another week. We leave her with cash and batteries and blank cassettes.

The airport is gray and bleak. Concrete floors, many of the

windows boarded up. Young paratroopers stand around, wearing khaki jumpsuits and blue berets, large knives at their belts. The runways are dark, with no aircraft in sight. Patriotic choral music—women's voices—reverberates under the high ceilings. Enough people have gathered to fill up a plane. Everyone paces, most people smoke. Two hours go by. I am cold, stiff, dull, just bored. This is a long way from the end of the movie *The Year of Living Dangerously*—Mel Gibson as a radio journalist who bluffs his way through the Jakarta airport to escape Indonesia after a coup. He's been clubbed by a soldier, his eye is bandaged. He leaves his equipment and tapes behind, and Sigourney Weaver waits at the door of the plane.

At last a Lufthansa jet appears. A clean, white, warm plane. We leave Romania. The *Financial Times* of London, *USA Today*—European Edition—the *International Herald-Tribune*. There's German beer, free. Steak and sushi for dinner, and Colombian coffee. It's the best meal we've had since leaving home. And I'm sitting next to a woman who will be our last interview. She opens a portfolio and shows me photographs of the revolution, of the people on the streets, especially the young mothers with children. She tells me how important the Gypsies were, and the actors. She was taking the photographs to be exhibited at Leipzig. We taped a quick interview at Frankfurt Airport, while waiting for the luggage to arrive. It became part of our last story.

shattered glass being swept up

NOAH: In Romania the broken glass is everywhere, and fire-blackened buildings. Romania even without the damage from the revolution, especially at night, is like a country after a nuclear war. It's cold and dark. Gas is rationed. There are people with rifles guarding the railroad bridges.

It used to be against the law in this country to hoard coffee. You could go through a whole winter without ever being warm. A hot bath would be an unthinkable pleasure. The previous regime even censored the weather—there was a rule that said you didn't have to work if the temperature fell below a certain point, but it never did, according to the weather office.

Romania was a country ruled by a tyrant king. He wrote the words to the national anthem. He kept original paintings in his home and had copies made for the museums. He had people imprisoned for speaking out, and in the last fight it was said children were killed in the hospitals. One of my colleagues on this trip told me Ceausescu was "insane on purpose."

As I left Romania, a woman I met at the airport told me some more about the young people who had taken part, boys and girls, twelve to fifteen years old. Unspoiled, unsophisticated.

WOMAN, IN ENGLISH: Once they stood alive after this danger, they have nothing to be afraid of any longer. They have such an extraordinary courage and such a self-conscious in the best sense of the word that they cannot be stopped any longer. So I imagine that the youth won't *resignate* and they won't make compromises.

Sunday, January 14, Washington, D.C., 1990

There's nice sunlight through the windows of our house; the rooms still full of unpacked boxes, mostly books. I'm up early again—it's a difficult adjustment after all the time in Europe. I've been falling asleep at 9:00 P.M. and waking at 5:00 A.M. We got back on Tuesday evening and I had to go in and do the program on Wednesday. Stayed up last night to watch Harry Connick, Jr., on "Saturday Night Live," and I'll try to take a nap later today. Connick's quickly become a

jazz superstar—albums, concert tours, a role in the film
Memphis Belle—and Neenah and I have been watching
with pride. We brought him to Saint Paul two years ago to
play on "Good Evening." He was twenty-one years old and a
phenomenal presence at the piano, just lighting up the theater. We took him for an Afghan dinner after the show, and
on the way back to his hotel he said, "Thanks for a great
time. By the way, do I get paid for this?" I guess his agent
didn't really want to tell him it was only three hundred
dollars.

It's nice being home. The coffee's better, a friend has sent
us some grapefruit from Florida, and I'm having fresh green
salads twice a day.

Friday, January 19, Washington, D.C., 1990

There's been violence in the Soviet republic of Azerbaijan,
fighting between Azerbaijanis and the Armenian minority.
The story's hard to cover; we talk with experts in the United
States and Ann Cooper reports from Moscow. Then, we find a
freelance reporter in Yerevan, who talks with Robert over a
wonderfully clear phone line—it's a portable satellite
uplink telephone. This one is owned by the Armenian National Assembly. One can assume the Assembly gives the
reporter access to the phone to be sure that at least the Armenian side of the story gets out to the West. It's going to be
tough to give equal coverage to the Azerbaijani position.

Robert points out later that these portable phones could
be a big factor in guerrilla fighting and revolutions. It's always said that if you're trying to overthrow a government,
the first thing is to gain control of the national radio station—now a coup planner would do well to steal all the satellite phones in the country. You can easily imagine Mikhail
Gorbachev and his staff sneaking up to the roof of his dacha
to make a satellite call during the August '91 takeover attempt.

The system weighs only seventy-five pounds, fits into a couple of suitcase-size boxes for traveling. You just unfold the umbrella antenna, aim toward the right satellite, listen for a dial tone, and make the call. The phones cost about $55,000, and that's nothing if you're CNN and you have Peter Arnett in Baghdad during the fighting in the Gulf. The CNN anchors in Atlanta would talk to him every day— by way of satellite phone—and we'd see a still picture of Arnett speaking into a handset, with the antenna in the background.

Soon it's going to be possible to talk with anybody, anyplace, about anything. And some people would probably even now like to return to the days when journalism was a less frantic endeavor—the first wars, for example, were covered by reporters who "corresponded" by mail with their editors. In New York City, foreign news was once gathered by people who would go down to the docks to talk with arriving passengers about events in Europe.

Three significant deaths on the wires today: former Supreme Court Justice Arthur Goldberg; the Bagwan Shree Rajneesh, in India; and Myles Horton, the founder of the Highlander Center, a community-organizing workshop in Tennessee. How many obituaries should one program do? We decide to cover the Bagwan in the newscast, Robert does an interview about Justice Goldberg, and I put together a story about Myles Horton, using tape from a previous interview.

I had visited Highlander a couple of times, and I especially remember a Sunday evening a few years ago. Horton fixed us some black bean soup and ceviche for supper, and talked about farming techniques in Nicaragua, and the history of the War on Poverty in this country. He had a small house and a garden on the hillside above the Center. You could see the Great Smoky Mountains off to the south. Twenty-five years earlier the state of Tennessee had shut down what was then called the Highlander Folk School, selling at auction 175 acres and the buildings and a 5,000-volume library. The school had been under attack because of its civil rights activities. Horton and his staff reorganized—he always said Highlander was really just an idea.

As part of the obituary, we played one of my favorite pieces of tape: Horton's soft Appalachian-accented voice talking about some people in Bumpas Cove, Tennessee. They were trying to fight against a toxic waste dump in their town, and had come to the Highlander Center for advice. But it was not the Highlander way to be experts, to tell people what to do. Horton and the staff believed that the people who have the problems are the ones who have the answers.

HORTON: There are strategies that can be used, and they used them in Bumpas Cove when they couldn't get the officials to stop the dumping of chemicals there that was poisoning the stream—they blocked the roads with their trucks and stopped the dump trucks from coming in. And the women and children got up on the mountain and rolled rocks down on the trucks. Now, nobody had to tell them—those are mountain people, they know rocks roll down hills, you know, and there's plenty of them. So, they do things, we didn't—even if we'd tried to work out a story, we probably wouldn't have thought of anything like that.

NOAH: Back in the summer of 1927, when Myles Horton was a senior in college, he went into the mountains to organize vacation Bible schools for the Presbyterian Church. He said later that he liked what Christianity was *supposed* to be. He stayed in East Tennessee, started a labor-organizing school, teaching, holding workshops, helping people empower themselves. And then in 1952 Highlander decided that the problem of civil rights simply had to be addressed, that segregation was getting in the way of what they were trying to do. Many of those who would become leaders in the movement had been to Highlander for other workshops; it was one of the few places in the South

where blacks and whites could get together. The
Highlander staff believed that blacks should take the
lead in the struggle for civil rights.

HORTON: A lot of people realized that, but we were the first
people in the South to say that the blacks had to do it
themselves. And that wasn't popular with blacks, any
more than it was popular with whites, so it wasn't a
popularity contest we were getting into, we were
getting into what we thought was a real, honest
analysis of the situation. Then when I say that to the
black people, they would say well, why should we, who
are being oppressed by the white people, have to be the
ones to take the responsibility for solving the
problem? And my only answer was ... it's not just, but
it's the *only* way. Because there's nothing in history
that suggests, or gives us any clue, to anything
happening any other way.

music fading in, singing

My life will be sweeter
So sweet some day
Ain't you got a right
To the Tree of Life

Ain't you got a right
Ain't you got a right
Aint' you got a right
To the Tree of Life?

I had a deep respect for Myles Horton and the work he had
done, but I'm aware than I can tend toward the romantic in
my writing, especially when it comes to older men. One Sunday night years ago in Kentucky, we stopped in the small
town of Versailles to talk with A. B. "Happy" Chandler, a
former governor and U.S. senator, and the commissioner of
baseball in the late 1940s. Chandler was in his eighties already, a charming teller of stories, and still a consummate

politician. He had been educated at Transylvania College in
an era when young men were proud to recite poetry, and to
sing, and over the years he'd become famous for his rendition of Kentucky's state song. So at the close of the interview
I said, "Governor, I wonder if I could ask you to sing a verse
of 'My Old Kentucky Home'?" "Hell, son, I'll sing it all," he
said, and stood up and closed his eyes and sang in full voice.
Before he finished, tears were coming down his cheeks.

When Chandler died in the spring of 1991, I put together a
remembrance that included the tape of his song and some
of the interview, but perhaps I let him take a little too much
credit for breaking the color barrier in big league baseball
by letting Jackie Robinson play for the Dodgers. That honor
of changing baseball rightfully goes to Branch Rickey, the
Brooklyn owner. Chandler, as commissioner, decided to support Rickey against the wishes of all the other owners. In
our interview he said he told Rickey, "I have to meet my
Maker someday and if he asks me why I didn't let this boy
play and I'll say it's 'cause he's black, that might not be a
satisfactory answer. These kids are fighting and dying and
offered to fight and die for the country at Okinawa and Iwo
Jima and all these places, then we come back here and
they're told, notwithstanding the fact they got great talent,
that they can't play the American game of baseball. I don't
think that's fair, I don't think it's just, and I think it's something that ought not to be perpetuated, and I said you bring
him on in and we'll make the fight."

Quite often our letters from listeners contain the finest
obituary tributes. In October 1991, I heard from a friend in
Florida that Gamble Rogers had been drowned. Gamble was
a folksinger, I think he liked the term "troubadour." He'd
been on our program quite a lot back in the seventies and
I'd seen him several times in different cities over the years. I
made some calls to confirm the news—he was camping with
his wife near the ocean, and tried to rescue another man
who was drowning—and we found some time in that eve-

ning's program for a brief obituary. A week or so later a listener in California sent along what would have been a truer comment on Gamble's death. Tom Brislane of Santa Cruz recalled:

One day while I was working in a guitar shop in Chicago, late in the afternoon, a slender fellow strode in and eyed our collection of vintage jazz guitars. He said he'd to try one. Now, in the manner of jaded music store employees, we'd heard all this before. So you can well imagine the awestruck silence that greeted a virtuoso rendition of "Cannonball Rag." For the next two hours we were regaled with a tour de force of Merle Travis tunes, interspersed with verbal riffs and comments that turned our little shop into an impromptu nightclub. I surely will never hear "The Sheik of Araby" without thinking of him.

And Mr. Brislane concluded:

He was a man of a certain elegant, patrician reserve that I always associated with the long departed southern aristocracy. I thought of him as Faulkner with a six-string. He travelled light and friendly, often staying with friends and fellow musicians, for they were everywhere. So now there are small and empty stages in places like the Earl, in Chicago, The Inn of the Beginning, in Sonoma, McCabes, in Santa Monica, and a thousand other half nameless places where the slim man with the beat-up Guild D-50 on his hip will be missed.

And I was pleased by this letter a year or so earlier, from Benjamin L. White, Jr., of Fairfax, Virginia:

A few times before this has happened, where I am so moved by a piece on "All Things Considered" that I become consumed by emotion and need to pull off the road. Once when you reported on AIDS babies this happened, once when you reported on the singer Maura O'Connell and her heart-piercing Scottish soprano. This time it was your piece about the passing of Leonard Bernstein. A woman conductor [Rachael Worby of the Wheeling Symphony Orchestra] described in great and visceral eloquence her love for the man and his music and how he had transported her since she was six. As I listened I was driving home from work on a back road through the Virginia countryside near Middleburg. The October sun was low and lighting up the just-turning sugar maples with a golden light. The music, the praise of this man, the light and the trees fit just right. This moment of sanity seemed the most blessed of good medicine, antidote perhaps for the sadness and world pain that listening to your program faithfully (and being well informed) brings.

Obituaries can be problematic: you have to move fast, confirm the death, start making calls (carefully, because our call could be the first notification), start doing interviews. Sometimes I'll talk with two or three people, trying to find someone willing to put their own ego aside long enough to talk about their friend or colleague who's died. If it's an entertainer who's died, I usually ask the desk assistants not to bother calling Milton Berle—he tells good stories but he's awfully unpleasant to deal with. And he'll say to an interviewer, "No, that's a dumb question. Ask me this: Say, 'Mr. Berle, did you think so-and-so had a chance to make it in show business when you first saw him in Kansas City in 1939?'"

Many thousands of people loved the folksinger Steve Goodman, and his music. It was known he had leukemia, and the day of his death you could sense our audience taking a deep, sad breath together. Scott Nearing, the back-to-the-land activist, died at home in Maine; he had just turned one hundred years old. Helen Nearing proudly told us about the memorial service and their lives together. In a book she published later, *Loving and Leaving the Good Life,* Helen described Scott's death. He had been robust: "Old age for him was a time of fulfillment. Scott kept his strength and bearing all through his last decades: his seventies were not elderly, his eighties not decrepit, his nineties not senile." (Nearing finished his last book at ninety-two.) But he lost strength, he was sometimes confused, and Helen writes:

Scott wanted to go before his powers began to fail too far. He wanted to go of his own free will and accord, consciously and intentionally—a death by choice, cooperating with the process.

A month and a half before Scott went, a month before his hundredth birthday, while sitting with a group at the table one day, he said: "I think I won't eat any more." He deliberately and purposefully chose the time and the way of his leaving.

For a month Scott took only liquids, at first juices and then water, until "he was completely detached from life."

Scott Nearing died at home, without doctors or medication, with Helen at his side. And she was pleased that he had done well: "Leonardo da Vinci wrote in 1500: 'As a well-spent day brings happy sleep, so life well-used brings happy death.'"

The death of Kim Williams, in Missoula, Montana, was a difficult time for all of us. She had been a commentator on our program for about ten years, mostly on the subject of wild foods but always about her exuberance for life. In 1986 we learned that she was dying of cancer, and Susan Stamberg called to have a conversation with Kim on "All Things Considered." It was a sad, good-humored discussion. Kim was feeling tired but spirited, said she was "getting ready to move on to new dimensions." Kim was doing without chemotherapy and radiation. In a book she had written earlier she included a chapter about dying, and thought the subject was too often evaded in today's society, that the "empire of medicine" allows people to avoid talk of death. Kim said she didn't want any letters or flowers, that "after a while it gets like Grand Central Station around here," and she wanted time to think. Susan thanked Kim, and they both said goodbye, and so did the listeners.

Friday, February 2, Washington, D.C., 1990

News from South Africa. President F. W. de Klerk an-
nounces the unbanning of the African National Congress
and the imminent release of Nelson Mandela. We have seven
stories and interviews, the entire first third of our program.

And a fun interview with Bill Melendez, the chief anima-
tor for the Charlie Brown television specials. Melendez is
also the voice of Snoopy for the TV shows; he does all the
barks and growls and whimpers. He's seventy-three, works
every day either drawing Snoopy or sounding like him.

I'm a little concerned about my conversation with Mike
Sagar, who wrote an article for *Rolling Stone* about "ice,"
crystal methamphetamine, a new popular drug, especially
in Hawaii and on the West Coast. The interview included a
description of the drug as providing "durable erections and
delayed orgasms." Seems now, on second thought, to be almost an advertisement.

We had this same concern a couple of years ago with a
story about teenage suicide and spent a lot of time talking
with experts. Is it possible that a program about suicide
could be too suggestive for teenagers, could discussing it
give someone the idea to do it? No, was the unequivocal
answer. Well then, how about the subject of "autoerotic as-
phyxiation"—young men accidentally dying of strangula-
tion, hanging themselves to decrease blood flow to the brain;
it's said to enhance a masturbatory orgasm? This gave us
even more pause, but again the answer was: it's an important part of the story; tell it, but don't sensationalize it.

Sunday, February 4, Washington, D.C., 1990

A rainy day at home. Kept a fire burning all day. Neenah's getting ready to go to Pennsylvania for a television shoot about a man who makes turkey calls. I read *Fast Fade,* a book about David Puttnam's time as head of Columbia Pictures.

Two hundred thousand people on the streets of Moscow, on the day before the Party Congress. It's the biggest crowd there, it's said, since the 1920s. ABC has Peter Jennings in Moscow, and Ted Koppel in South Africa, in anticipation of the Mandela release.

Friday, February 9, Washington, D.C., 1990

We bring home some Thai food and two movies tonight. The dogs like the movie nights; one is on the couch, the other nearby on the floor. We watch *Mean Streets* and about half of *Earth Girls Are Easy.* Then "Nightline" from South Africa. I've tried to watch three "Nightline" shows this week but always fall asleep. As I get older, I'm beginning to agree with the folks in the Midwest—the late news should come on at 10:00 P.M. instead of 11:00. Someone told me once that if you're flying over Minneapolis you can see the lights going out in houses all over the city, at just about 10:35.

NPR now has three additional people in South Africa, and one more on the way. That's a lot for us.

Sunday, February 11, Washington, D.C., 1990

Dinner tonight with Susan Stamberg and her husband, Lou. Susan's just back from San Francisco and work on a story about European Jews who fled to China before World War II.

The Nelson Mandela release was set for this morning, so Neenah got up early and made a fire, and I fixed some waffles for breakfast, and we watched television and listened to the radio at the same time. It started to rain in Soweto Township, and I knew I would soon hear reporters saying that the rain "failed to dampen the enthusiasm" of those waiting for word that Mandela was free. And I did. Although NPR's Phyliss Crockett pointed out that in Africa, rain is traditionally something to be celebrated.

All the TV networks used the same pool video coverage from South African television. When Nelson Mandela and Winnie were walking out of the prison, a commentator said, "Let's just let this picture speak for itself." I counted only seven seconds of silence.

Mandela's speech in Cape Town was delivered with absolute strength and no showmanship, closing with his own words at his trial, April 20, 1964, when he spoke of a democratic and free society for South Africa. "It is an ideal I hope to live for and achieve, but if needs be, it is an ideal for which I am prepared to die."

Wednesday, February 14, Washington, D.C., 1990

A long telephone conversation today with Mangosuthu Gatsha Buthelezi, chief of South Africa's Zulus, leader of the Inkatha movement (his office said he likes to be addressed as Dr. Buthelezi). I asked about his calling the African Na-

tional Congress "Marxist," and he didn't back off, although
he refers to the ANC as "brothers." These telephone interviews—from other countries—can be either satisfying or
frustrating in direct proportion to the quality of the line we
manage to get—a good clean phone line is a joy. Before the
interview starts we often beg the patience of those we talk
with, taking extra time to electronically equalize the phone
line to help the voice come through more clearly. The engineer at the audio console separates the signal into different
frequencies and makes adjustments, boosting the high frequencies, for example. Extraneous noise is removed. You
can do a lot but you can't work wonders, and several people
said later that Butholezi was difficult to understand.

Also, a performance-art interview—along with audio
from a videotape showing the work of a group called Blue
Man. Three young men in New York, two of them working
daytimes as caterers, comprise Blue Man; they perform in
clubs around town and sometimes on the streets. They have
a slick, androgynous look. Bright blue bald heads. And they
often perform *with* art: lots of different colors of paint and
toothpaste and Jell-O splashing around. I asked one of the
three, Chris Wink, to explain a word I had to spell for the
radio.

WINK: Rheology. (*Laughs*)

NOAH: I've never heard that, what is that?

WINK: That is the study of the flow and deformation of
matter and we came across that, I used to work for a
Japanese science magazine synopsizing articles—we as
Blue Men, actually, as Blue Man, are interested in
colors that ooze. We have paintings that literally paint
themselves, it's usually toothpaste gel we find the most
beautiful. Comes from behind holes in the canvas, and
the painting literally paints itself. Now, how did we get
onto the rheology? Well, we were fascinated with
studying different ways that things could ooze, or

explode—colors could explode or swirl in our little
world that we're creating in the shows—and so we
have turned to different scientific places for
inspiration, fluid dynamics, chaos science, and
rheology.

NOAH: And also, what kids would do with a lot of food,
and a lot of paint—

WINK: Absolutely. For every bit we go into a sort of
esoteric world of science or art, we try to go to the
other way to the same degree into what children would
do. Now that's because we want to get the creative
experience down to the lowest common demoninator.
There's an exuberance of creation a child has, they
don't have to be told about it, or taught it. And we're
trying to get back to that.

NOAH: In which category would be the part in your
performance that I read about where the Blue Men—or
Blue Man—sits down at a table and starts to eat what
is described as "claylike pablum" from plates, and then
the pablum comes out from holes in their shirts and it
goes back on their plates and they eat it again?

WINK: Well, that's a little more complicated. The childlike
playfulness is when we're creating an actual piece of
art. But this is a different point we're trying to make
there. With that piece, we have a delicate refined meal,
there are wineglasses, there are candelabras—and then
the Blue Man character, because of his unique
physiology, is unable to delay the waste product. In
other words, what he eats, the waste part come right
back out. Now, I don't want to—it sounds on the radio
like it's maybe disgusting. It's actually done very
tastefully and very beautifully.

> *music from Blue Man video, Ravel's* Bolero, *and
> audience laughing wildly*

WINK: The pablum, actually it's bananas. What we were hoping people would see is that by shortening the loop, the Blue Man could be a character to personify something that happens with the human being. He eats something, in a beautiful setting, but the tribal nature of it, of the waste, comes right back out to haunt him, and he doesn't quite know what to do, and that's where the humor is in that piece, the delicate setting and the waste confronting him immediately. Two of us are caterers—one of the things we noticed is that there's this waste product, an inevitable byproduct of consumption, and what we tend to do is delay or postpone or put it out of sight out of mind. But it does come back. We swim in it later in the summer or it may end up in a fish or some of the pollution in the groundwater or whatever. It does come back to us, and the waste product of our consumption will come back to haunt us.

Sunday, February 25, Washington, D.C., 1990

Chilly, cold, down to zero in the suburbs, they say. But yesterday it was warm enough to wash the car, and I've been thinking of planting peas and lettuce soon. The white snowdrops are out, and some crocuses.

I made a meat loaf and we watched *Do the Right Thing* on tape. I should be working on a proposal for Olympic stories. The Winter (France) and Summer (Spain) games are coming up fast and I'd like to get to know some athletes and start doing stories about their training.

There's a fascinating piece in Sunday's *New York Times Magazine* about an opera singer named Teresa Stratas. She's reclusive; she lives in an "eerie old building" within walking distance of the Met. It would make a great radio story. A friend of hers is quoted describing her performances, "You acquire the kind of radiance that Teresa brings to the stage by also soaking in the darkness." Probably she wouldn't talk to us.

This story reminds me of a story that stayed on the ATC list of story ideas for about two years. "High-Tech Gypsies" was something I read about someplace and thought we should find out if any of it was true. In the old days in Europe, it is said, when a Gypsy woman passed away, one of her dresses would be left hanging in the forest as a tribute to her memory. Nowadays, in California, it was reputed, when a Gypsy woman dies, in a city, one of her dresses is taken to the dry cleaners and then is never picked up. We didn't try to do the story, didn't make the first phone call about it, but it remained on our list and soon most of the staff forgot what the story was about.

Another quite possibly apocryphal tale involves NASA and a cure for jet lag. A former astronaut, Rusty Schweickart, was heard (not by me but by a friend, you understand) to mention at a seminar that NASA studied the effects of jet lag, found a way to allieviate the symptoms, but then withheld the information from the public. The answer was orgasm—as close to landing as possible. I first brought this up at an ATC editorial meeting in the late 1970s. "That's wonderful," everyone said. "Let's call up NASA right away. Wonderful." Then the meeting broke up and NPR's news director, passing me in the hall, said, "We don't really want to do that jet-lag story."

I still mention this idea at editorial meetings about once a year, usually at a moment when everyone's bored and enough new people have joined the staff to make it worthwhile, but I don't sell it very hard: I guess I have more fun with the idea in concept than in reality, and probably one phone call would destroy the myth of the story. And maybe it's okay to keep on wondering if Teresa Stratas would actually agree to an interview.

Tuesday, February 27, Washington, D.C., 1990

It would be great to be in Nicaragua this week. Violeta Chamorro has won a big upset victory against the Sandinistas, and both sides are demonstrating in the streets. Hardly anyone thought the National Opposition Union—*UNO*—could win, although we did find an article in *Harper's* that predicted a Chamorro victory. The polls were also wrong, but it would have taken some extra courage to tell someone you were planning to vote against the government.

An executive decision today about the semantics of the proposed merger of West and East Germany. Is it "unification" or "reunification"? Both terms have political weight. I had been slightly in favor of "reunification," since the countries had once been together, but then I learn that Bill Buzenberg, the managing editor for all the news programs, has ruled, after much discussion, in favor of "unification." NPR also uses "abortion rights" and "anti-abortion" to describe the two sides of that conflict, as opposed to "pro choice" and "pro life," which is how the respective groups might prefer to be identified.

It's a policy that took a long time to develop and there's now a large sign on the wall of the newsroom reminding everyone of the usage. There is much talk these days about "African-American" instead of "black," with the former being favored especially for first reference in a story. (I recall one reporter who, after agreeing with her editor to use "black" in a particular sentence, would go into the studio and change it back to "African-American.") You'll also hear discussions about "gays and lesbians" in place of "homosexual." And there's sentiment among AIDS activists that the term "victim" is inappropriate when referring to someone with AIDS. The politically correct term is "people with AIDS." But that shouldn't rule out the use of "victim" when talking about those who have died from the disease. (The date is now lost to memory, but I recall when we decided that we could just use the acronym, AIDS, and didn't need to follow it with "acquired immune deficiency syndrome.")

Most of these matters are worked out over time at a daily editorial meeting, where editors and producers talk about stories and assignments. Our listeners also have a lot to say. It was the public and not the media, you might remember, who caused the wording "the terrorist group has *taken credit* for the bombing" to be changed to *"claimed responsibility* for the bombing." Enough people finally wrote enough letters to enough news organizations. Sometimes we just make mistakes—once or twice a year you can hear "confessed homosexual," or worse, "self-confessed homosexual." Or someone will refer to "Israel's occupied territories," instead of "the Israeli occupied territories."

In a *Washington Post* story about the effects of the Exxon oil spill in Alaska, reporter Jay Matthews used the word "fishers" to mean people of both sexes who fish. I knew the *Post* had just published a new edition of their style manual, so we asked that book's editor to come in for an interview. "It took a little courage to use 'fishers' instead of 'fishermen,' I started. "What?" he said. "We don't use 'fishers.' That's not a word. We wouldn't do that." End of interview. No point in going on to other recent style changes. I began to doubt that I'd seen the word, but soon the editor called and said, yes, a weekend editor had indeed changed Matthews's "fishermen" to "fishers" and it stayed for a couple of editions before someone noticed. Later I had a chance to ask Matthews himself. He had lived in Alaska for a time, and assured me that some of the women who fish there do indeed prefer to be called "fishermen." "Fisher" once was indeed a useful word, especially in the Bible, and it's still offered without qualification by *Webster's New World Dictionary:* "1. a person who fishes; fisherman." But my Oxford English Dictionary, 1961 edition, says: "now *arch.;* superseded in ordinary use by FISH-ERMAN."

Sometimes it's difficult for a radio organization to arrive at a pronunciation standard. I've always preferred "a-PART-*hate,*" but others pronounce apartheid as "a-PART-*hide.*" When Nelson Mandela was released from prison, I was pleased to hear that my pronunciation of the word agreed with his.

"Harassment" became another problematic word, during the Clarence Thomas hearings. "Ha-RASS-ment," said the NPR style memo that was soon issued, in the interest of consistency. "HAR-ass-ment." said Bob Edwards, determinedly, every day on "Morning Edition." This was the way he'd always pronounced the word and some dictionaries backed him up. The memos continued, and Bob finally gave up using "harassment" in copy, finding ways to write around it rather than—in his view—mispronounce it. He wasn't alone; even the Senate Judiciary Committee seemed divided on the pronunciation.

Another food interview today. Polish donuts—*paczki.* This is Fat Tuesday, the last day before Lent begins, and people were lined up early outside Detroit's Oaza Bakery. Raymond Poplawski helped us learn the word.

POPLAWSKI: "PONCH-key" is pronounced just like I said it. That's the Polish pronunciation for what we generally in the United States call a Bismarck—a jelly-filled doughnut. Normally, they're filled with jelly throughout the year, but during the festive season of *paczki* we fill them with *better* preserves. That's raspberry, blueberry, strawberry, prune—which is a tradition in the Polish people—and then custard and lemon.

NOAH: Powdered sugar on the outside?

POPLAWSKI: Powdered sugar—here's what we use: we use a strawberry glazing, a regular glazing, granulated sugar and powdered sugar, and chocolate, to top the various different doughnuts that we make.

NOAH: And how many did you make?

POPLAWSKI: Well, in the last seventy-two hours, somewhere's in the neighborhood of fourteen thousand dozen. Not doughnuts, fourteen thousand *dozen.*

NOAH: What time did you come to work this morning?

POPLAWSKI: All right, I worked twenty-two and a half hours straight.

NOAH: Just for this one day?

POPLAWSKI: Well, it's two days. So you're talking forty-four, forty-five hours the last forty-eight.

NOAH: Wow. Just to make the *paczkis.*

POPLAWSKI: This is all we made, now. Nothing else in the sweet-good line has been made for the last seventy-two hours.

NOAH: Do people buy a dozen at a time?

POPLAWSKI: They buy more than a dozen. You very seldom see one box go out. It's three and four and five.

NOAH: Could you at this point, having been working on it a couple of days, could you possibly eat one of these *paczkis?*

POPLAWSKI: Right now? Looking at them is sufficient. (*Laughs*)

NOAH: Well, what do you want for lunch, do you want some chili or something like that?

POPLAWSKI: No, I think a nice egg sandwich would do real well.

Friday, March 2, Washington, D.C., 1990

I talk with one of our producers, Ira Glass, in Chicago, about coming back to help do something special at the Washington National Cathedral, for this fall. After almost a century of construction, the cathedral is to be finished in September. It's a vast mystical structure, with lots of good possibilities for sound, and I've been thinking that we could write, or commission someone to write, a science-fiction drama. It could be set in the cathedral a hundred years in the future. We'll do some research. I've missed working with Ira; he decided about a year ago to go out to our Chicago bureau and to do more reporting on his own. NPR also has offices and studios in New York and Los Angeles, and in London at the headquarters of the BBC Foreign Service. The Canadian Broadcasting Corporation helps out up north; we have satellite uplinks at fifteen NPR member stations around this country, in most of the major cities, so we can usually find a studio wherever we need one.

I have the first real pronunciation failure of my career today. I've interviewed Josef Škvorecký, the Czech writer, about his new detective novel, *The End of Lieutenant Boruvka.* Škvorecký emigrated to Canada in 1968 and now teaches English at Erindale College, University of Toronto. When I taped the interview—he was at the CBC in Toronto—I asked him to pronounce his name. Twice. Slowly. I thought I had it, but today I can't say it, can only come close. "Sch-var-etsky" is the best I can do, and I don't trust myself live, I have to go into another studio and tape the introduction while our program's on the air. I'm also laughing a lot while I try to pronounce it.

I suspect we all have certain words we have trouble reading out loud. I can't hardly say "rural" or "reservoir," and will sometimes frantically grasp for words that come close to meaning the same thing. I'll always change "particularly" to "especially," and I have to write out "strategic" as "struh-tegic." And my colleague Robert Siegel—who usually loves hard-to-pronounce words; when he was a newscaster he'd go out of his way to include the most difficult foreign names—is never pleased to see "judiciary" come up in copy. He had a difficult time with the Nixon impeachment story years ago, there being no way to avoid "Judiciary" when it belongs between "Senate" and "Committee." Lynn Neary hates "synthesizer" and is never quite sure how to say "drawer." Bob Edwards can stumble over "antiballistic missile system" and so would rather refer to the "ABM Treaty." We all prefer "CFCs" to "chlorofluorocarbons." Elizabeth Arnold, who worked as a reporter in Alaska, found "molybdenum" troublesome but essential in stories about Alaskan mining. And Scott Simon can say "al-u-MIN-nium" but not "a-LUM-i-num"; he'd be okay with this on the BBC.

I once wrote a commercial for a garden tractor; I described it as "indefatigable." Six syllables with a twisty pronunciation. The spot was read live during the broadcast of the high school football games, every Friday night. The radio station's owner was the color man for the games—his enthusiasm usually made up for his lack of on-air inexperience, but he never should have tried to say "indefatigable." He never did make it and the rest of the station staff would gleefully tune in at halftime, waiting for him to try it again. He wouldn't give up. I would have changed it to "tireless" in a flash.

Sunday, March 11, Washington, D.C., 1990

Last night we went to see the U.S. Women's Olympic Volleyball team, playing the Soviet team at George Washington University. The U.S. lost three games to nothing, but the Soviet women didn't seem to be that much better.

I've finally finished filing my expenses for the trip to Romania; it was a mess, in three currencies and languages. Neenah is packing now for a three-week trip to Mozambique. She'll be working as a freelance producer with NPR's Ted Clark, doing stories about children orphaned by the civil war in that country.

It's a warm day, and we buy some some oakleaf lettuce and arugula seedlings at the nursery. It's good to have something green in the ground early.

Friday, March 16. Washington, D.C., 1990

In the early afternoon, I go over to Lafayette Park near the White House to cover a ceremony marking the fifth anniversary of Terry Anderson's kidnapping. It's all for the media—about twenty video crews. Also taking part: Tom Brokaw, Dan Rather, Larry King, and Tom Friedman of *The New York Times*; they all make brief remarks. It's surprising to see journalists as participants in an event like this, even though Terry Anderson is a colleague, the Chief Mideast Correspondent for the Associated Press. (Anderson was taken hostage in Beirut in March 1985, and was the last American to be released, on December 19, 1991.) We use tape from Peggy Say, Anderson's sister, and some comments from Father Lawrence Jenco; both sound strong and sincere. Also we talk with a seventh-grade student who said she thought the hostages would be freed soon, because the world is changing so fast. Her history book is brand new but she realizes it's out of date.

A report today from the Committee to Protect Journalists. Fifty-three journalists were killed on assignments last year; 1,164 more were assaulted, and 60 expelled from different countries.

Back at the office, sitting with several people having lunch, I mention that Brokaw and Rather and the others had spoken at the ceremony, and there's a discussion about whether it's right for a journalist to take such a role. Is it okay for NPR reporters to make an abortion rights speech? Probably not. Would it be okay to join an abortion rights march? That would also be discouraged, but many would argue that you don't give up being a citizen when you become a reporter.

Margot Adler, one of our veteran reporters, is a witch, and the author of an authoritative book, *Drawing Down the Moon: Witches, Druids, Goddess-Worshippers and Other Pagans in America Today.* Once, at a naturist convention, Margot gave a speech without any clothes on. I thought it was wonderful. She also loves baseball and was especially fond of Bill Lee, the somewhat rascally pitcher for the Boston Red Sox and then the Montreal Expos. Margot used to stay at my apartment when she came down from New York, and on certain days I noticed she'd seclude herself in the bathroom. "What are you doing?" I'd say. She'd laugh. "I'm doing a little magic for Bill; he's pitching today." (Margot told *The New York Times,* on Halloween 1991, that she was beginning to focus her attention on the " 'goddess spirituality' movement. I'm more involved in that now than I am in 'the craft.' " It's a good bet she's still interested in baseball.)

Later in the afternoon, I have a chance to talk with the Reverend László Tökes. This is the one interview everyone wanted when we were in Romania; no one could find him then. Now he's come to Washington to meet with the President and Secretary of State James Baker. Tökes was at the very center of the December uprising in Romania. He is an ethnic Hungarian, the pastor of a church in Timisoara. His sermons calling for equal rights for all minorities drew the attention of the Ceausescu government; he was arrested by the *Securitate.* Tens of thousands of demonstrators—all ethnic groups together, Germans, Hungarians, Serbs, Gypsies, Romanians—demanded his release. Shots were fired by police, people were killed, the revolution began.

Father Tökes talked with me about his early hopes for

Romania's new leadership, the National Salvation Front. Promises were made, full rights for every minority. But, he said, several groups in his country are working against that.

> TŐKES: Mostly the National Peasant Party which is against the Hungarian full rights, and mostly there is an organization, a fascistic Ceausescu organization, *Vata Românească,* "Romanian Fireplace," it comes in English, and that is vehemently attacking the democratical forces and it wants a "Great Romania" without minorities. They advise us to leave Romania, to go in Hungary. The extreme part of Romanians participate in this organization.

(The Bush administration continued to express concern about human rights in Romania. In the spring of 1992, the State Department did note that local elections held in Romania in February met "generally accepted international standards." But the national elections promised for the summer of 1992 were postponed; the National Salvation Front seemed reluctant to give up power.)

Monday, March 19, Washington, D.C., 1990

A lucky chance to talk with Will Steger, who's just finished a successful expedition across Antarctica—with skis and dogsleds, almost four thousand miles across the continent. They started on August 1, arriving at a Soviet base on the eastern coast on March 3. I've spoken with Steger quite a lot in the past; a few years ago he called us every week or so during a long training trip in the Yukon. And he phoned today from his hotel in Australia—his team traveled there by boat, the first part of their trip home from the Trans-Antarctica Expedition. We had an ordinary, cheerful conversation about an extraordinary adventure. Two weeks later I went over to the National Press Club for a luncheon honoring Steger, and Quin Dahe, Keizo Funatsu, Geoff Somers, Jean-Louis Etienne, Victor Boyarsky; six team members from six countries. They all looked wonderfully healthy. And I got to pet Sam, one of Will's favorite dogs. I took along some daffodils that I bought out on the street, and Will posed with them, for their *Washington Post* photograph.

When he talked with me from Sydney, Steger mentioned that he had already eaten a nice ripe avocado, and he'd been thinking about spring, and about rain.

STEGER: One of my dreams during the long trip across Antarctica was the sound, and the feeling of rain. Especially a springtime rain. This was like coming back to life today. I was walking around the streets, in the rain; it wasn't raining that hard, just to feel it and smell it and hear it. It was ... ah, you really miss life when you're on a plateau for such a long time like that.

NOAH: The temperatures you were encountering near the end, the last month or so, how bad were they?

STEGER: We raced, literally raced winter across the plateau; we had such a long distance to travel. But I was very concerned about arriving too late and having the winter catch us on the plateau. The temperature rapidly started dropping, a lot of times four or five degrees Fahrenheit a day, and every day; it was getting down to fifty, then sixty below.

NOAH: Had you worried about the timing; I was really impressed to notice that you started in August, August the first, you said it would be seven months, and you did that almost to the day.

STEGER: Yeah.

NOAH: Was that luck?

STEGER: No. It's planning. It's very simple, actually, almost mathematical. You lay out the strategy; it's a game, almost.

NOAH: Yes. Most of us hearing about the conditions of the expedition would think it impossible to survive it, but I'm going to guess here that the hardest thing would be something that we would not even think of. Is that true?

STEGER: Yeah. To me, I knew I could get across Antarctic. I never really questioned that. Some of the storms, my hopes slipped a little bit to the bottom, but I knew we could do that. To me the challenge, the immediate challenge, was getting across with six people and being very close friends at the end. Most people say you couldn't do it. I look at the psychological challenge as much greater than the physical. I think our real strength as a team was two things: one, our diversity and nationalities and culture. That was very powerful. We didn't need to communicate by speech. Our speech was restricted. Because of cold weather, sometimes because of the limited use of the English language. But we communicated back and forth a lot just by the feeling. But the diversity was in our favor, and also we have an average age of forty. All of us are well established, with ourselves and the fields we work in, and there was no competition for leadership or for recognition, we were basically very mature men, and that worked in our advantage.

NOAH: Are you all there together in Australia?

STEGER: Yeah, we're very close. We actually, tonight we have separate hotel rooms, and I've been sleeping next to men for eight months and it seems so funny to have a room to myself. We've been, you know, just sardines. (*Laughs*) But we socialize together, we gravitate together when—now, on a tour like this, usually when

you're tired of people and you've been with them for
eight months, you have a tendency of gravitating away
from each other when you have the freedom, but it's
quite the opposite.

Wednesday, March 21, Washington, D.C., 1990

I saw a note in a magazine this winter about the body of Jan
Paderewski, the Polish pianist and composer, national hero
and statesman, which lies waiting at Arlington National
Cemetery. Paderewski died in New York in 1941. He had
wanted to be buried in Poland and President Roosevelt said
that Paderewski's remains would be brought to Arlington
Cemetery to rest, temporarily, until such time as Poland is
free. The casket is not buried, but rests inside a cypress box,
sitting on a cart, it could leave on a moment's notice. And
this week with the visit to Washington of Tadeusz Mazo-
wiecki, Poland's new prime minister, we thought it was a
good time to go over across the Potomac River and do the
story. The maintenance people were cleaning the floor of the
U.S.S. *Maine* Memorial, and the ammonia fumes were so
strong we could only stay inside for a minute or so to record
that part of the interview. Kerry Childress of the Arlington
Cemetery staff talked with us about the renewed hopes for
Paderewski's repatriation, but also pointed out that not all
of the remains could be sent home.

NOAH: His heart was taken and eventually wound up in
    Doylestown, Pennsylvania?

CHILDRESS: That is correct. It is a custom of the church,
    and it was also by request from the family that his
    heart be removed and placed in a shrine in
    Doylestown, Pennsylvania. Furthermore, the family
    has specifically stated that the heart will not return to

Poland but will remain in the United States. Primarily this is to symbolize Paderewski's long-standing devotion to the United States and the work that he had with the United States as well.

(Paderewski's casket was flown to Poland in June 1992; he was buried in St. John's Cathedral in Warsaw.)

Friday, March 23, Washington, D.C., 1990

We've had snow in the mornings; big wet flakes. There's nothing prettier than snow on daffodils, and the first tulips—red and pale yellow and white—and the new lettuce in the garden. Last year I thought about proposing a garden journal for "All Things Considered," a weekly essay about the garden's progress through the season, but I was discouraged somewhat by a letter our executive producer received: "After listening to tonight's 'cherry blossom' feature with Noah Adams, I feel a bit disappointed. Why spend precious minutes on a 'radio production 101' piece when your talented journalists could report on news? I don't care to learn what someone is having for breakfast while they're looking at the blossoms. I must say I think Noah's folksy interviews are depressing."

Tonight there was one of those "I wonder what it would be like..." interviews. I've been especially curious lately about the people who *jump* off high places—for fun. People have been talking about a recent Reebok television commercial: two men, each strapped at the ankles by strong, stretchy "bungee cords," leap headfirst off a bridge into a gorge. The jumper wearing Reebok shoes is brought to a stop by his cords. As for the other jumper, all that remains is an empty pair of Nikes, swinging in the wind. Reebok has pulled the TV spot, at least temporarily; a lot of viewers objected to its grisly implication.

The stunts in the ad were done by two brothers, John and Peter Kockelman, of Bungee Adventures in Palo Alto, California. Peter tried to reassure me—he said he's also an engineer.

KOCKELMAN: To try to let people jump off of bridges two hundred to a thousand feet high, there's a lot of engineering behind that.

NOAH: Yeah, I'd be somewhat reassured to have engineers at the other end of the deal. What's the highest you've ever jumped?

KOCKELMAN: Off of the, let's see, there's a bridge in West Virginia that was about eight hundred feet high. I forget the name of it. Also the Golden Gate Bridge, about two hundred and thirty feet.

NOAH: When you jumped from the Golden Gate, how close to the water did you come?

KOCKELMAN: About twenty feet, one time, and my brother did a "toe-hang bat drop" by one ankle and dipped his body into the Bay.

NOAH: He did a what?

KOCKELMAN: He was tied to the bungee cords by one ankle; he hung by his toes underneath the structure of the bridge, and he let go of his toes and he dipped his whole body in the Bay. (*Laughs*)

NOAH: Tell us about the commercial for Reebok. This was off of a bridge, over Puget Sound, right?

KOCKELMAN: Yeah, off Deception Pass Bridge, up there, north of Seattle.

NOAH: How many times did you have to jump?

KOCKELMAN: We did a total of seventy-seven jumps for the week.

NOAH: You and your brother, were there two of you, three of you—?

KOCKELMAN: There's two of us that were doing the jumps for the commercial, we also had a gentleman that—Chris Konkrite, who's a sky diver, and he takes videos of people that jump out of airplanes. So he jumped off, attached to bungee cords ten feet next to us, to get some of the shots.

NOAH: Shots of you falling?

KOCKELMAN: Yes.

NOAH: So when we watch that Reebok commercial, we're seeing sort of composite pictures from all seventy-seven jumps, or in theory we are. But in the commercial, of course, the joke is—well, not really a joke to some people—that somebody falls out of their tennis shoes and into the water.

KOCKELMAN: Yeah, well, if people are attached and the cords break or they fall out of their equipment, it happens normally when they're at the lowest point, so if I was to have fallen out, I would have fallen out eight to ten feet above the water. So what people don't realize is that you don't basically jump off a bridge and end up falling and hitting the water at whatever speed you would have accumulated. You're greatly slowed down or stopped by the time you're at the maximum force on your body, so—

NOAH: —Okay, let me try to understand. The slowing-down part is a very gradual thing as the shock cords begin to take effect.

KOCKELMAN: Correct. It takes you eighty feet to stop your body. From when the cords start to pull on you.

NOAH: So there's not a big snap at the end of—?

KOCKELMAN: No, it's very gradual.

NOAH: It's also very dangerous, is it not, really?

KOCKELMAN: Yeah, it's very dangerous undertaken by amateurs or people just saying, I want to go out bungee jumping. You really gotta go with some people that know what they're doing, 'cause it can be very dangerous.

Since that interview the bungee record has been rapidly ascending, with jumpers leaping out of hot-air balloons, cords more than 1,000 feet long tied to their ankles—the cords then can stretch to twice that length. A professional jumper said in *Outside* magazine, "You're going to see 5,000-foot bungee cords before long." And John Kockelman, Peter's brother, has been talking about a jump off the Golden Gate Bridge *without* a cord. The jumper would use a concussion bomb to dispel the surface tension of the water, dropping it just before he hits.

Wednesday, March 28, Washington, D.C., 1990

Robert talked again today with Vytautis Landsbergis, Lithuania's president, about Soviet threats against his republic's commitment to independence. He is patient as we arrange for a Lithuanian interpreter on another phone line. Landsbergis speaks English, but because he's making policy statements to the West (and likely will be heard at the State Department), he wants to formulate his answer to Robert's questions in his own language. He sounds calm, yet determined in his opposition to Moscow.

I get some time away from the program to clean up my office. It's a mess of newspapers and files and about a hundred books. And Neenah calls from Mozambique. After she talks with her editor, the call is switched in to me for a minute. She's in Maputo. Their trip went well, up into the country by small airplane. They are a bit dehydrated, can't buy bottled water, only Coca-Cola. Think they'll be able to go to South Africa tomorrow.

Friday, April 6, Washington, D.C., 1990

We ran an interview tonight that I'm beginning to regret. I talked with John Waters about his new film *Cry Baby*. The conversation was fun, but not enlightening; the movie was fun for a while, but lurid and unappealing—I was relieved when the screening was over. The interview was already scheduled, and so almost by inertia it got on the air. I always feel that listeners take it as a recommendation when they hear an interview about a movie, or a record, or a book; that we have found something interesting, something of value. And I really couldn't recommend this movie. This is a special problem with movie publicity people, who call and say you've got a chance to talk with a director, an actor, and they demand a firm date for the interview. It's hard to say, I'll do it but only if I like the film.

The dream is to have a great actor, great movie, great access; and—for me—that's only happened once. A friend of mine was having dinner with Jodie Foster, who said, "Why doesn't 'All Things Considered' ever call me? Do you know anyone there?" This was just before *The Silence of the Lambs* was released. Foster was working in Los Angeles, editing the first film she's directed, *Little Man Tate*. We found a couple of other stories to do in California, and asked for a morning's worth of Foster's time. Her publicist said, "How about lunch?" Great, we thought, she wants to meet us for lunch, but then we realized they meant the interview would take place *during* lunch—that's the way the magazines do it. But it wouldn't work for radio, talking in a noisy restaurant, and Foster graciously found a quiet mixing room at her production office, and we talked for more than an hour. I almost—but only almost—broke a personal rule and asked for an autograph, which actually wouldn't have been for me but for our desk assistant, Jill Crawford, who, come to think of it, quit her job and moved to Los Angeles within just a few months.

Jodie Foster ran into some publicity trouble later in the year when *Little Man Tate* was released. She canceled a "Today" interview because they planned to show videotape of the Reagan assassination attempt as part of the introduction to her segment. "Today" had agreed not to ask about John Hinckley and his obsession with Foster, but felt the subject should at least be mentioned. " 'Today' does not allow its interview subjects to set ground rules," the Associated Press was told. I had seen an earlier "Prime Time Live" story on Foster, which focused quite a lot on the shooting and the aftermath—even though they didn't ask her about it directly—and not much at all on *Little Man Tate*. I don't recall any real ground rules for our interview, although it's long been known she won't talk about Hinckley—she told the whole story several years ago, writing in *Esquire*.

Linda and Robert and I rarely run into difficulty with book interviews. We insist on reading the book before we set a date to talk with the author. And we each read several books a year that we decide aren't worthy of an interview. No one assigns us books—the choices are ours, and are very subjective. If you have to spend your spare time reading a book, it had better be something you like.

There's now starting to be a lot of pressure from publicists. There are fifty thousand books published every year and a mention on "All Things Considered" is significant. A Los Angeles bookseller told me that while Susan Stamberg was on the air one evening interviewing Bret Easton Ellis, he could watch the cars pulling up and stopping outside his store. He quickly sold every copy of *Less Than Zero* that he had in stock.

Early this morning I stopped by to see the public relations

director at the Washington National Cathedral about our idea of staging a science-fiction radio drama. She said, in effect, are you kidding? There's no way a work of fiction would be approved, and especially science fiction. The projects that win the cooperation of the cathedral are all designed to further the goals of the Church, I'm told. She spends a lot of time turning down ideas—television production companies in particular like the idea of filming there.

And for this evening's program my turn came to talk with Lithuania's President Landsbergis; I told him that Robert was away at a conference. He said that if Moscow wanted to govern Lithuania with military force, then we were back in the Stone Age.

Thursday, April 12, Washington, D.C., 1990

Finally we get in touch with David Lynch, the director whose series *Twin Peaks* has just started on ABC Television. *Twin Peaks* is dark and spooky, and funny—as different as television has ever been. We've been trying to interview Lynch for months, and so has everyone else. He's working in Hollywood, editing his new movie *Wild at Heart;* we send an engineer to his editing room and we do a short "tape-synch" interview. He talks to me by phone; the engineer records his side of the conversation. Later she uplinks the tape to Washington and it's synched with the other half, my side. It was a short interview because the tape recorder's batteries ran low, but we had enough to make an interview work. David Lynch sounds a great deal like Special Agent Cooper, his lead character in *Twin Peaks;* he has the same youthful enthusiasms. He told us about the certain look that he's been trying to create for his television show, a murder story in the Pacific Northwest.

LYNCH: There's a lot of wood, and I wanted it to be very warm, even though it was raining outside, it needs a cozy, warm feeling. We used like, kind of, turquoise and orange, brown and green, you know, some sort of strange fifties warm colors out there in the woods.

NOAH: The music, too, seems to be sort of warm and fuzzy.

LYNCH: It's kind of a hip, sort of happy fifties, sixties, you know, music. It's a little bit of a modern kind of jazz thing in the woods. It just needed to give kind of a modern feel to the woods thing.

NOAH: The scene I wanted to ask you about is the doughnut scene—I don't know why, it struck our fancy here—Special Agent Cooper, the FBI agent Mr. Cooper, comes into the local police station there and I think it's about midnight, is it not?

LYNCH: Right.

NOAH: And he walks in and there is a spread of doughnuts on a table—

LYNCH: A policeman's dream.

NOAH: He says, "This is a policeman's dream." My question is: why are the doughnuts on individual plates, stacked up on individual plates as opposed to a big heaping platterful of doughnuts? Did you have a discussion about that?

LYNCH: Well, yes. Lucy's a particular type of person. And she's very organized and pays attention to details—

NOAH: She runs the police station.

LYNCH: Well, she takes care of them, yeah, and she, like Harry, Sheriff Truman says, Lucy sets this out for the guys every night. She kind of like stacks them in groups of two, then that night she had special jelly doughnuts out for Agent Cooper.

NOAH: They'd be used to coming in and having two doughnuts.

LYNCH: Well, they could have two or four or six—you know, you feel happy when you see many doughnuts, and so the spread needed to be ... large.

NOAH: And then there's a great deal of conversation about Agent Cooper's clean motel room that he's going to go to with the reasonable rates.

LYNCH: Right, well, he's interested in economy and cleanliness, for sure.

NOAH: Was there ever a time, Mr. Lynch, on this set when the actors or the director or anybody else started giggling?

LYNCH: Yeah, there was always a feeling of having fun.

NOAH: Well, I was thinking more along these lines, that it seems to be almost to the point of parody but not that far and I was wondering if—

LYNCH: It really is not to me in the parody category. It's absolutely *Twin Peaks* and a *Twin Peaks* reality. It has to be this kind of way to be this ... wonderful dream.

NOAH: Why do you say it's a wonderful dream?

LYNCH: Well, you see, at least I want things to be this way, I want this mood and this feeling and, you know, I love these characters and I, we, fell into this world and it was like a dream. It had its own set of rules and logic.

NOAH: Did you make any sort—I've heard that ABC has treated you very well with regard to this series—did you make any sort of compromise, though, to television, to do the series?

LYNCH: You put on a different sort of hat when you work in each medium, and with the television hat automatically you stop yourself from thinking too far out in certain directions.

NOAH: Too far out in directions of sexual scenes, or—

LYNCH: Or violent things—

NOAH: Putting that aside for the moment, if somebody had said to you in midstream, "Let's make it a feature film instead of a television production," what difference would that have made?

LYNCH: There's a certain sort of innocence, and a safer, nicer feeling in *Twin Peaks* that you'd be forced, I think, and probably wrongly so, to think in harder ways for a feature film.

NOAH: You are writing, I've read, small movies to fit inside the commercial breaks.

LYNCH: You have to design things to fit into eleven-minute segments. At first, I thought it would be, you know, sort of impossible. But it's a beautiful structure to me now.

NOAH: You don't mind the commercial interruption at all?

LYNCH: No, I even thought about making a feature where you'd stop and maybe sell doughnuts in the middle of a feature. A rest sometimes is so good, then you start up again.

Monday, April 16, Washington, D.C., 1990

A good night of music at the Birchmere, watching Rodney Crowell, two and a half hours of high-energy rock and country. He's coming in Wednesday for an interview. I'm sure he's forgotten, but I first talked with him ten years ago, in a Georgetown hotel room. He was playing The Cellar Door. Now he's an authentic country star with a list of number-one singles. I've read that Crowell's a fan of Raymond

Carver's writing; and I'll try to remember to give him a tape of the interview with Tess Gallagher about Carver's last poetry.

And a conversation today with Marti Leimbach, the author of *Dying Young*. She was in a studio at WBUR in Boston, and in this case it would have helped if I could have seen her. She's twenty-six years old, has received a huge advance—$500,000—for a very good first novel (the book later became a movie, starring Julia Roberts and Campbell Scott), and is probably quite suspicious when she walks into an interview. It would have been nice to exchange a smile. That's something that Robert Pirsig certainly understood—he came to WBUR's studio for an interview about his new book, *Lila: An Inquiry into Morals*. This was his only broadcast interview and he refused to do it by satellite; he insisted that I be present. He wanted to see his "interrogator," as he put it.

I've been wondering about Pirsig since 1974, when I read *Zen and the Art of Motorcycle Maintenance*—no picture on the book jacket; he's been reclusive. And it just happened that I had a trip planned to Maine and then down to Cambridge, so I agreed to stay over and talk with him in person. I expected quite a difficult interview, but he was charming, honest, forthright. His new book is difficult to understand in parts, and I told him so, and he seemed frustrated, having worked fifteen years to make this discussion of metaphysics as clear as he possibly could. He thought *Lila* was a more important book than *ZMM* (as he calls it). *ZMM* still sells 100,000 copies a year. (Realizing that Pirsig is from Minnesota, I decided to include his name in my personal pantheon of cultural heroes from that state—a list of people who have greatly affected American culture. Six on the list now: Bob Dylan, Judy Garland, Garrison Keillor, Charles Schulz, Prince, Pirsig. No one ever guesses them all. Sometimes they want to add Hubert Humphrey, but if I'd put a politician on the list it would be Eugene McCarthy. F.

Scott Fitzgerald and Sinclair Lewis also come close, and perhaps in time Robert Bly, if the "men's movement" continues
to build.)

Sometimes, though, the distance of a satellite can help.
Usually no one gets to be in the same studio with Ted Koppel, on ABC's "Nightline," everyone is watching everyone
else on monitors. It makes it easier for Koppel to control the
conversation, interrupting smoothly if it's necessary. And
quite often I'll feel more comfortable being alone in the studio. Once I was in New York working on some stories; I had
an interview scheduled with Norman Mailer about *The Exe-
cutioner's Song.* I could have met him at our New York
studio. But I was so intimidated by Mailer's reputation for
being gruff and difficult that I went back to Washington
early just so I could be in my regular place in my home
studio. Turned out to be a silly decision—Mailer was easy; he
sounded like a soft-spoken accountant from New Jersey.

Marti Leimbach, in her interview, is pleasant but hesitant
as we discuss *Dying Young,* a love story involving a young
man who has leukemia and is refusing therapy.

LEIMBACH: He probably could have lived quite a bit longer
if he had done everything that the medical advisers
would have told him to do.

NOAH: Victor has decided not to have chemotherapy and
that is the way he met Hilary, advertised in the *Boston
Globe,* in the classified ads?

LEIMBACH: Right, he had decided he didn't want to
continue treatment and as a result gotten so much
friction from his friends and his family that he kind of
escaped from them, more or less, and he went and hid
out in Hull, Massachusetts, and he's hired this
woman—Hilary—because he anticipates that as he
gets sicker, he's going to need people to do things for
him. And then when the book opens they've already
established a love affair.

NOAH: You know what I really liked about the book, what I appreciated so much, was that there are conversations with Victor, who is dying, about just that—the fact of his dying is up front, on every page, in every moment of his relationship with Hilary.

LEIMBACH: Yeah, it's right out there in front, and I think it was a difficult balance to have at the one time always the—I mean, as a writer it was difficult to, on the one hand, always have his looming death available and being reminded of it; on the other hand not to sentimentalize the book and not to make that death become something that's overdramatized. Death comes up as jokes, death comes up as poetry, death comes up in discussion as an excuse, as a trait, as a part of a philosophy—it really is very much a part of the book—and yet the book isn't what I'd call morbid, in that sense that you might suspect just by that description.

NOAH: Have you heard of comparisons—have comparisons been made with this book to a book that I guess is now twenty years old: *Love Story,* by Erich Segal?

LEIMBACH: Yeah, I think those comparisons are inevitable because you have a love affair in which one of the characters is dying. One of the big distinguishing points that has been made about *Love Story,* versus *Dying Young,* is that in *Love Story* the people—both the guy who is not dying and the woman who is dying—become somehow angelic, perfect people, and this tragedy has sort of fallen onto them. And in the case of *Dying Young,* the characters aren't perfect people. Victor is difficult, you do see that sort of anger about his being sick come through. You see Hilary's ambivalence about having joined up in his life, his final year—and these people are not perfect.

NOAH: After *Love Story* came out and it was so successful
and it was made into a movie, I recall a great deal of
criticism about that book. People saying it was too
simple, it was too manipulative in a way and that any
writer could write this sort of thing—I don't recall
anybody else actually writing that sort of thing,
having a book that successful.

LEIMBACH: Well, I wasn't around when it first came out, I
wasn't reading, but I have heard lots of different things
about the book. It seems to me it's remembered very
fondly and I see that happen over and over again with
books. A book comes out and people all jump on it and
then it's remembered as, like you know, the most
incredibly great book, ten years later everyone tells
what a great book it was and then compares the
writer's third or fourth novel to that great book that
happened years ago that they didn't even recognize as
great when it came out.

NOAH: How are you doing about the money part of all
this? You got an advance, I've read, of five hundred
thousand dollars, everything included?

LEIMBACH: Yeah, there's a lot of money involved. And I
have a funny relationship to it in lots of ways. I always
thought of myself as sort of a quiet, literary writer, and
when all this money came around I was as surprised as
anybody about it. I hope it doesn't obscure the work
itself; I hope people can put to one side that I got paid a
lot for this book because, after all, when I was writing
it I wasn't being paid and nor did I anticipate that I
would necessarily be paid.

Writers have so little control over what their work
brings to them financially, I could have no more
predicted whether I'd get five thousand dollars or
whether I would have gotten five hundred thousand
dollars . . . it's just a bit of a roll of the dice. I was very

happy, of course, to have so much enthusiasm by my publishers about the book, both here and abroad, and it's enabling me to take time, time that I really do need, writing the novel I'm writing now, which will be the second novel that I'll publish.

Thursday, April 19, Washington, D.C., 1990

A black-tie affair tonight. A twentieth-anniversary celebration for Washington's WETA-FM, held in the old Pension Building. A reception, dinner, champagne, a string quartet. Robert Siegel was a graceful master of ceremonies. Stan Freberg came in from California to talk about the good (and funnier) days of radio's past. He complained to me later about the sound in the Pension Building; an interior courtyard, four stories of empty, echoing space. Why, he asked, would a radio station want him to talk about "rr-r-r-radio" in a room with such terrible acoustics? No one quite says "radio" like Stan Freberg, and he's entitled. He was one of the best radio actors, the last comedian to have a network radio show; he replaced Jack Benny on CBS, and while it's actually a record album, his classic *Stan Freberg Presents the United States of America* is wonderful radio.

For our first national broadcast of "Good Evening," in Minnesota, we asked Freberg to come and help us recreate some scenes from that album. He was pleased to be asked; he came and worked hard and, even though he can be irascible, he was especially generous with the younger members of our staff, helping the band with the song arrangements, teaching our director the proper way to format a radio script. We did have our difficult moments leading up to the broadcast. He wanted to do "Take an Indian to Lunch" (it was Thanksgiving), a great piece of musical satire and one of my favorite songs from the album, but we thought it would be inappropriate for our first show. "Look, Stan," I'd say, "you're

going to see homeless Indians here in Saint Paul on your
way from the hotel to the World Theater." "Don't worry, it's a
national broadcast," he'd assure me; but eventually he gave
in.

We spent many hours discussing our discussion, the conversation Stan and I would have on the broadcast, just
before the skits. We'd talk about the old days of radio (he
agreed to do some of his "Abominable Snowman" character;
he interviews the Snowman, making the creature's voice by
forcing breath backwards—against the advice of his doctor—through his own vocal chords) and about the record
album and his long career in advertising. I had thought we'd
just go out on stage together and see what happened; I've
always felt you can over-prepare for these things. "Not so
fast, Noah," Stan said. "The words 'wing it' are not in my
vocabulary." So we wrote and rehearsed and rewrote, even
the answers to such questions as "So, Stan, how'd you get
your start in radio?" I felt a bit foolish during this part of
the broadcast, but when I heard the tape later I realized—
Freberg sounded great! It was just as he had said: "Noah, I'm
a scripted kind of guy."

There was also a small problem with our microphones.
The Neumann U-87 condenser mike has been around for
years, we use it in the NPR studios, Stan used it on the
United States album. "Where's the U-87?" he said, when we
went on stage for rehearsal. "Well, we use different mikes
here in the theater, we find they work better." "Well . . . " he
said, "if you want Freberg . . . ?" So we set up a couple of
U-87s.

I was reminded of that moment a year or so later watching the movie *Tucker,* the story of Preston Tucker, whose
futuristic car designs threatened Detroit. He couldn't raise
enough money to build his cars and, to reassure investors,
he was forced to bring in an outside expert to run the company. Tucker didn't realize he'd given up control, and soon
the manager decreed: no rear engine, no disc brakes, no fuel
injection, no seat belts. Tucker complained, screaming. The

manager, Mr. Bennington, said, "May I remind you you have
no voice in matters of policy here. You can't have Falstaff
... and have him thin, Mr. Tucker."

We had another larger-than-life performer come to Saint
Paul for "Good Evening." Another great radio actor, William
Conrad. Thirty years ago he did *all* the voices for one episode
of the "CBS Mystery Theater" titled "The Waxworks." (The
script was what they call a "two-hander," two actors doing
all the parts, but the other guy got drunk and didn't show
up.) Conrad was thrilled by our call, and our plans to restage
"The Waxworks." "Would you come for three hundred dollars? That's union scale, that's what we pay everyone on the
show." He must have smiled. "Sure," he said. And he caused
quite a commotion in Saint Paul, gathering crowds along
the street, or in the hotel lobby, fans of the TV shows *Cannon* and *Jake and the Fatman*—he's by far the most recognized celebrity I've ever been with.

After the Saturday broadcast we took everyone out to a
fairly hip restaurant in Minneapolis, the New French Café.
Conrad makes quite an entrance, even to dinner, but the
people at the other tables pretended not to notice him. Then
the waiter came, bringing drinks and a basket of the New
French Café's justifiably famous bread. Conrad took a bite,
then another, telling me, "This is good, I really like good
bread." Then he said, in his famous and quite loud actor's
voice, "This is the best fucking bread I've ever had!"

The WETA dinner in Washington was a far more decorous
affair. It didn't really seem much like a public radio gathering, but it doesn't hurt to wear a tuxedo once a year, and
Neenah and I had a great time. It was an evening designed to
raise money and to thank a very loyal listenership.

The public support for NPR stations around the country
is increasingly gratifying; it's a thrill to be at a station in a
small town at fundraising time and to hear the phones ringing and realize how much the service can mean to a community. Local people helped put the station on the air, and they

want it to work. And to get better. That means more money, and that's the challenge for public radio—how much success can it pay for and still be thought of, quaintly, as noncommercial broadcasting? Already now you hear the word "sponsor" on the air. Public stations will talk about their "sales" staff. I've heard the actual voices of the underwriters giving their own credits on the air. The notion of "enhanced" underwriting continues to be tested. The Federal Communications Commission once had some questions about the wording of a credit that appeared, inadvertently, on WVXU, Cincinnati; the ID was really intended for commercial stations: "This traffic watch update is brought to you by Jiffy Lube, now offering a discount on air conditioner recharge with a Pennzoil oil change and 14-point lube check." The issue is identification versus promotion. This example helped clarify the Commission's viewpoint, and it's now understood that "discount" is not a concept favored by the FCC, nor is talk of interest rates, special gifts, or calls to action ("Come on down and see us"). My all-time favorite funding credit comes from PBS: "*Sesame Street* has been brought to you by the letters G and N, and by the number 19."

It's tough for local stations to pay the bills and to offer decent wages. And costs keep going up, especially the program fees—NPR is a membership organization, the stations pay for the programming they use; the larger, more prosperous stations are charged the most. WAMU, also in Washington, paid NPR $226,000 in 1992, mostly for "Morning Edition" and "All Things Considered." This is usually, it is hoped, a fair trade: WAMU raised $1.2 million from listeners during the same period.

Many of the stations find it easier to raise money when there's something important and exciting going on—the Persian Gulf war coverage found an especially appreciative audience. The following August, KCRW, Santa Monica, held a subscription drive while the coup attempt was under way in the Soviet Union. The pledge total was $344,655; "The phones just never stopped ringing."

You'll see some interesting new techniques to raise

money for public broadcasting. You might receive a SWEEP-STAKES envelope in the mail, bright yellow with blue letter-ing: YOU MAY ALREADY HAVE WON A FABULOUS 1992 HONDA ACCORD LX. YOU HAVE 354 CHANCES TO WIN. OPEN IMMEDIATELY! I was both-ered by this at first; it seemed far too commercial. But if you believe in public radio and want it to continue to grow, why not see if some more aggressive fundraising could work?

Friday, April 27, Washington, D.C., 1990

A couple of field trips this week. Wednesday I went over to the Air and Space Museum to interview Paul Garber. And to watch him fly a kite. Garber is now ninety years old—his job title is Historian Emeritus. When he was a boy in Washing-ton, he was flying a kite one day and Alexander Graham Bell stopped by to watch and give him some advice. On May 21, 1927, it was Paul Garber who sent a telegram to Charles Lindbergh in Paris, to congratulate the flyer on his solo At-lantic crossing, and to make sure the *Spirit of St. Louis* would be delivered to the Smithsonian Institution. On this morning Garber didn't meet us at ten o'clock. We waited Finally I called his office. He was almost frantic, apologetic. His kite had broken and he didn't think he could fix it right away. No story here.

Today's adventure—trying to get my lawn mower sharp-ened—turned out better. And we hurried back to NPR to cut the tape and quickly write a script. Smokey Baer, my tape editor for this story, finished seconds before it had to go on the air. Probably fifteen seconds. He ran from his editing machine, past the producer's desk into the control room. Somebody no doubt held the door open for him. Smokey could be the best tape editor in the business and he's proud of it. He will tell you that he's "better than anybody who's faster and faster than anybody who's better." Whatever that means.

Editing audio tape is a simple, old-fashioned craft. Using a splicing block and a razor blade, you make diagonal cuts in the tape, drop the unwanted part on the floor, and tape the ends back together. A stumble can be taken out of a question, a wordy sentence can lose a clause, a boring forty-minute interview can become fascinating at seven minutes. And if you do it right, no one can tell the tape's been touched.

Zbigniew Brzezinski, the historian who was President Carter's National Security Adviser, doesn't like to be edited, and as part of the bargain is quite capable of giving you a concise three-and-a-half-minute interview.

I went to California to talk with Edward Teller about President Reagan's proposed Strategic Defense Initiative—the Star Wars plan. Teller ("Don't call me the 'Father of the H-bomb,' I'm not the father of anything") was quite brusque, demanding to known the questions in advance ("Stupid," he characterized one of them). Then he said, "What's the longest *unedited* answer you will use on the air?" "Forty seconds," I told him. "Okay, begin," he said, finger poised—he would time with his own watch. I dutifully asked the first question, he started his stopwatch and started talking. When he finished, he said, "There. Thirty-nine seconds. You owe me one second." I've since noticed that Edward Teller is always quoted precisely in newspaper and magazine articles: you never see the usage, "Dr. Teller believes . . ." or, "Dr. Teller feels . . .", but I'll always regret giving in to his demands so readily. I was fully prepared for the interview, had even read two books about Teller himself, and I also think he would have been a far more effective spokesman for SDI had he simply been willing to have a conversation about it.

Finally, it is NPR's policy that presidents remain basically unedited. We're not allowed to do any *internal* editing of a President's remarks, a policy that I've had to ignore a few times in the past, especially in the Ford administration, just to help White House statements make grammatical sense.

We have four or five tape editors working on each day's

program. After a couple of years they often go on to other jobs, but Smokey has stayed since almost the beginning, coming to Washington from WBFO in Buffalo in 1973. He's in his late thirties, tall, athletic, more interested in everything than the rest of us but for shorter periods of time. Smokey's been known to sit around, watching the clock, just waiting for the pressure to build, and sometimes to throw things and yell, but he never misses a deadline and his tapes sound great. Working fast, he cuts by instinct, spilling tape on the floor without even having heard it all first. It was easier for our lawn mower interview since he came along for the taping.

This story grew out of my frustration with seeing a big red and green pile of broken lawn mowers at my neighborhood hardware store, all waiting for service. I'd been thinking about a new gasoline mower, but it seemed there were too many in the world already. Could I possibly find someone who knows how to sharpen the blades of the old *push* mower I'd found as trash by the curb? Dick Garvin, at Piney Branch Hardware, was qualified and waiting.

NOAH: What does it say here on the handle? F & N Lawnmower Company in Richmond, Indiana. So you've seen one of these before?

GARVIN: Oh yeah, it's not unfamiliar.

NOAH: Is it worth fooling with?

GARVIN: Yeah, if you're going to use it.

NOAH: We take my mower down into the basement. Dick Garvin puts on his blue apron. First, he takes off the handle, then the wheels, then the roller. He works on about fifteen push mowers every week. The best ones—in case you find an old mower at a garage sale—the best ones are the heaviest ones. And the more blades, the better. There's a lovely old Scott Silent

mower here waiting to be sharpened. It has six blades
and a wonderful wooden handle.

clunking sound

It's nice to see my mower coming apart. This is accessible
machinery.
Okay, there goes one wheel.

GARVIN: That has ball bearings in it. Now that is unusual.

NOAH: I'd say that's good, though, wouldn't you?

GARVIN: Yeah, it should be.

NOAH: Mr. Garvin also removes the bed knife—that's the
plate that comes up under the blades. And he mounts
the reel on a sharpening machine.

grinding starts up

NOAH: The sparks flash up in the dark basement. Dick
Garvin's hand moves slowly, guiding the grinding
wheel along the curving edge of each blade.

(TO GARVIN): How much of a chance would a fellow have
to do this without a machine, but to do it with a file?

GARVIN: You could do it. Take your time.

more raspy grinding

NOAH: The next step, the bed knife has to be sharpened.
That's a different machine, sort of looks like a lathe. It's
a Model 50 Ideal Bed Knife Grinder, made in
Plymouth, Ohio.

cranking sound

NOAH: Now, we're cranking the grinding wheel down on
the bed knife.

grinding sound

NOAH: Then the reassembly. The old gunky grease and dirt are scraped off, the wheels are freshly lubricated, the bed knife goes on, and the roller. Then Dick Garvin picks up a small sheet of newspaper, to test his work. He wants to adjust the blades so the paper is just barely snipped off. It takes some doing.

(TO GARVIN): You want to feel it grab that newspaper?

GARVIN: Yeah, should grab it. Actually, it should cut it, on these.

blades rattling

GARVIN: Just a little ... bit more.

blades turn once

GARVIN: Take it.

spins blades

NOAH: And it's over. The investment is twenty-nine dollars and fifty cents. And my time to look and to learn. I've got a working lawn mower. But as I said, I've been lucky. It's hard to *find* a lawn mower, and harder still to find somebody like Dick Garvin, and he's talking about retiring. And perhaps I'm being too sentimental about the whole thing anyway. I remember a man in my neighborhood when I was growing up. He would come around to cut people's lawns, using a beautifully maintained push mower. The sound of the blades *shimmered* in the summer heat. Then he would go home and clean up and change clothes and come back just before dark, to knock on the doors and collect his money.

mowing, fading

I liked this feature; it had good sounds, it was short, and in a way it was reassuring, like a familiar piece of music, "Guy Goes to a Hardware Store." Actually the story was a bit too short. After "All Things Considered" was over, I asked Smokey, "Where was that part about Sears?" "I had to take it out for time," he said. It was the last thing to go and it was good tape—Dick Garvin talking about the lawn mowers he's seen from Sears; some of them needed sharpening when they were brand new.

Saturday, April 28, Washington, D.C., 1990

A hot morning out in the country; it's weather I've been dreading all week. Several NPR folks are running in a 10K race, from Flint Hill, Virginia, along the Fodderstack Road into the small town of Washington—I'll finish behind Smokey Baer, Art Silverman, Michael Sullivan, and Neal Conan. The race starts at 10:00 A.M. and it's almost eighty-five degrees, with a strong, dry wind. I run along far in the back at a conversational pace, passing the first mile mark with a time of 9:30.

There's plenty of water along the way, people handing you paper cups, a hose left running by the roadside. The eponymous Fodderstack Hill comes up at four miles and it's tough. Within twenty-five yards of the top, I have to stop and walk up. I'm in fact walking faster than I was running. The rest of the race is fun, down to Washington. I finish at the courthouse, as the timer yells out sixty-seven something. I'm last among the NPR group. Michael Sullivan, our producer, has our best time at 48:26. He claims to enjoy the hills, sees them as an opportunity.

It's a nice feeling, after the race, walking around town to cool off, drinking water. We've brought a picnic lunch to have on the church lawn: fried chicken, deviled eggs, and asparagus.

Monday, April 30, West Virginia, 1990

The distant ridge is West Virginia. You can see the state coming for a long time as you drive out from Washington. At Front Royal there's a bridge that crosses both the north and the south forks of the Shenandoah. The natural traffic in this valley—boats, pioneer wagons, Civil War troops, trains, and now sixteen-wheelers—has been vertical, between the slanting lines of the Blue Ridge Mountains and the Alleghenies, but if you want to do some driving, follow Route 55 on up into the hills to the state line and beyond. WELCOME TO WILD AND WONDERFUL WEST VIRGINIA, says a blue and gold sign, and your ears pop before you get there.

I'm starting to worry about the deal I made last week with my producer. The Senate will soon vote on a new Clean Air bill; it's certain that a lot of coal miners will lose their jobs, and I've been asked to go to West Virginia to check on the reaction. Sure, I said—I was tired and eager to get out of town—easy story. And I even proposed more. I'll do the coal story and I'll also do an audio journal—I'll just take the whole week and drive around the state with no special plans, finding stories along the way. A romantic notion on Thursday morning, and now a tough prospect on Monday afternoon.

I stop at Wardensville to read the posters and notes in the window of Twitty's IGA. I've missed a revival; Bennie Smith was the speaker, from Dunn, North Carolina. There were some ramp suppers over the weekend: ramps are pungent wild-growing bulbs, sort of like onions but much stronger. Churches and fire departments put on ramp feeds every spring to raise money. One of the earliest stories I can recall hearing on "All Things Considered"—almost twenty years ago—was about ramps (the reporter was Jennifer Roth, now the general manager of WBFO, Buffalo), and it's probably time to do another one.

I pass a truck that could be a short story. It's parked, abandoned, it looks like. And it's somebody's carnival ride. Beat-
up yellow octopus cars waiting on the trailer. Farther along
in a yard, there's a Corvair up on blocks, and one fellow has
three old Pintos for sale. I cross another ridge of mountains,
the small towns quiet in the high valleys. VOTE PUDGY FOR
MAGISTRATE. NIGHTCRAWLERS—$1.50 A DOZEN.

Some canoeists are just coming off the river—the North
Fork of the Potomac—and they're happy to be interviewed
about rapids and eagles and drinking beer. And at Seneca
Rocks, I sit out on the porch of The Gendarme climbing
shop and talk for a half hour or so with Tom Cecil; he's running the shop this afternoon but he's also a climbing in-
structor. He's maybe twenty-five, five feet ten inches, slim,
wearing a dark blue pullover and black pants. Spends his
summer here and the winters at Joshua Tree National Mon-
ument in California.

Seneca Rocks is nationally ranked as a climbing spot, the
edges of sandstone almost a thousand feet above the valley
floor. Tom Cecil could take me up there, roped to other be-
ginners. I'm intrigued by climbers. There's a sign in the
shop: IF YOU DIE WE SPLIT UP YOUR STUFF. It reminds me of a
T-shirt I saw in a book about competitive rowing: A young
man's shirt read: ON THE WATER NO ONE CAN HEAR YOU SCREAM.

Two hours more driving, again across the ridges, and up
into the Canaan Valley. We've been cross-country skiing
here once. No snow at all in Virginia and you can drive up
here and find fifteen inches. The Canaan Valley is 4,100 feet
high. Most of the pioneers left it alone and went on to settle
Ohio, Indiana, and Illinois.

I find a room at the lodge in the State Park, and have a late
supper—spaghetti—while reading about Harper's Ferry,
West Virginia, and the beginnings of the Civil War.

Tuesday, May 1, Ohio, 1990

After breakfast I make some calls from my room. I'm going through the Clean Air file, for the first time really, and getting puzzled. The coal in question is high sulfur. The high-sulfur coal seems to be in Ohio, not West Virginia. I call Senator Robert Byrd's office—he's the senior senator from West Virginia. His press secretary says, yes, that coal is mostly in the Ohio River Valley, and the mines to the south in West Virginia are low-sulfur coal. In fact, West Virginia mining is likely to get a boost if the higher-sulfur coal can't be burned for electricity. I am two hundred miles and one full day out of place for this story. It's the first time this has ever happened, that I've left Washington without a clear idea of what I was doing. I decide to drive on across West Virginia and then head north to the Ohio River.

I'll probably have to give up this idea of doing a travel journal, but I sure do keep finding interesting things. There's homemade butter at the M & R Market on Route 32, and I hear about wonderful examples of "naive art" over in Braxton County—murals painted on walls in old houses. A folklorist found them. One is said to be a fantastic painting of sea battles, by a man who was hiding from the law; the paintings were to pay for his room and board. And, curious about homemade protest signs along the road, I stopped in Philippi to do some interviews about a local trash issue. An out-of-state company wants to dump out-of-state trash, ten thousand tons a day from Pennsylvania and New Jersey. I talked with a woman who was leading a fight against the landfill proposal. The other side of this story would take some time to locate, so I drive on up into Marshall County. Deep valleys and high ridges; the road goes through a couple of towns that are now almost deserted, the houses collapsing, but most of the farmhouses along the way are freshly

painted white, with the grass and backyard gardens invit-
ing in the clear light. Above Moundsville the road drops
down to the Ohio River, and I find my way a few miles east
to Wheeling.

It's been seven hours of driving today and I'm worn out,
don't know where to stay, and suddenly I'm on the Interstate heading into Ohio and ten miles later there's an exit
with a Red Roof Inn, and a Bob Evans restaurant nearby,
and that's good enough for me. I go out for a run and take a
shower and have a beer and then have chicken-fried steak
and mashed potatoes and watch a little of *Tap,* on television,
the movie with Gregory Hines, but I'm still pretty discouraged when I call home to let Neenah know where I am.
It's two days now and I haven't even started this story.

Wednesday, May 2, Ohio, 1990

On the phone early to Beth Vorhees, the news director for
West Virginia Public Radio in Charleston, to let her know
I'm in her territory working on a story, but mostly for
names and numbers—she quickly gives me five or six con-
tacts in the Wheeling area. Robert Murray's on the list; he's
the owner of Ohio Valley Coal. Murray's in Washington
today, I'm told when I call, but maybe we can do something
in a day or so.

I spend an hour in Wheeling at the headquarters of an
anti-Clean Air Act coalition. Their position: why can't the
government give us a few more years to clean up the emissions from the power plants? There's a new study coming—
paid for by the government—that will prove there's no such
thing as acid rain. The older men can't be retained and there
wouldn't be any jobs for them anyway.

shopping mall sounds

NOAH: I talked with a miner's wife at a shopping center in St. Clairsville. She'd come by to sign up for information on how to fight the Clean Air legislation.

WOMAN: You can't say the power plants and these coal emissions and all that stuff is doing all this, you check these cars out there that pass you, that smoke's just flying by like crazy, and these big old trucks going by. I mean, crying out loud, you smell that like crazy, and I see nothing from the coal mines, or from your power plants.

NOAH: From up there on the hill, can't you see a haze out in the valley?

WOMAN: Not all the time, no.

NOAH: But some of the time?

WOMAN: Oh, some of the time. But that has always been with that valley. I mean, my husband—I look at it this way. My husband is, he's forty-nine. And he dropped out of school and coal mining is all he knows. So what is he going to do if this closes him down? What is that man going to do at age forty-nine? Who's going to hire him? He's too close to retirement in the coal mines, really. And it's just going to be a hardship on a lot of people.

I also talk with the president of Local Number 6, United Mine Workers. Larry Ward's theory is, in part, that there are people in Congress who would benefit financially from the collapse of the coal and steel business in this country. It seems you can always find conspiracy theories.

outside sounds, birds

NOAH: It's farm country in southeastern Ohio, green
    hillsides, golden with flowers and springtime, small
    quiet towns with old white houses. It doesn't look like
    coal-mining country; you have to go looking to find a
    mine. But the coal companies are essential to the
    economy. The mine workers average thirty-five
    thousand dollars a year, and you can *buy* one of those
    white frame houses for twenty-five thousand.

Friday, May 4, Ohio, 1990

The interview with Robert Murray was fine. And I realized
how lucky I was to find him. Normally, you wind up talking
to some vice-president downtown and not getting much you
could use. Murray got his start in the business as an underground miner. He's worked for several coal companies, and a
couple of years ago, he managed to borrow $55 million to
buy this one and run it himself.

MURRAY: I graduated from high school thirteen miles
    from this coal mine. And my grandparents lived just a
    few miles from this mine. So I think the Lord has a
    plan for us here and we've been able to grow from
    about two hundred employees here to nearly four
    hundred now, and I don't know what I can do in the
    autumn of *my* life that's more important than to see
    these families thrive when they were really living off
    the dole or just barely surviving because they couldn't
    get employment other places.

It always happens—the best comments come right after
you turn the tape recorder off. Murray was more upset than
I thought, and as I was leaving his office, he took my arm

and told me that sometimes he feels like he's ready to take up a shotgun and secede.

Then he asked if I wanted to go underground and see the mine! Usually that would take months of negotiation back and forth, but it's Murray's mine and he said it was okay. They put me through a pretty thorough safety briefing, and gave me coveralls and boots and a hardhat with a light, and a self-rescuer unit in case of trouble, and soon we were in the elevator going down.

We traveled several miles underground, mostly in the electric shuttle cars. I got to watch the roof bolters working in one tunnel, and then they took me up to the face to see the continuous mining machine. The sound was wonderful, heavy clankings and ominous rumbling, and hissing; I just wished I'd brought along an engineer and some better audio equipment.

grinding, machinery sound

NOAH (*loudly*): What's it like running this? Is it just like when you were a kid and had one of those remote powered cars?

MINER (*laughing*): They didn't have those when I was a kid.

NOAH: What can you make this do now? What can you make this machine do with these knobs?

MINER: Anything you can do by running it manually. You can start—it starts your electric motors, this is a hydraulic raising head and shear—

more electric sounds start

MINER (*yelling*): This will start the cutter motors and that will start the scrubber in a few seconds.

blast of motor and water sounds

NOAH: There is a spray of coal dust and water vapor, and the continuous mining machine with its

carbide-tipped steel teeth takes a ten-foot-wide bite
into the coal face. The crunched-up coal runs on a
conveyor belt to the back of the machine, where a
shuttle car takes it away.

This coal will be sent to Cleveland and burned there,
and if the new Clean Air regulations go into effect, that
may not be possible after 1995. The concern is acid
rain, the sulfur *deposited* in wet form. It is feared acid
rain could sterilize lakes and waterways, it's believed
acid rain hurts the trees, and even buildings, and
breathing the sulfur in the air is said to be harmful.
The utility companies will have a choice: switch to
natural gas, find some low-sulfur coal to burn, or
install scrubbers to burn the high sulfur more cleanly.
That choice will be made well before 1995.

Later, in Washington, I talked with Richard Ayers of the
National Clean Air Coalition. He says perhaps five thousand
people could lose their jobs if the new legislation passes (one
highly speculative industry figure is three and a half million), but that the time has come to make the changes and
the technology is ready.

AYERS: The acid rain issue is really all about a set of
    power plants which have escaped pollution control
    now for twenty years under the Clean Air Act. For
    twenty years the utilities have managed to stave off
    cleaning up this dirty fuel, and by the time they finish
    cleaning it up, it will be thirty years since the first
    Clean Air Act came into being. I think what they're
    really playing for is the time to complete the full life
    cycle on these old power plants, and retire them, and
    never have to put pollution control on them. I just
    think what the environment is telling us is it can't
    stand that—it can't take another fifteen or twenty
    years of this kind of assault.

I left Ohio thinking mostly about the coal mine. The air was cool and seemed heavy, and the light was eerie and it could get claustrophobic and it certainly is dreadfully dangerous work, but there was something comforting about being down in the mine. It seemed calm and quiet in a way, and far away from anything above ground. Miners always tell you that it gets in your blood, that it just becomes a way of life, and I'm a little closer now to understanding that. Or they will say, as Lewis Henson just did a few hours ago, "I can leave my doors unlocked at night here. And I know everybody. I went to college for a couple of years. I lived in Columbus and I lived in Athens and it's not for me. This is where I live and this is where I'm going to die."

Most of these phrases are indeed heartfelt, but we've heard them so much they've become useless. When someone mentions "way of life," a lot of reporters will just stop taping, figuring this person has nothing more to say and is now just repeating something that he or she has seen on television. One day in the studio during "All Things Considered," while a report from one of the member stations in the Midwest was on the air, Linda Wertheimer yelled: "Eeeek!"

"What is it?" I asked.

She looked at me sternly, "One of those farmers just said, 'way of life' "

Linda's been around long enough and on enough political reporting trips to have a very low tolerance for that phrase.

I made it home just before midnight, driving east on the Pennsylvania Turnpike and then south to Washington. You can't get any AM stations on the radio these days, just the local FMs as you pass by. I couldn't even pick up the fifty-thousand-watt signals: KDKA in Pittsburgh, WLW, Cincinnati, or any of the stations from Boston or New York. It may just be my radio, but I've noticed it in other cars as well.

I left Ohio right after an early supper at Mehlman's Cafeteria, outside of St. Clairsville. "Your best food is over there at Mehlman's," they said (the advice of Jane and Michael Stern,

authors of *Roadfood*, is not to ask, "Where should I eat?" but
rather, "Where do you eat?"). I had a baked pork chop and
lima beans and coconut cream pie that I thought was banana but ate anyway. I had missed lunch, down in the coal
mine. All the miners of course brought their dinner, but I
hadn't even thought about getting a chance to go underground.

Saturday, May 5, West Virginia, 1990

> NOAH: In the springtime of the year, in North Carolina,
> Virginia, West Virginia, Pennsylvania, people gather in
> parking lots outside of fire stations and American
> Legion halls and churches, standing in line, getting
> hungry, waiting to eat ramps.

> EUGENE MORLAND, MT. STORM, WEST VIRGINIA: We usually go
> to about three or four ramp dinners a year,
> recommend them highly. I'll tell you what I found out,
> some people say they smell on your breath, but that's
> saying it very mild. (*Laughs*) This odor just oozes out
> of all of your pores.

I'm back on the same road I traveled Monday, going out to
West Virginia for a ramp supper at the Petersburg Volunteer Fire Department. I took a day off at home to go through
my tape and notes from Ohio, then decided to do the ramp
story after all—the notice for the supper was posted at a
grocery store out in Seneca Rocks.

The Clean Air Act piece will be fine, I guess, and I'll get
something useful about ramps, but I regret the stories I
missed: the mysterious farmhouse murals, the out-of-state
dumping issue. I even thought I could have done some interviews about a sign I saw in a grocery store: "Prom gowns
for sale, sizes 7 to 12." I also wanted to go south in West

Virginia, to Summers County. The health department there is broke, can't even afford Pap smear testing anymore, and the director has asked for foreign aid from Britain, France, and the Soviet Union. I've interviewed him by phone; he's serious and he's got a serious problem.

I spend two hours in the Petersburg fire hall, surrounded by smiles and pleasant accents, and smells of cooking. It's all-you-can-eat: five dollars for adults, four for children. Soup beans and hash browns and ham—plus the ramps. You can have them plain, or cooked with bacon, with eggs, or hamburger. Iced tea and coffee and homemade cakes. There are plates of fresh raw ramps on every table. The word "ramp" comes from the Old English *hramsa*. They resemble wild onions, and grow in the woods at elevations close to five thousand feet. The men from the Petersburg fire station had to drive about seventy miles back in the mountains to dig their ramps this year. The taste of ramps is said is be over-powering, especially when you eat them raw.

NOAH: How many raw ramps would you sit down and eat?

MAN AT TABLE: Oh, last Saturday evening I had about three dozen, and I suppose I'll probably eat a dozen or so this evening.

NOAH: You had three dozen in one sitting?

MAN: Oh, yes. My preferred way of eating them is: take the raw ones, put it between two slices of buttered bread, salt and pepper, and chow down. Some people complain that they swell after you eat them, but I have no trouble with that at all.

NOAH: That you swell?

MAN: Absolutely, it causes you to bloat, but I don't have that problem. (*Laughing*).

WOMAN NEARBY: I don't know, John, I never ate them raw, I'll tell you.

Everyone seems to have a ramp tale to tell. A ten-year-old
boy tells me he prefers ramp suppers to the fast-food places
in town because ramp suppers don't do any damage to the
rain forest in Brazil. And there's an old story about a newspaper called the *West Virginia Hillbilly*. One spring Jim
Comstock, the publisher, decided to print an issue with
ramp juice in the ink. The post office made him promise not
to do it again. "Do we know that's true?" Brooke Gladstone
asked me while she was editing this piece. I made a couple of
calls but couldn't confirm that he actually used real ramp
juice in the ink, so we changed my copy to read: "It smelled
like ramp juice, anyway."

At the fire hall the time eventually came for what's
known in the business as "gratuitous participatory journalism"—I ate a couple of ramps, raw. They were much milder
than I'd expected, a peppery wild onion–garlicky taste.

My real fondness for this story has to do with the volunteer firemen, and the ladies' auxiliary. Some of the men had
been standing there for hours over pans of ramps frying in
bacon grease. They said they need $37,000 this year to pay
for a new rescue truck; the fire station only gets $1,000 a
year from the county, so they always have to raise money.
The Petersburg fire hall is also well known for its pancake
and sausage breakfasts.

frying sounds

TIM PARKS: We'll take a whole hog, and dress it out, have it
   dressed out, and Paul Ott over here, he's the butcher,
   and he'll make it all into sausage. And then we'll have
   a carnival, we have a carnival coming up the last of
   this month, going into June, as well. There again, the
   cooks that are here will be cooking hamburgers and
   hot dogs . . . it's an uphill proposition for a small
   company.

I leave the supper after cake and coffee, and drive north
for a while and then turn east over the mountains, still

wanting something even sweeter. And on the road between Moorefield and Wardensville, I find it: it's almost dark and the Pink Flamingo glows like neon beside the road. The Pink Flamingo is an ice-cream stand, an old one; under new ownership and just now painted hot pink, with plastic flamingos gathered in the driveway and over by the picnic tables.

"Where'd you get the paint?" I asked the man through the window as he fixed my vanilla cone. "At the hardware store, no problem." He laughed. He and his wife had just moved here from California; I'd noticed the license plate on their older model Cadillac, a pink Cadillac. At least, that's the way it is in my memory. Maybe it was just an ordinary car, but it was late and getting dark and near the end of a long week, and I guess I really wanted it to be a pink Cadillac.

Monday, May 7, Washington, D.C., 1990

Back at work, trying to finish a story that producer Peter Breslow and I recorded last month about the FBI training academy. We spent a day at Quantico, Virginia, watching the new agents go through role-playing exercises, making arrests, chasing down suspects. Haven't had time to even listen to the tape and now we're late—the story's been in some newspapers and in *People* magazine last week. The FBI has built a "training town" at Quantico: several downtown streets, a bank, stores, a warehouse, gas station. You can see just a bit of "Hogan's Alley" on screen in *The Silence of the Lambs.*

A call from the United Mine Workers Union. Out in Ohio I was asking union people about this rumor—did the UMW and Rich Trumka, the president, make a deal with the Bush administration? The union is not protesting, not making all that much of a fuss about the proposed Clean Air Act, and I'd heard that they agreed to be quiet in return for help in ending the almost year-long strike against the Pittston Coal Group. A federal mediator was called in and soon there was a settlement. "That's not true, where did you hear that?" the union man said. He was cordial but intensely curious. I'd heard it mentioned by one of the Clean Air Coalition organizers, in Ohio, and really didn't plan to use it on the air unless I could move it past the rumor stage.

Monday, May 14, Washington, D.C., 1990

Ted Clark has a long, quite sad report tonight from Mozambique, entitled "Manicu's Story," about some of the thousands of children left homeless by fourteen years of civil war. It's one of the stories from Neenah's trip with Ted to Mozambique and South Africa.

A couple of weeks ago Robert Siegel talked with an attorney in Ohio, who was one of those wounded in the Kent State shootings. It was the twentieth anniversary of Kent State. And today is the anniversary of another shooting: on this night twenty years ago two students died at Jackson State in Mississippi, as police opened fire on a group of demonstrators. Gene Young, who's now on the Jackson State faculty, was a nineteen-year-old sophomore at that time, active in both the civil rights and anti-war movements.

> YOUNG: Not only did we have some returning veterans on campus, but I personally was very much aware of the fact that if my grade point average wasn't kept up and I was able to stay in school, the local board would have been more than happy to send me to Southeast Asia. And that was one of the points of contention, too; not only the war in Vietnam and the escalation of the war by the U.S. troops invading Cambodia, but all-white local boards are making some life-determining

decisions on the lives of young black men in Mississippi.

NOAH: At the night of the fourteenth, past midnight, actually the fifteenth of May, the third night of demonstrations—were those protests and demonstrations on your campus related—I believe they were—to what happened at Kent State?

YOUNG: Surely enough. There was the war in Vietnam; I recall posters around campus saying: "Remember Kent State." "Remember the Augusta Six." You might recall that after Kent State there were several blacks who were shot in the back in Augusta, Georgia. Surely enough, students were politically aware at that time, not only about international events but also what was going on in this country.

NOAH: Tell us where you were that night.

YOUNG: That night I was sitting in front of the wing of Alexander Hall, which was bullet-riddled later. And a friend of mine decided, you know, that it was just going to be a repeat of the previous evenings where students would just protest and protest and eventually go home, but as we rounded the wing of the building to go home late that evening right before midnight, the bullet fire started. People said that there was a bottle to be heard bursting on the concrete pavement there on the street, and after that it was just a barrage of bullets being leveled at the students who had assembled there in front of Alexander Hall.

NOAH: The amount of fire—I've read that every window on the street side of the five-story building was blown out by gunfire.

YOUNG: By shotgun blast and buckshots, and there are some pictures that have gone around, and I think once people see that picture it's a miracle with the number of students present that only two students, tragically, Phillip Gibbs, a student here, and James Earl Green, a local high school student on his way from work that evening, crossing campus, were the only ones to be killed that evening.

NOAH: What did you do when you heard the firing start?

YOUNG: I stopped immediately and listened, and as I listened, I'm saying, my God, it's been a wholesale slaughter around there, just listening to the gunfire. And then after the gunfire had ceased, I went back around there, smoke was in the air, students were crying and screaming, and in an attempt to try to calm the tensions there someone gave me a microphone and I just started reciting some words from Dr. King's "I Have a Dream" speech. And it had a little bit of a calming effect, but people were traumatized and terrified by what they had just experienced and witnessed.

NOAH: What was the rest of that night, that morning, like for you and your fellow students; did you think, for example, that the students were under attack, that there would be more bloodshed on the campus?

YOUNG: Initially, there were some people who wanted to march downtown at midnight to protest, but cooler heads prevailed and we stayed on campus right there on front of the lawn of Alexander Hall. Then most of the students came out of the dormitory—the weather was still warm and beautiful here in Mississippi—and we all camped out on the lawn there on blankets and sat down, and people tried to find out as much as they could about their fellow roommates and classmates. And we sang and prayed throughout the morning until the break of dawn, and at dawn students returned to the dormitories to collect their items because the university was officially closed, commencement had been canceled, classes had been canceled, and most students returned home.

NOAH: Dr. Young, have you ever tried to put yourself in the place of the policemen that night, twenty-two policemen facing hundreds of students, there was the bottle being broken, firefighters earlier in the evening had been attacked by people throwing rocks? Have you tried to figure it out from the other side of that?

YOUNG: I can't—you know, this is Mississippi, and we were used to blacks being victimized by white violence in our society, and again, if they wanted to just disperse those students, some other kind of methods could have been used. Advancing with bayonets, or tear-gassing the students could have been used rather than such lethal force, so in that regard, I can't, twenty years later, justify the action that took place on this campus twenty years ago.

NOAH: It's been speculated that the authorities in that town, Jackson, wanted to demonstrate that they could control the students on the campus.

YOUNG: This is Mississippi, and it has a historic image of how it deals with the blacks who speak out against the system. Again now no one has ever served a day in jail for the death of Medgar Evers, no one ever served a day in jail for the death of Emmett Till, or Mack Charles Parker, and were it not for the fact that Michael Schwerner and Andrew Goodman were with James Chaney, little or no attention would have been given to his death in Philadelphia, Mississippi, in 1964. But because he died along with two other white civil rights workers, James Chaney's death was noted, because even in the process of looking for those three civil rights workers, several black bodies were found which had been unaccounted for, or unnoticed during the summer of 1964 here in Mississippi. So again, what

little attention Jackson State received is due primarily
to the fact that it came in such close sequence to the
deaths, the similar deaths of protesting students at
Kent State University.

Tuesday, May 15, Washington, D.C., 1990

An interview with a friend tonight. I've known John Gorka
for a few years now, and think he's a great songwriter. The
question comes up: because I know him, should I *not* do the
interview. But John's never been on "All Things Considered." He's just released his first album on a major label
(Windham Hill), plus he's fun to talk with. I've gotten to
know several musicians and writers, and sometimes, just
for that reason, it seems right not to interview them about a
new project. I passed up Peter Ostroushko's latest album.
Some friends in Maine have written a book about their
coastal farm, and I'll recommend it to one of the other NPR
programs.

My wife, Neenah, produces albums for Red House Records, in Saint Paul, Minnesota, so I skip the Red House artists, including Greg Brown and Claudia Schmidt, but not
without misgivings—it should be the quality of the work
that matters most. All of us worry about doing book interviews with friends and acquaintances. What if the book's no
good? What if the *interview's* no good and can't run—what
do you tell your friend? There's another factor. I do better
interviews with people I don't know at all. I think I'm just a
bit too comfortable with people I've met before, not eager
enough to challenge them. Interviews need to have an edge
of uncertainty.

Today, one of our previous stories turns out to be not only
uncertain but a complete hoax. I had interviewed—two
weeks ago—a florist in West Virginia who said he was being
persecuted because people thought he had AIDS. Now the

state Human Rights Commission says, after an investigation, that Bill Grealis "perpetrated a fraud on all of us, and the media, too." Grealis has checked himself into the psychiatric unit of a local hospital.

We later told our listeners about this development, and received, among others, a letter complaining that "One man's testimony, with the help of NPR, was allowed to embarrass and falsely accuse an entire community before the nation." "In all my travels," Stephen Taylor wrote from Berea, Kentucky, "I have never found people so sincerely friendly, kind and generous as those in West Virginia."

Listeners were right to be upset. Although the story was originally on the AP wire from Charleston, and we did call West Virginia Public Radio to check on it—we gave up too soon. We should have called somebody in Campbell's Creek, the small mining community where Bill Grealis had his business. And I should have been more skeptical during the interview. Grealis, however, sounded very convincing. He said he'd been ill and lost weight. A rumor started that he had left his wife for a man. The threats began, letters, phone calls; people wanted him out of Campbell's Creek.

GREALIS: I actually began to wonder myself, well, maybe I do have something wrong with me. So I went to my doctor and he did run an HIV, which is the test for the AIDS antibody—

NOAH: And you posted the test results in your shop?

GREALIS: That's correct, they're posted there now, and I've invited anyone to come in to see them, and I have yet had the first person to come in. In fact, I had a woman come to my door last week. She owed a bill: she opened my front door and she threw a check into my shop on the floor, slammed the door, got in her car and squealed her tires as she was leaving.

NOAH: Why do you figure the reaction to this idea that you might have AIDS has been so strong?

GREALIS: People up here are, in my opinion, are extremely
uneducated. They're afraid of the word "AIDS," they're
afraid to have any contact whatsoever with anyone
that has it—I see people in the grocery store that I
have known for years, I've lived up here twenty-three
years—and they see me coming, turn their shopping
carts around, and head in the opposite direction rather
than pass me.

This is the most fooled we've been, that I can recall, although every year there seems to be some sort of minor
hoax out there—and, in the fall of 1991, quite a major hoax
was uncovered. *The Education of Little Tree,* A True Story
by Forrest Carter, had been on the paperback best seller lists
for several months. Booksellers loved *Little Tree,* readers
loved *Little Tree.* "I cried all the way through it," you would
hear. But the story, which purported to be from the memory
of an orphaned boy who grows up with his Cherokee grandparents, was in fact from the imagination of Asa Earl Carter,
a well-known white supremacist who once wrote speeches
for George Wallace. I interviewed Dan Carter, the Emory
University history professor who revealed the deception.
Carter maintained that much of the philosophy expressed
in *Little Tree* was in fact not inconsistent with the beliefs of
Asa Earl Carter. Soon *The Education of Little Tree* was
removed from the nonfiction lists, and then became a fiction best seller. I had already made arrangements to do a
story about the audio version of *Little Tree,* to be recorded
by the actor Peter Coyote, but we decided to drop that idea
for a while.

Scott Simon's program "Weekend Edition Saturday" was
the target of a prank in January 1992. An interview with a
man who wanted to sell one of his kidneys for $25,000
turned out to be phony. "Thomas Frey" was really Alan
Abel, a veteran hoaxer; he's fooled the media before and
probably will again. And CNN almost announced one day
that President Bush was dead. Mr. Bush had fallen ill at a

banquet in Tokyo; a man claiming to be his doctor called CNN and said the President had died. "This just in to CNN Headline News," the anchor in Atlanta said, "And we say right off the bat, we have not confirmed this through any other source . . . " Then the audience heard an off-camera voice, "No, stop!"

And NPR has—on April Fools' Day—confused some listeners on purpose. People still ask about Scott's report ten years ago concerning scientists who discovered that coho salmon could talk, and even sing. Scott also brought us a fine story one April 1 about a hardworking family who owned a pickle ranch (this, in the tradition of the BBC's classic story about a spaghetti farm).

On April Fools' Day 1992, the "Talk of the Nation" staff crafted a masterpiece: RICHARD NIXON RUNS FOR PRESIDENT. They enlisted Rich Little to impersonate Nixon; a legal scholar and a political expert were guests on the program, and for an hour John Hockenberry took calls from all over the country. The callers became part of the hoax: "Of course, it's an April Fools' joke," they were told. "And we want you to go on the air and play along." They did, happily.

We mention our more serious errors in editorial judgment in our "Letters from Listeners" feature on Thursdays; many of our corrections come directly from the audience. And I think it's best to simply say you were wrong, give the correct information, and not bother to explain *why* or *how* you messed up. (I've long admired *The New Yorker*'s attitude; their occasional mistakes are mentioned under the heading, "Department of Amplification and Correction." My favorite *New Yorker* amplification was written by John McPhee: "Attention has been called to a slice of turbot that I mentioned on page 88 of the February 19th issue of this magazine, in a profile of a chef named Otto. Referring to a slice of turbot he consumed at the restaurant Lutece, Otto was quoted as follows: 'The turbot is delicious, very fresh, perfectly cooked. My guess is it was frozen.' Otto guessed wrong.")

John Gorka, I trust, is telling the truth, mostly, in our interview.

NOAH: John Gorka's new album is called *Land of the Bottom Line*.

music fading in, Gorka singing:

Freedom for freedom
Call that an even scheme
Give me time to wonder and to dream
I'll take the money
They'll take the time
Down to the Land of the Bottom Line
To the Bottom Line . . .

(fading)

NOAH: John Gorka is thirty-one years old, with dark, curly hair, and a beard and a careful smile. He's spent most of his life in Pennsylvania. He went to college there in Bethlehem. And probably did not figure on being a performer. But he's now spent more than a thousand nights alone, with a guitar, on a stage. And his songs are conversations he might be too shy to have.

GORKA: Almost always it's the first line that triggers the rest of the song. And once I get that first line, I can kind of pull the rest of the song out of it, because I think a lot of times that first line determines—you know, it's like the germ of the song, determines the whole direction of the rest of the song.

music fading in, Gorka singing:

I saw a stranger with your hair
Tried to make her give it back
So I could send it off to you

> *Maybe Federal Express*
> *'Cause I know you'd miss it*
>
> *I saw another with your eyes*
> *The flash just turned my head . . . (fading)*

NOAH: The songs seem just a little bit offbeat, just a little
bit out of kilter, a little bit surreal, the rhymes seem a
little bit off—you know what I mean, coming in the
middle of the word sometimes. And they also seem
just a little bit sad.

GORKA: Well, I'm from New Jersey, so that might explain
some of that, and also I guess I always admired the
songwriters who kind of took a chance and the ones
who had a lot of imagination in their songs, people like
John Prine and Steve Goodman and Greg Brown. I
always liked the mix of the humor and sad stuff,
because I think there are certain moments that are all
sad and there are certain moments that are all funny,
but most of the time it's a mixture of the two.

NOAH: Thank goodness.

GORKA: Yeah, yeah.

> *music fading up, Gorka sings:*
>
> *The day we met is still a blur*
> *Though I remember just how nice you were*
> *And what you wore in Central Park*
> *And how you left before the darkness fell*
>
> *(Now) I cry over these strings*
> *This sentimental case of things . . .*
>
> *(fading)*

NOAH: I know that you spent several years, I guess, at
Godfrey Daniels's Coffeehouse?

GORKA: Yeah, I'm playing there as a matter of fact this
weekend. I first started coming there to go to the "open
mikes" and I would go there when I could afford to.
Being a college student I didn't have a whole lot of
money and sometimes I would go halfway through the
show because they would lower the price at halftime,
so I would get a little bit of a bargain but also get a
taste of the music, too.

NOAH: You've said that you're a singer now because of the
feeling that you had after midnight driving back
across the bridge to North Bethlehem after hearing
some music . . .

GORKA: Yeah, I think I was probably walking, I don't
think I had a car then. But I was just so inspired by the
people who came through there who were just great,
and I couldn't believe there was this whole world of
music that seemed like nobody else really knew about,
at least the other people in the dormitory.

NOAH: Can you recall a singular performance, one song by
one person one night . . . that stayed with you?

GORKA: Oh, there's just so many—I remember Stan
Rogers. He's one of my musical heroes. He's a Canadian
singer-songwriter. He was a huge guy; he's about six
foot four. He had this huge bald head, and this great
big voice, and I was the MC that night. I just remember
walking in and Dave Fry, the owner of Godfrey Daniels,
introduced me to him, and I was pretty star-struck, the
whole night I was kind of hovering around him, and at
one point, I guess I was making him a little nervous, he
said, "Have a beer, John." And I think I did and I asked
for a request, there was a song called "Harris and the
Mare," and it was the kind of song that I had never
heard anybody write before. It seemed like it was a
whole, a whole novel, or a whole short story in, like,
nine verses. And there was just so much detail and so
much passion in the song, I was just amazed by that.

So I remember he played it that night and he thanked me from the stage, he said, you know, he was thanking Dave Fry and Cindy Dinsmore for keeping the place open and the audience for coming out, and I remember him saying, "and thanks to our new friend, John, who's been so kind and helpful all night."

music fading up, Gorka singing:

I worked at a place
Where the bands came through
Some of them rang false
And some rang true
I'd stick around
After they played
To see how legends were made . . .

(fading)

Monday, May 21, Washington, D.C., 1990

Again, I'm in the wrong town. I'd been looking forward to meeting her, but Blair Brown was in our New York studio.

Blair Brown has become quite well known now because of *The Days and Nights of Molly Dodd,* first on network television and then cable. I first saw her in *Altered States,* with William Hurt. She spent ten years in theater before that, appearing in Canada, at the Guthrie in Minneapolis, the Arena Stage in Washington, D.C. Her new movie has opened, as they say, to mixed reviews. It's called *Strapless.* Brown plays an American physician, a cancer oncologist, working in England for the National Health Service; she falls in love with a mysterious, extravagant man she's met on holiday. I didn't like *Strapless* very much, but I'm never confident of my reaction to a screening in an empty theater at ten o'-clock in the morning. In the interview I tried to quickly move away from the story of the film. I asked Brown how she felt about the way she appeared on screen—many times she looked pale and tired. David Hare, the director, said, "I wanted Blair to look like a hardworking doctor who's contemplating middle age, not a movie star. I wanted to read real life in her face."

> BROWN: Well, I really liked it. I mean, I remember when I got my first jobs in California and I liked to sort of do my own hair and not wear very much makeup. I was fresh out of drama school and was very much of a—I took a very realistic approach to things. And, of course, all along the way I was dissuaded and sometimes forced into abandoning that. So, I think that in small-budget films, particularly European/English films, you have a chance to really do those kind of slice-of-life stories in a way—it's not a genre that we really appreciate here in this country. I think we need to look at a lot of French films, Italian films, you see people looking much more like life, and here it's considered bad cinematography, instead of people wanting to make a choice about that. So I welcomed it.

> NOAH: Somebody once compared you to, was it Katharine Hepburn, actually—

> BROWN: Oh, that's nice. Gosh, everyone likes to be compared to Katharine Hepburn.

> NOAH: —who said, "You look enough like me to be my daughter."

> BROWN: Oh, she did say that to me once a long time ago and I had come to audition for *The Glass Menagerie,* she was doing *The Glass Menagerie* on television. And I came down, I was doing a play up in Canada at the time, and I walked into the audition and the first thing she said was (*imitating Hepburn*), "You look enough like me to be my daughter." And I thought, I've got the job. This is it, I've got the job. I came back in the afternoon, we read, and she then turned to me and

said, "I'm not going to hire you for this part because you—actually somewhere deep inside you, you have a certain kind of confidence, that is apparent. This character doesn't have that."

And I was so astonished because, of course, I was a nervous wreck and quaking in my boots and felt completely weak and frightened. And left quite bewildered by the whole experience. But over time I've come to understand what she means.

NOAH: It's really quite a compliment.

BROWN: Yeah, it was. But it was so strange coming to me at a time when I felt so completely vulnerable.

NOAH: You didn't say, "Gee, Ms. Hepburn, I'm an actor, I can overcome that confidence?"

BROWN (*laughs*): Oh, sure. I think I did say that but, I—you know, when they make their mind up, they make their mind up. I remember years ago I was working on a low-budget film and I sat in on auditions and read with a lot of different actors when they came in. And wonderful actors. And it was a great lesson, 'cause I remember thinking, a lot of times when you don't get a job you don't get it; you've given a great audition, you can feel the magic in the room, it's the right kind of job for you to get at this time in your career, all that kind of thing, you don't get the job, and it was so clear that day watching that sometimes it isn't the person that does the best audition, sometimes for no reason other than instinct you say no, it's this guy, and he hasn't done as much and he doesn't seem as right. But that's the one, that's the one that [has] the certain *thing* that seems right for a character. So it's very magical, and capricious and mysterious, all of this.

NOAH: Yes ... What's the finest thing you've ever seen on stage or on the screen, in terms of performance?

BROWN: I think, actually, that it's the stage performances of John Malkovich. Having seen him in *True West,* the Sam Shepard play, and *Death of a Salesman,* and Lanford Wilson's *Burn This.* I—he's the most extraordinary stage actor that I have ever seen. I don't think that his particular magic is as strong on film, for me, but on stage I've never—it's almost like you have to blink because you can't believe you're seeing all that you're seeing from one moment to the next.

NOAH: And have you had moments on stage—I would assume on stage as opposed to film—where you felt that way about a performance of yours, if only for one night or for a couple of nights?

BROWN: Sure. Yeah, yeah, you have moments—I mean, I think it's interesting, the frustration in working on the stage is . . . you'll get a magic night or you'll get a magic scene and you think, "God, I wish this were on film." Because it evaporates, and it's only there in the memory of those people at that moment at that time, and it's a very strange experience to be involved in something so fleeting. And yet there are other times on film when you just really wish that this were not permanent (*laughs*), that you would have a few more tries at it before it goes down into history.

NOAH: Do you recall what play it would have been when you felt that way?

BROWN: Actually, some work I did at the Guthrie. We did *School for Scandal;* we did actually then tape it for PBS, but it wasn't the same as some of those nights—or years ago I was in *Threepenny Opera,* at Lincoln Center. And I went on as a dare, basically, the woman who—I had left the show by then—Ellen Green played Jenny, sang all those great songs, Kurt Weill songs, and she was ill and her understudy was ill, and I got a desperate call from the New York Shakespeare Festival saying there's no one to go on tonight, and the house is sold. I thought ... I'll do it. So I went and worked for about a couple of hours with Raul Julia, and I went in that night and I actually never saw the part on stage because when I'd been in the play earlier, I was on stage at a different time. And it was ... the *most* extraordinary night of my theatrical life. Because it was real kamikaze acting (*laughs*), it was away we went, and I sang all the songs and did this very torrid tango with Raul and it was ... wonderful. And I just wanted—you know, it's one of those things you wanted to say, to everybody there, this is the most amazing night ... of my life, you know? I don't know what the audience saw.

Wednesday, May 23, Washington, D.C., 1990

Missed a chance, I just found out, to talk with Feng Li, the son of Li Shuxian and Fang Lizhi, the Chinese dissidents who are still inside the U.S. Embassy in Beijing. Feng Li, who's a student in Detroit, hasn't given any interviews over this year. He made a statement yesterday here in Washington—he's organizing a letter-writing campaign—and I thought for a time we might arrange an interview, but now he's said no. Later in the summer, in June 1990, Feng Li's parents were allowed to leave China; they traveled first to Cambridge, England, and then settled in Princeton, New Jersey, where Fang Lizhi was given a fellowship at the Institute for Advanced Study.

In May 1991, Fang agreed to an interview and I took the train up to Princeton for a pleasant conversation in a classroom at the Institute. He talked about his time in the embassy—not as difficult, he said, as the time of China's Cultural Revolution, when, after being critical of the

Communist Party, he was sent out to work in the countryside, far from his colleagues and scientific journals. And
Fang spoke of astrophysics and cosmology, saying his study
of the origins of the universe convinced him that everyone
is equal, deserving of the same rights. I was surprised that
we could just walk right in to Fang's office—the building
was open, and he didn't have a secretary. Just another mid-
dle-aged researcher with a desk and a computer and a few
books.

Tonight a fun interview with a pilot named Oddvar Sand,
in Alaska. He had a Norwegian accent and the ironic humor
that comes from having survived a scary experience. He had
been flying on his regular route from Hoonah to Juneau.
This is a story about an airplane, a pilot, a passenger—and a
duck. It has a happy ending for everybody but the duck,
which was hit by the plane.

SAND: I had just dumped off a load of people and luckily
    was bringing one passenger only, and I was just
    reaching my cruise altitude at two thousand feet and
    my cruising speed was about a hundred sixty, a
    hundred seventy miles an hour, and I spotted a flock of
    birds, turned out to be migrating ducks, flying in a
    formation off to my right a little below me. It was a
    pretty sight and I kind of looked at it and the next
    thing I know there's just a shadow passing over my
    windshield and the next thing I hear is this shattering
    bang as my windshield breaks and the duck comes
    through and hits me in my chest, gets my mouth full
    of feathers, in fact.

NOAH: Pardon it [the pun], but it was a shattering
    experience to have that windshield break, I guess.

SAND: Well, when you go a hundred seventy miles an
    hour and a lot of wind suddenly comes in there—I was
    bleeding and stuff, but I never really felt any pain or

didn't even feel cold. I guess I didn't think about it, concentrating about controlling the airplane, because it turned out another bird hit the wing and left a gash in the wing. I never did see that until I was almost on the ground, though.

NOAH: You didn't have any trouble controlling the plane?

SAND: No, I just reached out for the throttle and slowed down the airplane.

NOAH: The duck wound up in the empty co-pilot's seat?

SAND: Exactly.

NOAH: And then what happened to the duck—it died?

SAND: Yeah, it just flapped its wings a few times, and its head came back, and its eyes started flickering and it died right there. In fact, I got the duck in my freezer right now; I'm going to have him stuffed.

NOAH: You're not going to have it for supper?

SAND: No, I'm not going to have him for supper, I'm going to save him—he's a pretty duck, you know. (*Laughs*) I know it sounds kind of weird.

NOAH: You came, I understand, from Norway to fly, to work in—?

SAND: —The States, yeah.

NOAH: Nobody ever warned you about ducks?

SAND: Nobody ever told me about it. I kind of had a feeling that these birds they don't give way for anybody—

NOAH: Sounds like you had a lucky day.

SAND: Yeah, thinking about it in retrospect, you know, I think I had.

NOAH: Have you flown since this happened?

SAND: Yeah, I flew the day after on the same route. I can never stop flying, that's all I want to do. So, takes more than just a bird coming through my windshield, I guess.

Monday, May 28, Washington, D.C., 1990

Memorial Day. There's not much going on. I spend most of the afternoon editing an interview with Allister Sparks, author of *The Mind of South Africa,* a very good history of the apartheid conflict. Neenah and I have been watching some movies about South Africa: *A Dry White Season,* and *Cry Freedom.*

Tomorrow's a day off. I'll try to get the car licensed in Maryland, the Virginia tags will soon expire. I also want to find a way to put our bird feeders up out of reach of the neighbor's cat. The cat's been eating high on the food chain this spring.

Then Friday, it's off to Kansas. This is a story I could easily mess up. It has echoes of the counterculture (a friend used to call it the "over-the-counter" culture), the feel of a folk festival with organic refreshment stands, with the marching orders of the sustainable agriculture movement. It all could get just a bit righteous and, as a reporter, I've never been as skeptical as I should be. But it's an important issue and a good ATC sort of story—just let the people who are doing it talk for a while.

Friday, June 1, Kansas, 1990

I was a little concerned, late in the afternoon waiting for Wes Jackson in his office at the Land Institute, outside Salina, that he would turn out to be as often described—

craggy, monolithic almost, a gruff scientist. But he walks in and he's a regular-sized guy with a good smile and an impish sense of humor; he looks more like a football coach than a professor.

We sit for a time before going out for a tour of the farm. And we mention his friend, my acquaintance, Wendell Berry, back in Kentucky. Wes says Wendell is thinking about not flying anymore, not going anywhere that requires that sort of speed, traveling around giving talks and readings and going to seminars, and that he's just thinking about "staying home and being decent." I'm reminded of Yves Chouinard, the mountaineer who founded Patagonia—the outdoor clothing company. Chouinard has decided that jet lag is too hard on the body and his traveling will only be latitudinal north and south, avoiding the time shifts. Makes sense, and there's lots to see from the Arctic to South America.

Irish fiddle music fading in

NOAH: On a weekend late in spring about five hundred people have come to the Land Institute in central Kansas for a Prairie Festival, for seminars and demonstrations, and a supper and a square dance on Saturday night.

Wes Jackson and Dana Jackson are the founders of the Land Institute, and they are truly *of* Kansas. Wes Jackson was raised on a farm near Topeka, his dad was a champion corn grower; Dana is from close to Abilene, Kansas, her father was born in a prairie sod dugout. The Jacksons have spent twenty years now wondering what American agriculture *could* be like. And for many of those years Wes Jackson has had a smiling sense of hope. It came in the form of a question that was simple, but quite radical. It came almost as a vision, and he has been almost a prophet. Here's the question: Why couldn't you domesticate the prairie grasses—Illinois bundleflower, eastern gamagrass, and the others? Encourage them to produce more seed and harvest that seed as grain? *Why couldn't you grow a prairie that could feed the world?* There is much skepticism about this idea; in the wheatfield of American agriculture Wes Jackson is a single stem of prairie grass standing against the wind. Yet everybody seems to agree—it's really a good question.

Dana Jackson and Wes walk us around the garden—it's about half an acre. I ask Wes what's the best way to tell people how big an acre is, and he doesn't have a ready answer, but the next day he's figured out that an acre is the size of a football field including the end zones. The garden feeds the Jacksons most of the year round, and the interns, who come in February and leave in December—they delight in huge vegetable stir frys, and cantaloupe feasts, sitting out in the grass by the garden.

DANA JACKSON: We planted cabbage and onions and peas in different rows. The cilantro comes up by itself and just spreads. Everything's on schedule; see we've got the cabbage worm (*laughs*), we've got all the little organisms that belong in the garden. And these are carrots and beets and tomatillos, there in the cage, rhubarb...

NOAH: Some of the plants in Dana Jackson's garden are annuals, grown from seed every year, and some are perennials—they just come up, and the Jacksons believe a perennial prairie could grow the same way.

car sounds, driving over fields

NOAH: In America most of what used to be the prairie was plowed up by the white settlers and is now called the corn belt. Wes Jackson has a few acres of prairie left.

WES JACKSON: Now here, look at that. There's pretty close to what Stephen Long and Zebulon Pike and all that

bunch that came across here . . . saw. The one that's
dominant right now is blue wild indigo, baptisia, and
the little finger mallow is in bloom. But see there's the
vegetative structure and what it was like before the
great plowing. They said it was like plowing through a
heavy woven doormat. Two and three yokes of
straining oxen. Every now and then they'd stop and
beat the plowshare back into shape. Some said it
sounded like the opening of a zipper. You imagine that
"shear" going across this continent making its zipper
sound.

We meet Molly, the Jackson's Border collie, and Bobbins, a
Schnauzer mix. Molly is shamed, having just attacked Bobbins who's back from the groomer's newly shorn and per-
fumed, and to Molly, unrecognizable. The dogs don't bark,
and no one talks about them, and they aren't at all important to the story about the Land Institute. Later, Melissa
Block, the producer, with hardly more than a lifted eye-
brow, convinces me to take my reference to Molly and Bobbins out of the first draft of the script.
    The sound of the wind is fascinating here. There's a high-
tech windmill spinning with metallic whirling sound. And
you can hear the wind high in the cottonwoods, always a
noisy tree, and in the prairie grasses. Wind is difficult to
record. It sounds great on the scene but in the studio it usually sounds like water rushing—just "white noise." Our engineer, Liz Buchal, tapes for about thirty minutes, from several perspectives, with an entranced look on her face.

Saturday, June 2, Kansas, 1990

In the morning the wind starts up hot and fast—as high as
fifty miles an hour. At the Prairie Festival registration desk
there's a sign: RUNAWAY TENT FOUND—EUREKA DOME. We go out

into the fields to talk with the Institute's plant breeder, and his wife, a plant pathologist. The wind is discouraging, enervating, and the interviews don't go well. A talk inside the greenhouse with the staff ecologist turns out the same way—he's been outside giving tours all morning and is exhausted from yelling. The Institute people pretend the wind's nothing to worry about, but then someone tells me that attendance at the festival might be hurt, that Kansans especially would sooner go out in the rain than to be outside in this sort of wind.

In the afternoon, I spend a sleepy few hours in the Institute's barn, listening to speeches, and question-and-answer sessions; then it's time for the Saturday night potluck supper. Everyone who's come to the festival has brought a dish—Melissa and Liz go into town to buy fruit and rolls as our contribution—and all the food's laid out on the tables in the Jackson's backyard and it works, there's plenty for five hundred people. I'm practically the last one in line and there's still cold asparagus and salad and pasta and apple pie. There's a nice post-hippie sort of feel to the evening.

At ten o'clock we decide to go back to the motel. We had been recording some music, an "ecological" folksinger who sounded fine here but would seem too corny on the radio, and we wanted to wait for the square dancing to start, but things were running late and we have to be back out here at sunrise. It's too bad—Liz wanted to dance.

Sunday, June 3, Kansas, 1990

6:30 A.M. Thank goodness the wind is down for the bird walk. About twenty of us have gathered around Jake Vail, who's on the Institute staff. Jake is less than thirty, has long, light brown hair, and carries binoculars and a *National Geographic* guidebook—it has both the eastern and western birds and central Kansas is right on the dividing line. A five-year-old boy wearing an orange sweatshirt goes cheerfully along with us, eating from his box of Crispy Crackers. We walk along the river and then out into a meadow. Blue-birds are about, and a red-bellied woodpecker, the yellow-billed cuckoo, brown thrasher, northern oriole. The birds' calls are pretty and the tape will be useful, but I realize it's a bit too much for all three of us to be out here this early.

Then a song service, to welcome the day. A circle of chairs on the grass, a couple of the interns with guitars. The songs are sweet, if a little ragged and off-pitch. One is about a planet, a garden, a harbor. Even more pleasing is to watch two blond girls in a sawdust pile nearby. A young father is supervising; his daughter is the one with no diaper on.

In the afternoon we talked with some of the interns. Al-most from the beginning the Land Institute has invited young people to come and help out and learn. They have a stipend of a hundred twenty-five dollars a week. They live in Salina, in town, and many ride their bicycles out to work. There were nine interns this year, with undergraduate de-grees in chemistry, botany, range management. One has worked on organic farms in Scotland, another has been an environmental writer. They all seem optimistic about help-ing develop a prairie that you could harvest, but they have their own agendas as well. Paul Muto, from New Jersey, is concerned about all the tractors and other machinery being used at the Land Institute.

MUTO: Yeah, there's a lot of power equipment and it does trouble me, a bit. And I think it's important that we try to do something about it because it does take away from your argument about sustainability if you can't practice it yourself.

Holly Ewing, from Oklahoma, explained her commitment to what she termed "sustainability in a broader sense."

EWING: That entails a more respectful relationship to the land, but also things like redistribution of wealth and a dismantling of the hierarchical structures in our

society: racism, classism, sexism, homophobia, all of
those things ... the treatment of the land is just one
more dimension of that.

We went to the barn to record the final talks. It's a working barn with haylofts and burlap bags of seed hanging
from the rafters. A couple of hundred folding chairs that on
Sunday evening will go back to the First Presbyterian
Church. If America is to turn away from large-scale and
highly fertilized farming, it would be people like these, gathered in this barn, who would do the work. They seem pleasant, serious. Older couples, mothers with two young children, farmers wearing coveralls and running shoes. The
people listen and ask questions: about farm politics, and
how did the Indians regard the land, can ecology and agriculture come together. A woman mentioned that she had
just bought a burial plot in Council Groves, Kansas, a town
on the route of the old Santa Fe Trail. Her grandparents and
great-grandparents were buried nearby. She paid forty dollars for an eight-person plot. Wendell Berry's name is
brought up often: his essays and poetry are all written from
his farm, his grandfather's land, along the Kentucky River.

Wes Jackson's closing speech was dandy; he could have
"made a preacher," as they say back home. We rarely can use
tape of someone giving a speech, it just doesn't sound right
on the radio, but there's thirty seconds here that should
work just fine. Jackson talks about all of us as "children of a
dying star." And about what young people need to study in
college if they want to become "homecomers": liberal arts,
statistics, and certainly Shakespeare. Shakespeare, Jackson
says, to recognize Hamlet and Macbeth situations when
dealing with bankers and corporations.

JACKSON: We also ought to study the *Odyssey,* and we
ought to know and have totally internalized, I think,
what it meant for Odysseus returning from the wars of
Troy, going to the cave of Calypso, with sexual delight

every night and eternal youth; but then choosing to go home, to farm, to grow old, and die; and recognize that the American culture is still wanting to be in the cave of Calypso. The shopping mall is simply a way of accommodating life in the cave of Calypso. (*Audience laughs*) And medicine, modern medicine ... (*fading*)

We had scheduled an interview with the Jacksons for five o'clock, when the festival was over. I'd planned to ask about rural communities, and I had some doubts about the perennial polyculture experiments. Wes's explanations turn out to be hard to follow, his metaphors obscure, and close to an hour goes by without much happening that we'll be able to use—it's just too dense and a touch pedantic. But then Dana lost patience with Wes as he started explaining how people would leave the towns and come to settle in rural communities. The conversation was suddenly alive and accessible. Dana was tired and distracted, but I suspect she would have fussed with him anyway.

NOAH: Dana, you've been shaking your head a little bit—you have some doubt about this talk about community, about rural communities?

DANA: Well, communities have to be a place where people want to be, and women in particular have had a lot of opportunities as a result of moving out of small communities, being educated and living in cities. (*Laughs*) Wes talks about this sort of simply, "we're going to do this, we're going to do this; the psychology of people is such that ... " There's a lot that has to happen that will make it a better place than it's been.

NOAH: For women?

DANA: For *women.*

NOAH: What about Dana's concern that women would move away from an interesting job in the city, come back to the farm and be simply cooking the meals for the guys who come over to do the harvest?

WES: Well, I don't think that it has to be that way. I mean, there's too much water that's gone through the turbines for us to ever go back to the threshing machine era in which men ate like a hay baler and the women provided the food. (*Laughs*) I don't think we're talking about that. I think we will have some labor-saving devices, and that there probably can be much more of a sharing in some of the work.

DANA: Well, for all the advances we've made, women still do most of the household work. And we haven't overcome that. Women go to work in the morning and work all day, just as their husbands do—*all over the world*—they come home at five-thirty; the husband sits in his chair and reads his paper, the woman takes care of the kids, does the housework: that's going on now. And if we haven't been able to overcome that now, I see a life based on a lot of physical work as putting us even more in that position. So, I wouldn't try to build a Utopia based on what the ideal situation would be for people in their relationships, that wouldn't work because it all has to be within the framework of the physical resources and the realities, and those are changing. We will not have the kind of world we've had because we will not be able to waste resources the way we have. I don't go off into feminist Utopias because I realize that, but I am afraid that we will lose some of the gains we've made, and I don't think we've made enough gains.

Monday, June 4, Kansas, 1990

By 9:00 A.M. we were looking right into a bison's eyes. We were on a hillside at the Konza Prairie, walking back to the biologist's Jeep, when he said, "Uh-oh, look here, who are you?" We had been watching a group of bison from a safe distance and now a bull was watching us from about fifteen feet away; he had just come up over the edge of the hill. There was a cow behind him. We were in the way. Liz had stopped several feet behind us to change tapes on the Nagra. The biologist said move slowly and try to figure out where he wants to go. We walked to the bull's right; he slowly moved ahead, making a low, grunting sound, going on up the path.

Gary Merrill had been kind enough to open the back gate to the Konza preserve, out by the Interstate, and take us on a quick tour. The Konza is the largest protected grassland left in the country; most of it's been grazed but never farmed. It's in the Flint Hills—the stone, the chert, was too hard for the pioneers' plows.

We went on over to the airport in Kansas City, talking about how we could fit the encounter with the bison into our story about the Land Institute. In fact, we did try to use the scene as the opening (Wes Jackson had brought some of his students to Konza some years ago, and it was then that he started asking himself questions about the prairie), but the story was running too long and we had to take it out. It was a nice image, and Merrill had talked about the prairie once being *dark* with bison; it could take days for a herd to pass by.

It was a two-hour flight back to Washington. We were tired, had missed some sleep on this trip. I thought a lot about the questions I should have asked, a book or two I should have read beforehand. But the story should be okay—some good Kansas voices on the air.

We'd been listening to "Morning Edition" in the car, starting just after six o'clock. I'd heard some news from China
over the weekend, reports of trouble on the first anniversary
of the killings in Beijing. And this morning Deborah Wang
was on the air with details: students attacked, reporters
beaten and arrested. A very long year has passed, and it still
seems close.

But Kansas provided some distance to the Beijing anniversary. On Sunday evening, after the last interview with
the Jacksons, we went back to the motel and cleaned up and
drove twenty miles south to Brookville. "Make sure you go
to the Brookville Hotel," people said, "for the fried chicken."
(And then they'd almost whisper, "but the mashed potatoes
aren't real anymore.") It was clear and cool. Dogs were barking, nighthawks were out in the evening air.

Brookville Hotel sits with historic pride at the center of a
small farming town that probably never was prosperous.
Some of the buildings downtown were boarded up. We were
perfectly hungry. But the man at the cash register said, "Oh,
but you're so late; we stop serving at eight o'clock." He hadn't
stopped smiling, though, and said, "What I can do is fix you
some chicken to take out. Would you like that?" Three
chicken dinners in boxes, and iced tea and biscuits with
butter and strawberry jam. We went across the street to a
small park and sat at a picnic table in the last few minutes
of Kansas sunlight and had our supper.

Acknowledgments

The magic works—radio waves do fly through the air. It's an effect achieved by the talent and concentration and courage of hundreds of NPR folks, in Washington and around the country and the world; and especially our ATC staff: Virna Phillips, Jean Durr, Akili Tyson, David Rector, Margaret Low Smith, Max Friedman, John Baer, Art Silverman, Peter Breslow, Marika Partridge, Bob Boilen, Patricia Hammond, Rosemary Shinohara, Teresa Fung, Melissa Block, and Ellen Weiss. They have my admiration and gratitude.

I have failed to make adequate mention in this book of Weekend "All Things Considered," Saturday and Sundays, a program with a separate staff. As the year of my journal indicates, quite often the biggest news happens on the weekend; it's reassuring to click on the radio at five o'clock. And I thank the NPR technical staff—for their determination and companionship.

Thanks to Ellen Weiss, Bill Buzenberg, Doug Bennet, and John Dinges for encouragement and time off. Thanks to my agent, Jonathon Lazear. Also, W. W. Norton's Hilary Hinzmann who made clear panes of glass from the sands of my journal notes (and to copy editor Ann Adelman who polished them). Neenah Ellis helped with research and fact checking, along with Kee Malesky, Rob Robinson, and Jyl Hoyt.

A word of thanks to Don Wheeler, who gave me my first public radio job. And a farewell to Robert Montiegel, who taught so many of us.

My final thoughts are with the NPR station in your town. "All Things Considered" exists each evening only as a tiny stream of electrons, amplified and made real by the station you're tuned to. We owe these stations our attention and appreciation.

Credits